Cosmopolitics and the Emergence of a Future

Also by Gary Banham

KANT AND THE ENDS OF AESTHETICS

KANT'S PRACTICAL PHILOSOPHY

KANT'S TRANSCENDENTAL IMAGINATION

HUSSERL AND THE LOGIC OF EXPERIENCE (*editor*)

EVIL SPIRITS: Nihilism and the Fate of Modernity (*Co-edited with Charlie Blake*)

Also by Diane Morgan

NIHILISM NOW: "Monsters of Energy" (*Co-edited with Keith Ansell Pearson*)

KANT TROUBLE: Obscurities of the Enlightened

Cosmopolitics and the Emergence of a Future

Edited by

Diane Morgan
and
Gary Banham

First published in 2007 by
PALGRAVE MACMILLAN
Houndmills, Basingstoke, Hampshire RG21 6XS and
175 Fifth Avenue, New York, N.Y. 10010
Companies and representatives throughout the world.

PALGRAVE MACMILLAN is the global academic imprint of the Palgrave Macmillan division of St. Martin's Press, LLC and of Palgrave Macmillan Ltd. Macmillan® is a registered trademark in the United States, United Kingdom and other countries. Palgrave is a registered trademark in the European Union and other countries.

ISBN-13: 978–0–230–00152–7 hardback
ISBN-10: 0–230–00152–1 hardback

Library of Congress Cataloging-in-Publication Data

Cosmopolitics and the emergence of a future / edited by Diane Morgan and Gary Banham.
    p. cm.
    Includes bibliographical references and index.
Contents: Cosmopolitics: law and right / Gary Banham – ConcateNations: globalization in a Spinozist context / Yves Citton – Cosmopolitic and its Sadian discontents / Meredith Evans – Nationalist cosmopolitics in the 19th century / Daniel Malachuk – The cosmo-body-politic / Jill Marsden – Goethe's "Enhanced praxis" and the emergence of a cosmopolitical future / Diane Morgan – Kant's logic of political transformation / Paula Keating – Human rights and public accountability in H.G. Well's Functional state / John S. Partington – Imagination and reason: an ethics of interpretation for a cosmopolitan age / David Rose – Towards a cosmopolitics of heterogeneity / Lasse Thomassen.
    ISBN-13: 978–0–230–00152–7
    ISBN-10: 0–230–00152–1
    1. Cosmopolitanism. I. Morgan, Diane. II. Banham, Gary, 1965–

JZ1308b.C69 2007
306—dc22   2006049326

10 9 8 7 6 5 4 3 2 1
16 15 14 13 12 11 10 09 08 07

Printed and bound in Great Britain by
Antony Rowe Ltd, Chippenham and Eastbourne

Contents

Outline of the Book

Cosmopolitics and the Emergence of a Future is set out in four parts, the first of which concentrates on the Kantian provenance of cosmopolitics. The first chapter, by Paula Keating, looks at the relationship between Kant's account of political revolution and the models of revolution that are embedded in the structure of his thought. Seminal in respect of the latter are the role of Ideas in Kant's thinking, and it is to these that Keating looks for a type of 'metaphysics of morals' that advances from Kant's own.

In contrast, Gary Banham looks at the relationship between Kant's reflections on the topic of perpetual peace and the response to these reflections provided by Jürgen Habermas. Habermas sets out an ambitious reconstruction both of Kant's original thought and of its application to contemporary situations. Banham's chapter presents a respectful commentary on this reconstruction that situates the ways in which this reconstruction does and does not improve on Kant's original project.

David Rose's chapter also engages with the territory of Kantian thinking, but in a way which differs from the approach of Keating or Banham. Opening the relationship between imagination and reason to renewed interrogation, Rose sets out some suspicions for the understanding of practical philosophy by means of reason. Drawing on the notion of imagination, partly in Kantian terms and partly outside of them, Rose appeals for an understanding of cosmopolitics that has a hermeneutical and dialogic flavour. Using the work of Vico, Rose suggests a new type of relationship between liberal principles of reason and hermeneutic appeals to interpretative protocols, opening *en route* a possible different transmission of Kant.

Part II turns to explorations of material diversity that complicate the question of cosmopolitics in ways which differ from the Kantian considerations informing the pieces of Part I. Meredith Evans' article takes seriously the Marquis de Sade's original version of republicanism. Deftly combining Sade's challenge to the more orthodox Enlightenment accounts with reflections on Derrida's late writings on cosmopolitics, Evans sets the political regime of desire alongside formal political theory to produce a rich response to the situation of cosmopolitical reflection today.

Yves Citton, in contrast, concerns himself with the location of Spinozist thought in response to the narratives of globalisation. Setting out from a reflection on the conditions of early modern philosophical thought, he contrasts Hobbes' political theory with Spinoza's, providing *en route* a sense of how, from early on, economic liberalism was faced with emancipatory challenges whose force and urgency have not diminished.

Jill Marsden's chapter on the cosmo-body-politic concentrates on how Daniel Schreber's reflections on his mental illness provide a way of thinking the integration of the human with the extra-human. This exploration of the cosmic positioning of reflection connects Schreber with the Nietzschean investigation of the 'will to power'. Marsden's reflection on organs and bodies presents an alternative to conventional philosophy that provides a vista on politics quite different even from that of Evans, at the same time indicating a conception of the cosmic that rivals the alternatives set out by Diane Morgan and Howard Caygill in Part IV.

Part III introduces three key topics which influence the shape, dimension and limits of cosmopolitical thinking. These are the nation, the world state and displaced persons. Daniel S. Malachuk reactivates an often-overlooked version of nineteenth-century nationalism, one which scuppers the oversimplified opposition between an affiliation to a particular nation and a wider allegiance to humanity conceived of as a whole. He thereby refloats the notion of a 'nationalist cosmopolitanism'. This interesting term could provide a more fertile and sympathetic ground for understanding recently emerged nation-states in, and on the edge of, 'New Europe' than the usual disdain for nationalism as irrational backwardness. However, it also implies limits and obligations which would have to restrain an unbridled and unprincipled patriotism.

John S. Partington gives us a clear exposition of H. G. Wells' blueprint for a world state which endorses and upholds human rights. In his 1904/5 *A Modern Utopia*, Wells had already made clear that, for him, the future will be global and that, in his eyes, individual nation-states will necessarily be superseded by the one world state. Wells would thus disagree with the views of Mazzini, Eliot, Whitman and Renan explored by Malachuk. His endorsement of a world state also provides a counterpoint to Kant's views on the subject. Kant rejected the idea of a world republic or of a world monarchy in favour of a 'federation of free states'. His fear would seem to have been that any sort of global state would lead to despotism because of absolute rule being in the hands of so few. He also perceived a global system as necessarily imposing a monolithic identity on all, thereby crushing the invigorating differences between peoples that he thought so important. In contrast, Wells provides a different account of the world state, one which presents it not as petrifyingly 'perfect and static' but instead as 'imperfect and dynamic'. Whilst acknowledging the unequal perfectibility of humans, the world state – as outlined by Partington – is to contribute to establishing basic equal rights among humans.

Whereas Malachuk explores certain nineteenth-century thinkers' negotiation of the intersection between national and cosmopolitical belongingness, and Partington explores Wells' replacement of national frontiers by the limitless world state, Lasse Thomassen continues with the topic of boundaries in his consideration of displaced persons. Drawing on the films of Theo Angelopoulos and the writings of Derrida, he explores the urgently contemporary topic of the *xenitis* (someone who is a stranger everywhere). In a world characterised by massive migratory movements and almost 20 million refugees, asylum seekers and displaced persons, Thomassen provides us with a timely analysis of those who are constitutionally heterogeneous. Moving beyond a politics of assimilation, he opts for a more radical form of politics, a cosmo*politics*, which not only renders visible the contingency and historical processes sealed up within the apparently delimited community or nation-state, but also puts into question the very site of the divide between those who belong and those who do not – that is, the opposition between an inside and an outside. Thomassen leaves us with the challenge of rethinking the home in a way that is neither nostalgic nor incompatible with the idea of a journey.

Part IV returns us to Kant. Both Howard Caygill and Diane Morgan examine the implications of his sustained attempts, from the early writings through to the late works, to think the human within 'the entire span of nature' wherein 'all is tied together' and 'all members [are] related to one another'. Caygill demonstrates how Kant's conception of the cosmos (as plural, dynamic, expanding and contracting) is intertwined with his understanding of human physiology. Consequently, rather than the 'starry heavens' representing a beautiful certainty which confirms the centrality of the self-righteous human, it becomes clear that Kant's notion of humans and their place in the universe is indissociably bound with cosmic matter(s) whose sublime beginnings and ends remain elusive and challenging. A possible cosmopolitical conclusion to be drawn from Kant's enquiries is that it is incumbent on humans to think about the world in ways which are non-anthropocentrically conceived and which recognise that life is universally interactive.

The principle of 'interactive global growth' also informs Morgan's reading of Kant via Goethe. For Goethe, Kant was a source of inspiration for thinking the world as a dynamic whole, as an evolutive cosmopolitical entity, to which humans belong as more than just parts. Reading Kant together with Goethe brings into focus their joint insistence on life as creative potential and as ecological responsibility. This combined focus provides a fitting conclusion to our exploration in this volume of cosmopolitics as the emergence of the future.

Notes on Contributors

Gary Banham is Reader in Transcendental Philosophy at Manchester Metropolitan University. He is the author of *Kant's Transcendental Imagination* (2006), *Kant's Practical Philosophy: From Critique to Doctrine* (2003) and *Kant and the Ends of Aesthetics* (2000). He edited *Husserl and the Logic of Experience* (2005) and co-edited *Evil Spirits: Nihilism and the Fate of Modernity* (2000). He is also the general editor of Palgrave Macmillan's 'Renewing Philosophy' series.

Howard Caygill is Professor of Cultural History at Goldsmiths College, University of London. He is the author of *The Art of Judgement* (1989), *A Kant Dictionary* (1995), *Walter Benjamin: The Colour of Experience* (1998) and *Levinas and the Political* (2002).

Yves Citton is currently Professor in French Literature at the University of Grenoble, having previously taught for twelve years at the University of Pittsburgh. He has published numerous articles on eighteenth-century authors such as Rousseau, Diderot, Potocki, Chénier and Charrière, on literary and political theory, and on the history of economic thought. He is a member of the editorial board of the journal *Multitudes*. His most recent books are *L'Envers de la liberté: L'invention d'un imaginaire spinoziste dans la France des Lumières* (2006) and *Portrait de l'économiste en physiocrate: Critique littéraire de l'économie politique* (2001).

Meredith Evans is Assistant Professor of English at Concordia University. Her current research focuses on literary representations of political community in early modern England.

Paula Keating is currently writing her doctorate on Kant and politics at the School of Philosophy, University of New South Wales, Sydney, Australia. She holds honours degrees in both arts and law from the Australian National University, Canberra. She is the author of the article 'The Conditioning of the Unconditioned: Kant and Derrida' (*Borderlines*, 2004).

Daniel S. Malachuk is a Visiting Professor in the Literature Departure at The American University and has taught political theory at Georgetown and George Washington universities. He is the author of *Perfection, The State and Victorian Literature* (2005) and several articles on nineteenth-century

British and American literature and philosophy. He is currently completing a book project entitled *A Higher Law: American Transcendentalism in the Human Rights Era.*

Jill Marsden is Senior Lecturer in Philosophy at the University of Bolton. Her main area of research is contemporary European philosophy and literature. She is the author of *After Nietzsche: Notes Towards a Philosophy of Ecstasy* (2002).

Diane Morgan is Lecturer in Cultural Studies in the School of Fine Art, History of Art and Cultural Studies at the University of Leeds. She is the author of *Kant Trouble: Obscurities of the Enlightened* (2000) and co-editor (with Keith Ansell Pearson) of *Nihilism Now! Monsters of Energy* (2000). She is currently working on a book entitled *Cosmopolitics and the Future of Humanism.*

John S. Partington is the editor of *The Wellsian*, the journal of the H. G. Wells Society. He is the author of *Building Cosmopolis: The Political Thought of H. G. Wells* (2003) and has edited *The Wellsian: Selected Essays on H. G. Wells* (2003) and (with Patrick Parrinder) *The Reception of H. G. Wells in Europe* (2005). He has also written the notes for two Wells novels for Penguin Classics, *The New Machiavelli* and *The Shape of Things to Come* (both 2005). He works as a bookseller.

David Rose is Lecturer in Philosophy at the Centre for Research in Knowledge, Science and Society at Newcastle University. He has published articles on Sartre and Vattimo and he is currently concerned with the issues of political legitimacy, justification and whether hermeneutics can be normative.

Lasse Thomassen is Junior Lecturer in Politics in the Department of Politics and Public Administration, University of Limerick. He is the editor of *The Derrida–Habermas Reader* (2006) and (with Lars Tønder) *Radical Democracy: Politics between Abundance and Lack* (2005). He is currently working on a research monograph on *Deconstructing Habermas.*

Introduction: Cosmopolitics and Modernity

Gary Banham

The suggestion of this volume is that the thought of 'cosmopolitics' is connected to an understanding of temporality. However, for this connection to be assessed it is first necessary to think of how cosmopolitics emerges from a past that we can generally summarize under the heading of 'modernity', as it will be indicated here that it is precisely because modernity is past that the notion of cosmopolitics arises for discussion.

In general terms, modernity could be said to have opened with the twin assumptions that politics is based on sovereignty and that the understanding of cosmology is in terms of a unified system of natural law that brings the various elements of the universe together into a mechanistic whole. Sovereignty is the capacity to organise and orchestrate power.[1] The way in which these two elements can in fact be regarded as integrally linked is easily seen in the work of Thomas Hobbes. Although Hobbes is best known today as a political philosopher whose work presents a case for thinking of sovereignty as absolute and undivided, he presented this view of the social contract through the prism of a conception of physics. Hobbes was clear that all physics could be summarized in the conception of 'matter in motion', a conception that tied him to viewing the cosmos as a set of interlinked natural laws that produce a deterministic and materialistic view of both matter and its laws.[2] The fact that this conception of the universe could be allied with the normative justification of absolute sovereignty is what permits Hobbes to be regarded as the 'founder of modernity'.[3]

Seeing modernity in this way allows for clarity concerning the relationship between cosmology and politics. Modernity in a more general sense can be said to be the era in which politics is viewed, in international terms, as no more than a 'state of nature' between states. The relation between states, that is, is one that is not governed by law.[4] In contrast to an international order divided between contending polities there is the steady growth of a scientific community which elaborates procedures permitting consensus and universal communicability. The conception of 'science' itself is formed as a prime product of modernity, and the nature of its formation has naturally been a source of great dispute among historians of modernity.[5] But what it seems to involve, as a minimum, is a conception of investigation that permits and even requires procedures of investigation that are capable of repetition and comprehension by all who are suitably educated and trained. This has even provoked some to think of the model of 'communication' thus taken to underlie science as a basis for a universal political solution.[6]

This is not to suggest that the dissymmetry between science and politics, the vision of political strife and cosmic unity, was acceptable throughout the period of classical modernity. Quite the contrary: there were constant attempts to overcome this bifurcation. Leibniz's notion of a 'universal jurisprudence' is one of the most complex of these attempts but was largely conceived of as an attempt to reunite Christendom rather than overcome the divide between emergent nations.[7] Kant's description of 'perpetual peace' has had greater influence on conceptions of international order and has been held to provide a model for the assessment of non-national political entities since the time of Woodrow Wilson.[8]

If the general pattern of modernity can, however, be formulated in terms of a unified natural order connected to a mechanistic conception of a social contract, then what would be meant by describing this period as now past? The challenges to the unified conception of natural order as propagated in the Galilean–Newtonian pictures of nature and science were formulated decisively over a century ago through the elaboration of new notions of time and space in the theory of relativity, and subsequently – and even more dramatically – in quantum mechanics. These systems of mapping time and space have been connected to extraordinary speculations in terms of many possible dimensions of temporality. With such potential proliferation of temporal axes the method of unification of both science and the 'nature' it allegedly accounts for has been thrown into a consistent situation of crisis that could be said to be indicative of the formation of a permanent state of non-'normal' science.[9]

If the situation of cosmology has been thus re-drawn, how could this be related to the question of the understanding of 'politics'? To address this, it is first necessary to mention another aspect of 'politics' different from that we have set out. Although the conventional pattern of political thought can be captured in terms of the centrality of sovereignty in political theory and the emphasis on the nation-state in political affairs, there has been a persistent tension between this model and the push to expand the boundaries of the political since these boundaries were drawn. One signal site of such problems with the boundary of politics has been the shift towards seeing the position of women both as a problem for the site of the political and as requiring a reconfiguration of many of its central concepts. One boundary that has often been thus questioned has been the one between what is 'personal' and what is 'political', a divide connected to, if also slightly distinct from, the one between ethics and politics.

Whilst the emergence of women as political agents has been a much-remarked element of a move beyond the political model of modernity, the general question of the space of the political has been less noted as something that has been not only progressively broadened but also insistently reshaped. Just as the emergence of women as political actors and subjects has created new tensions and strains in the arena of the political, so the cosmological has also intruded itself in certain direct ways on the human arena, pushing with it certain questions about the humanistic conception of the political. If the relationship between humanity and the environment is one obvious and burgeoning problem, the problem of the relationship between the human and its 'others' has come to place the very question of what it is to be human in the context of a question of whether there is any future for the human.[10]

The reshaping of humanity by technology and by the radical alteration of 'natural' conditions is what gives a new context to the question of how 'politics' could be thought today. If we connect this radical shift in the understanding of the political to that in the conception of nature charted by the advance of the new paradigms opened by and since Einstein, we arrive at the juncture that the editors of this volume think of as 'cosmopolitics'. Cosmopolitics would thus be the attempt to think the political in relation to the cosmos in a situation in which both politics and the cosmos have become plural rather than singular unified entities. This radical perspectival shift is what was promised in the Nietzschean thought of the 'will to power', and hence if cosmopolitics is concerned with the emergence of a future, as the title of this volume suggests, then the future in question will be one in which the will to power refigures the project of 'perpetual peace' perhaps to promote, perhaps to hinder, the emergence of a 'greater violence' (with the 'perhaps' here indicating a divergence that runs through this volume) than the upholders of a 'project of modernity' would wish to see.

Notes

1. See Thomas Hobbes' definition of sovereignty (1651, part II, chapter xvii, paragraph 13).
2. The very beginning of *Leviathan* already emphasises this, with Hobbes writing there of life as 'but a motion of limbs' and drawing an immediate parallel between the body and the state: 'For what is the *heart*, but a *spring*; and the *nerves*, but so many *strings*; and the *joints*, but so many *wheels*, giving motion to the whole body, such as was intended by the artificer? *Art* goes yet further, imitating that rational and most excellent work of nature, *man*. For by art is created that great LEVIATHAN, called a COMMONWEALTH, or STATE (in Latin CIVITAS), which is but an artificial man, though of greater stature and strength than the natural, for whose protection and defence it was intended; and in which the *sovereignty* is an artificial soul, as giving life and motion to the whole body' (1651, Introduction, paragraph 1). This extended comparison subsequently guides the first book of *Leviathan*, where Hobbes provides a naturalistic account of human motivation which is the basis of his description of politics and in which the types and varieties of mechanical motion are the foundation of all else.
3. For the general argument to this effect that is broadly being indicated here see Strauss (1952). Strauss' presentation of this conception of Hobbes is controversial but has recently been supported by Edwin Curley in his introduction to the edition of the *Leviathan* cited above. Part of what makes the Straussian interpretation controversial is its alignment of Hobbes with 'liberalism', an alignment that questions part of Carl Schmitt's conception of sovereignty. For the latter see Schmitt (1922), and for an influential philosophical description of the way in which concentration on politics is based on the conception of sovereignty that Schmitt has utilised see Agamben (1995).
4. Habermas (1997) presents a basic case for the view that classical political theory of international right is based on the acceptance of a state of war between states which is, he believes, incompletely superseded by the conception of cosmopolitan right.
5. The principal problems here concern the relationship between natural philosophy, 'science', experimental methods and the status of laws. For an overview of some of the central philosophical questions here and how they engaged the philosophers of the early modern period see Buchdahl (1969).
6. The relation of communication to politics is filtered through a conception of 'science' in a fundamental way by Marxists and under their influence has shaped conceptions of the Enlightenment. For an illustration of how widely diverse conceptions of the latter were and are see James Schmidt (1996). The model of universal communicability as a basis for political thought is associated with the work of Habermas (1984, 1986). The relationship between 'discourse ethics' and politics is a complex one which would require much articulation.
7. For a particularly intriguing discussion of Leibniz's jurisprudence see Caygill (1989).
8. The most striking appropriation of Kantian thought in the realm of international relations theory has been that by Doyle (1993). For a different account see Covell (1998).

---

9. Thomas Kuhn (1962) is the *locus modernus* of the notion of 'normal' science, but he formulates it precisely through the discussion of periods of rupture. The question that we are suggesting here is that this 'rupture' perhaps requires a new theorizing given that the model of unitary science may well no longer be plausible.

10. For a seminal discussion of the human as prosthetic, a discussion that calls into question the understanding of human 'mastery' by means of technology see Steigler (1994).

References

Agamben, G. (1995) *Homo Sacer: Sovereign Power and Bare Life*, 1998, trans. D. Heller-Roazen, Stanford: Stanford University Press.

Buchdahl, G. (1969) *Metaphysics and the Philosophy of Science*, Oxford: Basil Blackwell.

Caygill, H. (1989) *Art of Judgement*, Oxford: Basil Blackwell, pp. 110–27.

Covell, C. (1998) *Kant and the Law of Peace: A Study in the Philosophy of International Law and International Relations*, Palgrave: London and New York.

Doyle, M. W. (1993) 'Liberalism and International Relations' in R. Beiner and W. J. Booth (eds) (1993), *Kant & Political Philosophy: The Contemporary Legacy*, New Haven and London: Yale University Press.

Habermas, J. (1997) 'Kant's Idea of Perpetual Peace, with the Benefit of Two Hundred Years' Hindsight' in J. Bohman and M. Lutz-Bachmann (eds), *Perpetual Peace: Essays on Kant's Cosmopolitan Ideal*, Cambridge, MA and London: The MIT Press.

Habermas, J. (1984) *The Theory of Communicative Action Volume 1: Reason and the Rationalisation of Society* (1986, trans. T. McCarthy, Boston: Beacon Press.

Habermas, J. (1989) *The Theory of Communicative Action Volume II: Lifeworld and System: The Critique of Functionalist Reason*, 1987, trans. T. McCarthy, Boston: Beacon Press.

Hobbes, T. (1651) *Leviathan or the Matter, Form, and Power of a Commonwealth, Ecclesiastical and Civil*, 1994, ed. E. Curley, Indianapolis and Cambridge: Hackett.

Kuhn, T. (1962) *The Structure of Scientific Revolutions*, Chicago and London: University of Chicago Press.

Schmidt, J. (ed.) (1996) *What Is Enlightenment? Eighteenth-Century Answers and Twentieth-Century Questions*, Berkeley, CA and London: University of California Press.

Schmitt, C. (1922), *Political Theology: Four Chapters on the Concept of Sovereignty*, 1985, trans. G. Schwab, Cambridge, MA: MIT Press.

Steigler, B. (1994) *Technics and Time, 1: The Fault of Epimetheus*, 1998, trans. R. Beardsworth and G. Collins, Stanford: Stanford University Press.

Strauss, L. (1952) *The Political Philosophy of Hobbes*, Chicago, IL and London: University of Chicago Press.

Introduction: Parts and Wholes – Kant, Communications, Communities and Cosmopolitics

Diane Morgan

In his 1770 *Considerations on the Government of Poland*, Rousseau exclaimed:

> Whatever one says to the contrary, today there are no more Frenchmen, Germans, Spaniards or even Englishmen; there are only Europeans. Everyone has the same tastes and the same habits. (Rousseau 1990, 171)

The prospect evoked by Rousseau of a European identity superseding national differences probably seems remote to us today in the wake of the repeated rejection of the European Constitution (2005). Of course, to place the quotation in its context, Rousseau is himself not speaking in favour of an eventual European project: indeed, according to the sentiments expressed in this text, it seems he also would have voted 'no' in the referendum. The motivation for his essay is the wish to *affirm* the importance of specific national and cultural identities *against* what he sees as a dangerously formless abstraction. Rousseau regards 'Europe' as leading to a generalised state of decadent mediocrity. Uncannily echoing contemporary debates, he presents 'Europe' as smothering its inhabitants' individuality with its all-encompassing uniformity; for him it lacks the animation which properly pertains to a particular, robust and resonating 'national form'. He considers that the prevailing deregulated, liberalised Europe has spawned an all-pervasive lusting after the same materialist 'values'. Instead of being the site of shared, traditional, cultural activities, the marketplace is dominated by a reifying consumerism. Love of luxury, unscrupulous greed and the cultivation of hypocrisy undo any deeply felt loyalties and affinities between people, and, as a consequence, generalised prostitution reigns supreme.

1

Drawing his bleak conclusion about the nature of these new Europeans, Rousseau writes:

> What does it matter which master they obey, which state's laws they abide by? As long as they find money to steal and women to corrupt, they are everywhere at home [*ils sont partout dans leur pays*]. (Rousseau 1990, 171)

According to Rousseau, the new Europeans' mobile cosmopolitanism is a hollow, unprincipled lack of commitment to anything in particular – either to culture, to a homeland, to a people, or to a community – hence his willingness in this text to turn his sympathetic attention to a potentially re-emerging nation which might just succeed in resisting the debilitating trend. The Poles, who were at the time engaged in a life-and-death struggle with their rapacious imperial neighbours, provide him with a counter-example to the enfeebled and base humans of modern Europe.[1]

In his earlier essay on l'Abbé de Saint Pierre's *Project of Perpetual Peace* (1761), Rousseau, despite greatly appreciating the Abbé's worthiness and admiring his bold idealism, again wonders whether a European federative league is actually a desirable goal. He concludes:

> There is no prospect of federative leagues being established otherwise than by revolutions, and on this assumption which of us would venture to say whether this European league is more to be desired or feared? It might perhaps do more harm all of a sudden than it could prevent for centuries. (Rousseau 1927, 131)

Rousseau regards the idea of 'perpetual peace' at once as 'an absurd dream' – l'Abbé Pierre reveals himself to be somewhat childish in his belief that rulers might come to see that it is best to serve the public interest rather than foster private gains – and as a 'reasonable project' to be admired (1927, 129). However, for him such a pacific state of affairs can be brought about only by fearfully violent means, which leads him to conclude that it is perhaps for the best that the place, a confederated 'Europe', where perpetual peace would reign actually does not exist (131).

Kant, despite being an avid reader of Rousseau, gives a different focus to his considerations of perpetual peace and a different view of cosmopolitics. He is interested in a system wherein the 'violation of rights in one part of the world is felt everywhere', that is to say, wherein the *parts* – whether they be individuals, communities, nations or continents – communicate with and through a greater *whole* (1991, 107–8). Unlike Rousseau and l'Abbé Pierre, Kant sees that the project of perpetual peace cannot be limited to an international agreement between European states.[2] Such a eurocentric focus is too partial. The rapid development of long-distance trade and communications technology necessarily means that the scale of the project has to be at least global. As such, the utopia in question for Kant is no clearly demarcated space, tightly contained within recognised borders, such as the Corsican, Swiss and Polish models celebrated by Rousseau. On the contrary, Kant's utopian world of 'perpetual peace' is open, multiperspectival and dynamic.

The use of the terms 'openness', 'multiperspectivism' and 'dynamism' may give the impression that Kant has an unreservedly optimistic view of what the future might hold. This is far from being the case. The project of perpetual peace is presented by him with great ambivalence: it is both eminently desirable as the only way forward for humankind and yet also highly preposterous, profoundly unrealistic in its aims; therefore entertaining such fancies continually runs the risk of becoming a complete waste of time. Sometimes perpetual peace presents itself as an attainable goal towards which humanity is ineluctably progressing. Sometimes, however, it fades like a mirage, leaving one stranded and cynically musing on how, after all, the only place where humans are destined to find permanent peace in this world is the grave (Kant 1991, 93). This structural ambivalence, the volatility intrinsic to the very idea of perpetual peace, is produced by the faulty nature of human beings themselves. In 'Idea for a Universal History with a Cosmopolitan Purpose' (1784), Kant had already identified the source of the human flaw when he wrote that 'humans neither pursue their aims purely by instinct, as the animals do, nor act in accordance with any integral, prearranged plan like rational cosmopolitans' (1991, 41–2). It would thus seem that the world of humans is doomed to remain chaotic if the very building-blocks of any constructive project, humans themselves, are, by their very nature, resistant to any systematic organisation and impervious to schemes designed to improve them. Neither wholly determined by instincts like animals, nor ruled by reason like rational cosmopolitans (who would be the ideal citizens of a utopian state), humans unpredictably fluctuate in their behaviour, sometimes complying with civic regulations, sometimes selfishly opting out of any social contract altogether. The manifest nature of human beings would have to be transformed for a global community to take shape and to be maintained.

Like so many utopian schemes, the project of combining humans together into a world community is dependent on the extent to which human nature is regarded as capable of evolution or as needing change. Either utopias are seen to fail because human nature is deemed to be recalcitrantly set in its ways or, alternatively, utopias themselves are regarded as constitutionally flawed because they require a certain type, or certain types, of human for their fragile structures to perdure. It is evidently for this reason that many supposed utopias turn out in fact to be totalitarian dystopias wherein humans are coerced into abiding by fixed, socially useful patterns of behaviour by means of various disciplining devices. The 'brave new world' is thereby unmasked as a repressive society, often run by an elite who ruthlessly employ propaganda, the secret police, drugs and, in more modern times, genetic engineering to enforce the law on otherwise rebellious subjects. Kant himself has been accused of being complicit with such a regime.[3] The Prussian academic has been portrayed as restraining and restricting the human within coldly calculated faculties which prefigure the repression of a fascistic *Gleichschaltung*.

However, Kant can be seen as having a different conception of human nature from those pessimists who see humans as possessing predetermined characteristics which thwart all evolution. He can also be distanced from those ideologues who try to stifle all human potential for growth so as to enforce their regimented worldview.[4] While exploring the specificity of humans by *negative* instruction, by drawing up guidelines of what not to do (i.e. by establishing which intellectual pursuits are ultimately counterproductive, a waste of energy, for humans), he leaves open any positive, determining definition of the human. Similarly, the utopian project of relating *parts* (e.g. human individuals) together into and through a greater *whole* (e.g. humanity within an open global community) is conceived as the birthplace, the 'womb [*Schoss*] within which all the original capacities of the human race may develop' (Kant 1991, 51). Just as any tentative regularity one might be able to trace in human affairs is detectable only at the level of the species, and not to be generated among individuals, here too it is the human species itself, and not necessarily individuals, which can develop its hitherto unconceived and unconceivable potential once a 'universal cosmopolitan existence' is eventually adopted. Specific human individuals do not have to be converted, pacifically or coercively, to the utopian cause; they can remain devilish in their inclinations if they so desire (Kant 1991, 112).

Another important aspect of Kant's notion of cosmopolitics is that the *whole* (the open global community) to which humans as *parts* are to belong and to contribute is *not* conceived as a self-centred emanation outwards.[5] That is to say, the part (the individual and his/her immediate relations) does not relate to the wider world as if through a series of concentric circles.[6] Hence, the inter-communication of the *part* and the *whole* is no linear relation, no gradual consolidation of knowledge originally centred on or located in the individual and his/her intimates. In contrast to the belief of Kant's favourite poet, Alexander Pope, the participation and commitment of the world-aware human does not 'rise from individual to the whole' (Pope 1963, 546: IV, l. 362). Indeed Pope's ambitious analysis, in 'An Essay on Man', of the place of the human within an open – plural and evolving – cosmic system, although often quoted with apparent approval in *Universal Natural History and the Theory of the Heavens*, differs in important ways from Kant's own views.

One example of their divergent views is apparent in the following lines from 'An Essay on Man':

God loves from Whole to Parts: but human soul
Must rise from Individual to the Whole.
Self-love but serves the virtuous mind to wake,
As the small pebble stirs the peaceful lake;
The centred mov'd, a circle strait succeeds,
Another still, and still another spreads,
Friend, parent, neighbour, first it will embrace,
His country next, and next all human race,
Wide and even more wide, th'o'erflowerings of the mind
Take ev'ry creature in, of ev'ry kind (Pope 1963, 546–7: IV, ll. 361–70).

Pope describes how an affective radiation out from the centred self towards 'friend, parent, neighbour' should be followed by the more mental embracing of fellow countrymen and, yet further still, of humanity at large. Once the 'close and natural ties' of the 'family' (the biological family and its neighbourhood, the nation as extended family, and then the family of humankind have been embraced), the human can generously include 'ev'ry creature . . . of ev'ry kind' in his embrace. Hence this conception of the cosmopolitical whole is not only originally self-centred, but also anthropocentric. Despite often reminding humans of the relativity and partiality of their view of the world, by evoking, for instance, the point of view of a 'superior being' to whom the intelligence of a Newton would appear ape-like,[7] Pope's basic message is one purporting to be a consolidation of our notion of ourselves: 'The proper study of mankind is man,' he states (1963, 516: II, l. 2). Like Kant's crit-ical project, his essay insists on the limits of human knowledge, but his aim is, unlike Kant's, an ethico-theological one: he wants to expose the vanity of presuming to pass judgement on what we cannot know so as to 'vindicate the ways of God to Man' and, concomitantly, prove that 'whatever is, is right' (Pope 1963, 504, 540: I, l. 16, IV, l. 145). Kant, in contrast, does not want humans to be content with their lot and with the ways of the world. A passive acceptance of the status quo as the assuredly wise product of an omnipotent divine being would be akin to leading the peaceful pastoral existence of a golden age (Kant 1991, 45). It would leave unfulfilled the vocation of the human to be substantially self-constructing. The inter-communicating world of 'perpetual peace' is therefore not the originary, quasi-mythical state of nature towards which a Rousseau would have us turn (Kant 1991, 98). Kant's utopia is instead a cultural, artificial construction dependent on constant and careful mediation, given shape by the vigilant conversion process of the categorical imperative: 'So act that the maxim of your will could always hold at the same time as a principle establishing universal law' (Kant 1956, 30).

Also, in contrast to Pope's depiction of the cosmopolitical whole and the human's relation to it, Kant's is not predicated on concentric circles originally situated in the self. It is true that the way we understand the world around us, as our understanding is discursive not intuitive, 'must advance' doggedly from parts, amassing and subsuming them into a whole (Kant 1988, 63 §77). However, the utopian idea of perpetual peace is an emergent whole, a whole which is greater than the sum of its parts. As a consequence it *cannot* be understood as such, but then *it does not have to be*: we are to regulate our actions in relation to it as project(ion). This task is also supremely difficult for humans and it involves a stretching and straining of the self in relation to 'all rational beings'.[8] Indeed, the moral law is not to be generated from among us humans. It is not to be the product of a consensual agreement between human beings; it does not permit a comfortable accommodation with human foibles and weaknesses. In *Groundwork of the Metaphysics of Morals*, Kant therefore writes:

> it is not enough to demonstrate freedom from certain alleged experi-ences of human nature (though to do this is in any case absolutely impossible and freedom can be demonstrated only a priori): we must prove that it belongs universally to the activity of rational beings endowed with a will. (Kant 1963, 115)

The moral law stretches the human by appealing to his will, encouraging him to muster more than human strength. It applies to us (but not to us exclusively), directs us to act imperatively, 'although every propensity, inclination and natural bent were opposed to it' (Kant 1963, 93). The moral law acts in this demanding way upon us humans as it necessarily structurally encompasses the possibility of other, maybe more rational, creatures, less driven by sensuality, elsewhere in the universe. This appeal to other intelligent life possibly to be found on other planets is one which features throughout Kant's writings. It necessitates a putting into question of what it is to be human in relation to what could be a radically different life-form. It signals a break with earth-bound, strictly geocentric concerns. It also concatenates Kant's thoughts on cosmopolitics with his cosmological writings.[9] In stark contrast to Pope's generation of cosmopolitics from a homely, human base, Kant's analysis decentres the human, obliging him to conceive of himself in relation to a complex inter-splicing of different versions of the world. This obligation structurally to take into account multiperspectival approaches to an undelimited world, wherein each point of view cannot be known in itself, is alimented by technology. Indeed, technology plays a central role in Kant's cosmopolitical utopia: it is a constitutive part of the production of the human, with and against the grain of nature.

For instance, in *Answer to the Question: What Is Enlightenment* (1784), the technology of the printing press, the postal service and long-distance travel (or, to use a contemporary example, the interactivity of the Internet) all help to construct the public sphere of the 'world of scholars' wherein the 'private self', otherwise a 'mere cog in a machine' obediently carrying out orders in the workplace, is converted into a different sort of animal. By assessing and contributing to the cosmopolitan world of global information and ideas, the 'public' self can express itself and act more freely, by exploring the extension of the (personal and inter-subjective) self through telecommunications (Kant 1991, 56).

In *Idea of a Universal History* (1784), Kant openly admits that the world is often a 'hell of evils' (Kant 1991, 48). Crucial to maintaining the notion of a future-oriented cosmopolitics against such blatantly stacked odds is the cosmological vantage point. This is also informed – given form – by technological practices. One of the means, which becomes *an extension of ourselves as project* – a project which is *also* the fulfilment of our potential, of our 'original capacities' – is the telescope (Kant 1991, 51). Repeatedly Kant refers to the 'different angle', the 'large scale', the 'great world drama' in connection with seeing ourselves as terrestrials (Kant 1991, 41, 42, 53). Astronomical observations, made possible by telescopes, address the question of the formation of the cosmos, the nature and composition of the universe and the earth's place within it, and the possibility of extraterrestrial life and how it might differ from ours. These enquiries give us the perspectives requisite for thinking a *global* identity and *global* politics. Technology permits us to trace indications of how and when the universe was formed. It also enables us to assume a theoretical – or even, in more recent times, an actual physical – position in outer space which renders the conception of the planet *as a whole* possible. The information gleaned from such observations serves as an index for Kant of 'purposeful natural processes' which can bolster our faith in a development of human nature towards a general, shared interest 'in maintaining the whole' (Kant 1991, 50–1). A Kepler who 'found an unexpected means of reducing the eccentric orbits of the planets to definite laws' and a Newton 'who explained these laws in terms of a universal natural cause' are tool-using tools that enable us to create 'guiding principles' through which to conceive a 'universal history' that implicates us in the future, and past, of our planet and its denizens (Kant 1991, 42). Observation and exploration of the 'starry heavens' become an integral part of our definition of ourselves *and* of our responsibilities.

The microscope complements the telescope's opening-up of ever-larger 'worlds beyond worlds' (Kant 1956, 166)[10] with its revelation of the ever smaller. The technologically mediated realisation that, to cite *The Critique of Judgment*, there is 'nothing so small which in comparison with some still smaller standard may not for our imagination be enlarged to the greatness of a world' (Kant 1988, 97 §25) provokes a disorienting decentring of the human through which the 'feeling of a supersensible faculty within us', our autonomy – our freedom and its responsibilities – is concomitantly 'awakened'. We rely on technology to supplement the fallibilities of our senses so as to see and explore ever further, but technology also demonstrates the relativity and constructedness of our limited, particular world, of our *Umwelt*. However, it thereby triggers off a reaction in us, sparking a rethinking of ourselves, a reinscription of ourselves within the 'entire span of nature [*in dem ganzen Umfang der Natur*]' (Kant 1981, 194). This confrontation with the dynamic world of magnitudes opened out by technology wrenches us out of the world of anthropomorphised nature. No longer is the natural world conceived of as just serving our purposes.[11]

There are other important perspectives which Kant explores in relation to his cosmopolitical project. I can merely allude to them here.[12] There is the technology which permits us to see the earth as a limited, spherical surface (i.e. cartography, the construction of ships and aircraft). It is this view of the globe as made up of vast, alternating expanses of land and sea which gives force to the law of hospitality. Bearing this view in mind one can see that no one has a primordial right of possession to patches of the earth's surface. The frontiers of nation-states are visibly not anchored in natural – physico-geographical – law (Kant 1991, 106ff). Finally, there is the technologically informed perspective, not of the earth's surface this time, but of the planet's depths. The technologies of the earth sciences plunge below the earth's crust and their discoveries led Kant to dismiss attempts to read natural disasters as divine signs intended for humans. Instead of contorting himself (as others did) to reconcile the 1755 Lisbon earthquake with a presupposed providential harmony, Kant insists that earthquakes happen in supreme indifference to human affairs. The consequence of this relinquishment of the human need for signification and this appreciation of our insignificance as mortals should, Kant suggests, be to activate 'our love of humanity'; it should be to stimulate our sense of needing one another for survival and of belonging together as a community (Kant 1912b, 471).

To conclude, Kant encourages a multiperspectival view of the world, of our place within it and of the nature of the 'our', of human commonality, of human nature, through his analyses of extraterrestrial life, of the earth as a spherical surface, of our life as terrestrial denizens and of the earth as a fiery ball surrounded by a thin crust. This generation of radically different and irreconcilable viewpoints, viewpoints which cannot be fused together to form one overall picture, is part of his cosmopolitical project. We are to feel part of, and act responsibly within, an expanding, evolving whole which we cannot fully conceive of, let alone dominate. It is this cosmopolitical vision that this collection of essays tries to respond to, and make sense of, in terms of the actual present and of the emerging future.

Notes

1. Unfortunately the Poles' valiant resistance proved to be futile when Poland itself was soon afterwards wiped from the map until its eventual restitution after the Second World War.
2. Despite in effect rejecting a limitation of his project to European nations, he does, nevertheless, conceive of his new world order as a voluntary confederation of sovereign states. For Kant a world republic or a world monarchy would represent 'soulless despotism' as it would signal the collapse of (free) difference into (repressive) monolithic identity (Kant 1991, 113). For a discussion of the problems that this position causes for his project for a world community, see Bohman and Lutz-Bachmann (1997, 59–77). For a more nuanced and detailed account than Kant's of the possibilities opened up by the world state, see Partington's analysis of H. G. Wells' vision in Chapter 8 in this volume.

3. See, for instance, Nietzsche (1987, 140; 1990, 134); Adorno and Horkheimer (1979); Böhme and Böhme (1985).
4. For an analysis of Kant as a keen proponent of human character as potential, see Morgan (2001).
5. This latent 'ecological' consideration by Kant of the human as part of a much wider and diverse system of living and non-living forms was obviously of major importance for Goethe. See Chapter 11 in this volume.
6. For an informative analysis of the mereological discussion between Nussbaum *et al.* and a critique of the either (part) or (whole) nature of that debate, see Chapter 7 in this volume.
7. These lines are quoted by Kant (1981, 190).
8. This reference to 'rational beings', which is constant across the precritical/critical divide in Kant's writings, has received little attention up to now. For one exception, see Crowe (1986). See also Chapter 10 in this volume and Morgan (forthcoming).
9. For an extended discussion of the nature and stakes of 'concatenation', see Chapter 5 in this volume.
10. For an extended consideration of the famous paragraph to which this phrase belongs, see Chapter 10 in this volume.
11. This refusal to tie nature down to anthropocentric 'purposiveness' was one of Kant's main attractions for Goethe; see Chapter 11 in this volume.
12. For a full exploration of the importance of technology for Kant's notion of cosmopolitics, see Morgan, 'Angelaki', Vol. 12, No. 1, April 2007.

Bibliography

Adorno, T. and Horkheimer, M. (1979) *Dialectic of Enlightenment* trans. J. Cumming, London: Verso.

Banham, G. and Malik, S. ed. (2001) *Tekhnema: Journal of Philosophy & Technology*, Issue 6, 'Teleologies – Scientific, Technical & Critical', Paris: American University of Paris.

Bohman, J. and Lutz-Bachmann, M. (1997) (eds) *Perpetual Peace: Essays on Kant's Cosmopolitan Ideal*, Cambridge, MA: MIT Press.

Böhme, H. and Böhme, G. (1985) *Das Andere der Vernunft*, Frankfurt am Main: Suhrkamp.

Crowe, M. J. (1986) *The Extraterrestrial Life Debate 1750–1900* Cambridge: Cambridge University Press.

Kant, I. (1991) *Political Writings* ed. H. Reiss, trans. H. B. Nisbet, Cambridge: Cambridge University Press.

Kant, I (1988) *Critique of Judgement* ed. J. C. Meredith, Oxford: Oxford University Press.

Kant, I. (1981) *Universal Natural History and the Theory of the Heavens* ed. and trans. S. Jaki, Edinburgh: Scottish Academic Press.

Kant, I. (1963) *Groundwork of the Metaphysics of Morals* trans. H.J. Paton, New York: Harper Torchbooks.

Kant, I. (1956) *Critique of Practical Reason* trans. L. W. Beck, New York: Macmillan.

Kant, I. (1912a) *Die Frage ob die Welt veralte, physikalisch erwogen*, in A. K. Vol. I, Berlin: Academie der Wissenschaften.

Kant, I. (1912b) *Geschichte und Naturbeschreibung der merkwürdigsten Vorfälle des Erdbebens, welches an dem Ende des 1755sten Jahres einen großen Teil der Erde erschüttert hat,* in A. K. Vol. I, Berlin: Academie der Wissenschaften.

Kant, I. (1912c) *Von den Ursachen der Erderschütterung bei Gelegenheit des Unglücks welches die westliche Länder von Europa gegen das Ende des vorigen Jahres betroffen hat,* in A. K. Vol. I, Berlin: Academie der Wissenschaften.

Kant, I. (1912d) *Untersuchung der Frage, ob die Erde in ihrer Umdrehung um die Achse, wodurch sie die Abwechselung des Tage und der Nacht hervorbringt, einige Veränderung seit den ersten Zeiten ihres Ursprungs erlitten habe und woraus man sich ihrer versichern könne,* in A. K. Vol. I, Berlin: Academie der Wissenschaften.

Morgan, D. (2007) 'Kant, Cosmopolitics, Multiperspectival Thinking and Technology', in F. Morlock (ed.), *Angelaki General Issue.* Forthcoming.

Morgan, D. 'Kant, Cosmogony and the Interplanetary Perspective', in *Cosmopolitics and the Future of Humanism.* Forthcoming.

Morgan, D. (2001) 'The Discipline of Pure Reason: Dosing the Faculties', in G. Banham and S. Malik (eds), *Tekhnema: Journal of Philosophy & Technology,* Issue 6, 'Teleologies – Scientific, Technical & Critical', Paris: American University of Paris, pp. 72–89.

Nietzsche, F. (1990) Twilight of the Idols: The Anti-Christ trans. R. J. Hollingdale, Harmondsworth: Penguin.

Nietzsche, F. (1987) Untimely Meditations trans. R. J. Hollingdale, Cambridge: Cambridge University Press.

Pope, A. (1963) *The Poems of Alexander Pope* Twickenham Edition, ed. J. Butt, London: University Paperbacks.

Rousseau, J.-J. (1927) *A Project for Perpetual Peace: Rousseau's Essay* Bilingual Bilingual Parallel Text trans. E. M. Nuttall, intro. G. L. Dickinson, London: Richard Cobden- Sanderson.

Rousseau, J.-J. (1990) *Sur l'économie politique/ Considérations sur le gouvernement de Pologne/ Projet pour la Corse,* Paris: Garnier Flammarion.

Part I
Kant and Cosmopolitics

1
Kant's Logic of Political Transformation

Paula Keating

Kant clearly believes in the necessity of political reform. But he is on the oft-repeated record as outlawing revolution. What he does offer politics are a priori ideas of reason, specifically a pure republican constitution and a perpetual peace.[1] These are active ideas, they for our use, as per Kant's practical philosophy, that he first sets out in the *Dialectic* of the first *Critique*. In the *Metaphysics of Morals* Kant calls 'a perfectly rightful constitution among human beings' the thing in itself (TL, 6:371)[2] and stipulates that the idea of a pure constitution, 'if it is attempted and carried out by gradual reform in accordance with firm principles, ... can lead to continual approximation to the highest political good, perpetual peace' (RL, 6:354). Herein lies the apparent paradox of Kant's logic of political transformation: the progress towards the better seems to take place without any achievement. How are we to apply the ideas of reason, of noumenal status, as they are if we cannot ever attain them? What conditions, and what are the conditions of, political change? What plausible foundations are there for this asymptotic progress? Understanding Kant's account of political change is problematic because it seems as if there should be a passage from the specific imperfect condition to the perfect unconditioned condition, but he explicitly denies the possibility of such a transition.

I. The passage of pure revolution

The Metaphysics of Morals presents us with two teachings: on *Recht* and on virtue. And it is this correspondence between the two parts of practical philosophy – politics and morality – that I draw on to develop an understanding of the logic of Kant's ideas on political change. While the *Rechtslehre* attempts a rare systematic approach to politics for Kant,

I turn first to the teaching of the doctrine of virtue and how moral improvement is structured.

Practical philosophy is, of course, grounded in the idea of freedom. Kant explains that *Recht*, because its focus is the togetherness of humans, deals with external freedom, while virtue is concerned with the inner freedom of the individuals and their dutiful actions. The realm of inner freedom is where personal maxims are determined by the idea of duty itself. Thus, in the doctrine of virtue, Kant provides 'the duty to the self' as the 'duty of one's own perfection' in a practical sense, which means a duty to work on one's own moral perfection (TL, 6:387). These moral imperatives command one to 'be holy' and to 'be perfect' (TL, 6:446). But since human beings are 'frail', the duty is qualified to be one of enterprise: to 'strive for this perfection, but not to reach it'. Hence the determination of compliance with this duty can consist only in practical work, of a striving for it, which in turn represents a continual moral progress (TL, 6:446). In all of Kant's works there is repeated and emphasised reference to the human as a 'vernünftiges *Naturwesen*', a rational, natural being (see for example 6:379); this phrase serves to remind us always that it is only being in its ontological sense that can be totally rational, perfectly moral. The representation of the morally perfect in the duty to 'be holy' actually works in the same regulative way as practical principles. It is, asymptotically, in the seeking that the progress to the condition is achieved.

To help us further understand this method of attaining virtue by following the commands to be divine we can turn to a passage in *Religion within the Limits of Mere Reason*. For the rational natural being, Kant distinguishes two concepts. On the one hand, there is virtue in its 'empirical character', phenomenal virtue, which is 'acquired *bit by bit*, ... through the gradual reform of conduct ... But not the slightest *change of heart* is necessary for this; only a change of *ethics*' (Religion, 6:47). And we assume ethics here to represent the behavioural guidelines that are born of acting in accordance with maxims made in conformity with the moral law. On the other hand, the 'intelligible character' of virtue, that is noumenal virtue, where one is 'in need of no other incentive to recognize a duty except the representation of duty itself' (6:47), is acquired differently. This kind of virtue 'cannot be effected through gradual reform but must rather be effected through a revolution in the disposition of the human being'. Kant names such a transformation a 'kind of rebirth', a 'new creation' and a 'change of heart', which is achieved through a single unalterable decision to become moral (6:47). However, according to Kant, the noumenally virtuous person does not arrive at a final perfection but rather incessantly labours and becomes in an endless progress that is a unity, a condition that he equates with being a good person (6:48).

This presents an unproblematic relation between the phenomenal and the noumenal characters of virtue; they are distinguished from one another in terms of their different styles of effecting transformation. One the one hand, phenomenal virtue is achieved and mediated by behavioural ethics, while, on the other hand, progress to noumenal virtue is effected immediately. What is important to witness, however, is that the transition to noumenal virtue is not an end-point: the noumenally virtuous person has not reached a final state of perfection – he is still *at* work; the condition for having the noumenal character of virtue is being in the continual process – itself a condition – of its acquisition. If we compare this with the noumenal idea for politics – that is, a republican constitution where the idea of general will of the people is king – we would have to argue that to achieve noumenal political virtue a similar revolution must occur, a change of heart that sets the polity on the endless path of peaceful politics. I would call such a revolution pure because it occurs at the noumenal level: it is the decision that constitutes the change. My concern is not with a moral justification for violent empirical political revolution,[3] but rather to show that Kant believes in the cause of a moral metaphysical revolution, 'a revolution in the disposition of the human being' (Religion, 6:47), and that this is one of his grounds for political transformation.

By promoting a conception of revolution in the context of Kant's political philosophy, I am being interpretative given the absolute prohibitions on a right to revolution in the political essays. To further my interpretation I can mention the well-known fact that Kant praised the French Revolution at a time when all European governments would have been extremely concerned about the spread of subversive activities. What Kant approved was not the 'momentous deed nor crimes committed by human beings' (Conflict, 7:85), not the bloody and ugly events of the revolution, but rather its ability to express the moral spirit in humanity in general and a people in particular. This Kant called the 'mode of thinking of the spectators' and, given its universality, he denoted it as a real basis for hope in change. It is also of historical relevance to point out that Kant was censured by Friedrich Wilhelm II for contravening the anti-Enlightenment religious edict with his *Religion* text. Further, while I later contend that Kant's argument against granting a right to revolution is necessary to the potent dynamic of practical reason, I think that the sections of Kant's moral philosophy presented here permit me, by analogy, to say that perhaps the figure of revolution is not heretical to Kantian politics. Perhaps there is something like a revolution of the mind, a revolution for or towards the noumenal. Further, I would argue, the only plausible structure for such an activity is the one given by Kant's practical metaphysics. So we can advocate, with Kant, a passage to the noumenal level for politics that we cannot achieve through mere gradual reform. This presents a new context for revolution: it is a decision to follow the path of the ideas of reason, with progress measured by the diligence of the work towards them and not by their arrival.

II. Kant's political metaphysics

In the *Rechtslehre* we witness Kant's interest in creating plausible political theory. He states in the Preface to *The Metaphysics of Morals* that is an unfinished metaphysical system simply because as such it also necessarily includes its application. *Recht* is a pure concept and yet it is also based in and looks towards practice: a metaphysics of *Recht* is an infinite system.[4] Hence Kant advisedly renames the *Rechtslehre* 'the first principles of the doctrine of *Recht*' because he can give only an 'approximation' of the remainder of the system. Evidently Kant is concerned with the fundamental relation between formal purity and a specific conditioning of moral/political purity. What I am interested in is how Kant's account of politics works towards cultivating the condition of the ideal polity, how he sets up the praxis of bridging fact and idea. Thus politics signifies a state and a coming to be; it is a condition in both grammatical categories of the word condition, a noun and a verb. Kant's practical metaphysics, the *Rechtslehre* and *Perpetual Peace* in particular, is not simply about the application of the a priori ideas of reason to our imperfect world. Continual approximation of the highest political good – perpetual peace – is part of the metaphysical system itself. Thus, an ideal republican polity is at once both an ultimate state for politics and a condition necessary for achieving good politics. This is the action of Kant's practical metaphysics.

The domain of *Recht* is the social context of humanity. Reason determines that the external consequences of the will, called 'choice', should obey the law of external freedom and this is what founds politics. Thus Kant states, '*Recht* is therefore the sum of the conditions under which the choice of one can be united with the choice of another in accordance with a universal law of freedom' (RL, 6:230). The focus of *Recht* is humans in their world, the factual relations between people in a community.

A constitution based on the principle of external freedom gives us *the state in idea*, defined by Kant as 'a union of a multitude of human beings under laws of *Recht*' (RL, 6:313). This is the idea that justifies state formation and the civil condition. In disagreement with the orthodox social contract theory line, Kant believes that the state has an ethical a priori foundation, that it is not part of the necessity of history or of anthropology. A state should be republican in the sense that there is a strict division between the legislative, executive and judicial powers. The highest power of the state is the legislative authority, which must be the general united will of the people. But the united will of the people is also not an empirical concept; it too is an idea of reason (see for example RL, 6:263). Further, Kant asserts in *The Conflict of the Faculties* that the equivalency of the ruler and the ruled is the 'eternal norm' (7:90f) for politics.

The sovereign is obliged to issue just laws. As the sovereign is the outlet for the general will, we would assume that all laws are fair given that the people are not likely to issue laws that contradict what they desire. But if there is misfeasance, the people may not challenge the sovereign because this contradicts the conditions of *Recht*, a condition that cannot be suspended without fatal injury. The laws based on the supreme idea of *Recht* must be obeyed. The citizens can offer negative resistance through their ministers or through formal complaints (RL, 6:322). But there can be no right to rebel against an official abuse of authority. First, because this contradicts the rational separation of powers and strict regard for the rule of law that requires an independent judiciary (RL, 6:320), and, second, because it is conceptually 'absurd' to grant legal exceptions to the supreme authority of *Recht*, if there is an absolute posited political and legal power it is a contradiction to permit a provision for repudiation.

Kant states that change must be 'top down' (Conflict, 7:93), by which he means rightfully through the sovereign, who acts for the united will of the people. Kant prefers metamorphosis to palingenesis (RL, 6:340) as the style of gradual reform needed for empirical politics. And yet, if there is a new beginning forced by an insurrection, the new constitution and sovereign must be immediately instated as lawful as if there were no break in the condition of *Recht* (RL, 6:323). But for Kant it is essential that positive law be amenable to the step-by-step reform necessary for peaceful social relations. He writes, 'it must still be possible, if the existing constitution cannot well be reconciled with the idea of the original contract, for the sovereign to change it, so as to allow to continue in existence that form which is essentially required for a people to constitute a state' (RL, 6:340).

However, Kant specifically throws the polity a line from on high by introducing the 'spirit of the original contract' (*anima pacti originarii*) (RL, 6:340). The change that the sovereign is under a duty to create is the one most consistent with this spirit. It is this duty of the sovereign that I see as analogous to the duty in the doctrine of virtue to perfect oneself in a moral capacity, that is, to undertake what I call pure revolution. The spirit of the original contract provides the glittering if seemingly illusory path to the ideal itself. However, there is a problem for the sovereign in the empirical political arena to follow the commands of the spirit to the highest political good because for Kant the ideal republican state is without a physical manifestation of sovereignty. Sovereignty, in Kant's theory, is the a priori idea of the unified will of the people. Here is an example of the *Leitmotiv* problem of this essay: the apparent discontinuity between the contexts of the empirical and noumenal aspects of Kant's political theory.

Let me explain this with reference to the text. Kant alerts us to the complex relation between the metaphysical and empirical viewpoints when he distinguishes the idea of the head of a state, as a 'thought-entity' (*Gedankending*), from a 'physical person to represent the supreme authority in the state and to make this idea effective on the people's will' (RL, 6:338).[5] The personification of the idea of sovereignty is what we take to be the form of the state in terms of how the highest authority is configured – that is, as autocratic, aristocratic or democratic (RL, 6:339). But while the sovereign is under a duty to institute change according to the spirit of republicanism, Kant explicitly denies the sovereign the power to reform itself, that is to change, for example, from being aristocratic to democratic because 'it could still do the people a wrong, since the people itself could abhor such a constitution and find one of the other forms more to its advantage' (RL, 6:340). This then creates an exception to the 'top-down' rule for political change because the sovereign must consult the people when undergoing self-reform. And yet, such a change seems necessary if the sovereign is to meet its duty to follow the spirit of the original contract for the sake of achieving a perfect republican constitution. The confusion here around how a polity is to follow the spirit of the original contract while following actual political provisions for good governance illustrates the disjunction between the empirical and noumenal prescriptions in Kant's political theory.

However, if we return again to the detail of the text we can gain a deeper understanding. Kant qualifies the form of sovereignty as a mode of statehood to be only a superficial aspect of the state. The different forms of sovereignty are merely the '*letter* [*littera*] of the original legislation', they are only part of the empirical convention of constitutions, somewhat anachronistic, that will gradually be replaced with the rational form of government, the republican government, the only form of state that makes '*freedom* the principle and indeed the condition for any exercise of *coercion*' (RL, 6:340). What Kant deems to be 'literally a state' is the case where the only sovereign is *Recht* itself, where the will of the people needs no manifested representation as such because it is the sovereign itself (RL, 6:341). A pure republic, therefore, has no need for a form of sovereignty, or, to put it more precisely, sovereignty has no physical form. So, as soon as the sovereign 'also lets itself be represented, then the united people does not merely *represent* the sovereign: it *is* the sovereign itself' (RL, 6:341). Once the republic is established it 'no longer has to let the reins of government out of its hands' (RL, 6:341) as the sovereign may remain in its perfect form as the idea of the united will of the people. Thus, a right to revolution is superfluous because in the perfect polity the general united will of the people itself reigns supreme.

But it is exactly in the transformative act of the sovereign 'letting itself be represented' that the problem lies. Does the personified sovereign, with the permission of the people but not their violent coercion, simply dissolve itself? Kant appears to believe that such an event is possible if perfect politics is at stake. In lieu of a critique of power, what Kant presents us with in the *Rechtslehre* is an image of the strength of *Recht*, the reach of metaphysics into the empirical world.

To draw the analogy with the phenomenal and noumenal characters of virtue, we can see that a formalised sovereign in the empirical world is necessary to cleanly channel the will of the people and reform, bit by bit, the polity towards the ideal of a republican state. But the noumenal idea of a republican state needs no such medium of representation for the sovereign will of the people, so empirical revolution is redundant and no gradual reform is adequate to the task of instating an idea as ruler. The transition then to this ultimate condition could be achieved only by a revolution in the disposition of the polity, a non-empirical revolution, constituted by an irrevocable decision by the people to follow the spirit of the original contract by continually creating the conditions of a pure republic.[6]

Apparently, when Kant first heard of the declaration of the republic in France he cried, 'Now let your servant go in peace to his grave, for I have seen the glory of the world.'[7] And in one of Kant's final works, *The*

Conflict of the Faculties, released after the death of Friedrich Wilhelm II, Kant refers to the French Revolution as an 'experience in the human race, which as an event points to the disposition and capacity of the human race to be the cause of its own advance toward the better' (Conflict, 7:84). Even though Kant does not praise the bloody cost of the 'game' of revolution nor hope for its success, it is in the 'hearts of the spectators (who are not engaged in this game themselves)' that we find the pure cause that is capable of motivating humans towards the good (Conflict, 7:85). And it is this general spirit of the 'human race viewed in its entirety, that is, ... not as [a sum of] individuals ... but rather as divided into nations and states (as it is encountered on earth)' (7:84) that Kant is referring to as the agent of change. The French Revolution as an event is not simply about motivating the hope for progress, but, for Kant it also shows that the acknowledgement of the character of the spirit of change 'is already itself progress insofar as its capacity is sufficient for the present' (7:84). Here we find the foundations for political transformation – and their cosmopolitan scope – that appear quite straightforwardly in the ability of a people to think about and decide for 'the better'.[8]

Kant's ban on a right to revolution conditions the polity, educates it in how *Recht* should operate, which is by and for the people, where there is no need for public rebellion. Ideal politics, like noumenal virtue, is not an abstract, impractical perfect end-condition, but rather acts to excite us towards the highest political good, which is then achieved in the very act of cultivation.[9] It is indeed correct to say that granting a constitutional right to revolution is a contradiction, but this may not rule out revolution that is not justified by or even executed in the physical world. The pure revolution allows us to be led by the noumenal ideas, to work towards these ideas within our current reality. Such a change of heart makes peace between the limit and the ideal so the real work of change can begin. The pure revolution is a decision to be guided by the ideas of reason, which renders them plausible as agents of real political transformation. Thus, the foundations for Kant's politics – ones that encourage and permit necessary change – are revealed.

Notes

1. It is worth noting here a problem in Kant's political work, identified by Katrin Flikschuh, concerning the proliferation of ideas of reason in the *Rechtslehre* (e.g. republican state, perpetual peace, the general united will of the people, the social contract, original possession in common). Flikschuh (2000, 163) remarks that we are not advised as to the possible different status that they

may assume. Perhaps, for example, some may be derived from others or from the idea of Right itself, and, if there are lower-order ideas, do they have different functions? She asks whether they of the same order of apriority as the idea of freedom itself.

2. All works by Kant are cited in the text using the *Gesammelte Schriften* volume number and pagination. I refer to Part II of the *Metaphysics of Morals* as TL and Part I, 'The First Principles of the Doctrine of Right', as RL.

3. For such an argument see Korsgaard (1997).

4. Mary Gregor (1960) discusses the difference between metaphysics of morals as the 'pure' part of moral philosophy and as a priori knowledge.

5. Otfried Höffe (2001, 24) makes it clear that it is this distinction that causes confusion as to the right to revolution because in the case of the physical person who misuses their power, their metaphysical legitimacy as the idea of a sovereign is lost and so in the empirical realm we cannot rule out completely that a tyrant is morally protected from public censure in the same way the noumenal sovereign would be.

6. Interestingly, and in an analogy with the 'proof' of the idea of practical freedom, if the people do this, they are acting as if they were a united political will, and in this way they do assume sovereignty.

7. An acquaintance of Kant, Malter, wrote this to rectify Fichte's assertions that the French Revolution was of no interest to intellectuals in Königsberg. See Kuehn (2001, 342).

8. Another question concerns what form the manifestation of these activating political thoughts takes, but for a very interesting and convincing answer refer to Ellis (2005). She argues that it is public judgement that provides the motor for political progress.

9. Hunter (2002) argues this about Kant's moral philosophy.

References

Ellis, E. (2005) *Kant's Politics: Provisional Theory for an Uncertain World*, New Haven, CT: Yale University Press.

Flikschuh, K. (2000) *Kant and Modern Political Theory*, Cambridge: Cambridge University Press, p. 163.

Gregor, M. (1960) 'Kant's Conception of a "Metaphysic of Morals"', *The Philosophy Quarterly*, Vol. 10, No. 40, 238–51.

Höffe, O. (2001) *'Königliche Völker'. Zu Kants kosmopolitischer Rechts- und Friedenstheorie*, Frankfurt am Main: Suhrkamp, p. 24.

Hunter, I. (2002) 'The Morals of Metaphysics: Kant's Groundwork as Intellectual Paideia', *Critical Inquiry* Chicago, Vol. 28, No. 4 (Summer), 908.

Kant, I. (1996) *The Conflict of the Faculties* ed. and trans. Allen W. Wood, *The Cambridge Edition of the Works of Immanuel Kant*, Cambridge: Cambridge University Press.

Kant, I. (1996) 'Metaphysical First Principles of the Doctrine of Right', Part I, ed. and trans. Mary J. Gregor, *The Cambridge Edition of the Works of Immanuel Kant* Practical Philosophy, Cambridge: Cambridge University Press.

Kant, I. (1996) *The Metaphysics of Morals*, Part II, ed. and trans. Mary J. Gregor, *The Cambridge Edition of the Works of Immanuel Kant* Practical Philosophy, Cambridge: Cambridge University Press.

Kant, I. (1996) *Religion and Rational Theology* ed. and trans. Allen W. Wood, *The Cambridge Edition of the Works of Immanuel Kant*, Cambridge: Cambridge University Press.

Korsgaard, Christine (1997) 'Taking the Law into Our Own Hands: Kant on the Right to Revolution' in Andrews Reath, Barbara Herman and Christine M. Korsgaard (eds), *Reclaiming the History of Ethics: Essays for John Rawls*, Cambridge: Cambridge University Press.

Kuehn, Manfred (2001) *Kant: A Biography*, Cambridge: Cambridge University Press, p. 342.

2
Cosmopolitics: Law and Right

Gary Banham

Jürgen Habermas (1995) has attempted to address the question of how we should evaluate Kant's notion of perpetual peace given the political history of the last two hundred years and their effect on jurisprudence. The nature and scope of Habermas' corrections of Kant will be my theme and in the course of describing them I hope to evaluate the question of the extent to which Habermas enables a normative discussion that is more comprehensive than Kant's. It is worth noting initially, however, the nature of Habermas' description of how the notion of perpetual peace fits within the overall matrix of Kant's practical philosophy. Habermas writes that with this notion Kant introduces a jurisprudential innovation as alongside the account of the laws of states and international law there has now been produced a third element: 'the idea of a cosmopolitan law based on the rights of the world citizen' (1995, 113). Habermas' critical reconstruction of the thought of cosmopolitan law involves three stages. The first stage is where Habermas recasts the Kantian account by conceptually revisiting the manner in which Kant arrives at the goal of perpetual peace, the description of the project of it, and the solution to the problem that Kant posits to the problem posed by perpetual peace. The second stage is a confrontation of the reconstructed Kantian argument with the political history of the last two centuries, which enables Habermas in the third stage to articulate his own revised cosmopolitical project. I follow these stages in order to reach a conclusion concerning the extent to which a new form of cosmopolitical project would continue on the classical Kantian lines and the degree to which Habermasian reconstruction of these classical positions have been revealed to be justified.

I. The first stage: reconstructing Kant's concepts

When reconstructing the conceptual elements of Kant's account of perpetual peace, Habermas describes the goal in mind as primarily negative as Kant often refers to the horrible consequences of war. Kant has two different kinds of consequences in view: those inflicted upon countries fighting, in terms of destruction of property and life (what we might term the *physical* consequences of war) and loss of liberty and the necessity of resorting to spying (*moral* consequences). The description of the project of perpetual peace is in fact taken from Kant's first preliminary article in which the elementary condition for lasting peace is stated to be that the conclusion of any peace treaty should be that it includes no secret reservations for future wars. Habermas understands this to mean that the whole goal of perpetual peace is one that is specified in terms of a very specific conception of war, namely war of a limited kind between states and not world war or even civil war. 'Given the premises of limited warfare, the normative regulation of international law extends only to rules for the conduct of war and the settlement of peace' (Habermas 1995, 115). Specifically what Habermas thinks that Kant fails to describe in the basic setting of the notion of perpetual peace is the crime of *going to war*. Although Kant does not directly discuss offensive war, however, the fifth preliminary article of perpetual peace indicates that there could be no right to wage a war in order to interfere with another country's constitution or government. The discussion in Kant is of what types of rights exist in relation to war rather than what types of laws regulate the law. This distinction is based on the arrival of the conception of international law since Kant's time, and the structural consequences of it will be revealed to alter the landscape of Kant's discussion in many respects. What is clear with regard to the notion of the crime *of* war (as distinct from crimes *during* war) is that Kant really only allows for one such type of crime that is based on respect for the integrity of the moral personality of each state, a respect that forbids wars being waged for the purpose of constitutional alteration. In contrast, modern international law includes a provision not conceived of by Kant and thematised in the following way by Habermas: 'Now that wars are unlimited, the concept of peace has also been correspondingly expanded to include the claim that war itself, in the form of a war of aggression, is a crime that deserves to be despised and punished' (Habermas 1995, 115).

Hence, the first finding of Habermas' reconstruction is that the project of perpetual peace has to be expanded to encompass not merely limited wars but ones that are unlimited and, concomitant with this expansion, to officially recognise that the launching of wars that are to be regarded as constituting wrongs are not to be limited merely to the case of attempting to interfere in another state's constitutional and political arrangements. In fact, as we shall see, this proviso of Kant's that comes closest to recognising wars of a certain type as criminal in their nature is not merely expanded by Habermas, but the specific content of Kant's concern is precisely displaced by Habermas with very important consequences.

The description of the project of perpetual peace differs in various statements made by Kant. There are three instances in which Kant sets out an account of the type of political institution that could bring it about: (i) in the essay on theory and practice, (ii) *Perpetual Peace* and (iii) in the concluding sections of the Doctrine of Right. In each of these cases Kant draws a connection between the imperative that created the civil constitution and the need for an association that would transcend those of states. Prior to the civil constitution a state of nature existed and Kant's conception of the relation between states is that in their connection with each other they remain in a state of nature or one in which only private and no public rights can be asserted. The first treatment of this problem is given in the essay on theory and practice where Kant indicates the need for a cosmopolitan constitution, although he then modifies this by speaking instead of a federation that will still be decentralised in form, since placing all nations under a single head would lead to a potential for universal despotism. However least this seem an anodyne proposal it is worth citing the precise characterisation of the federation in the essay on theory and practice: 'the only possible remedy for this is a right of nations, based on *public laws accompanied by power to which each state would have to submit* (by analogy with civil right, or the right of a state, among individuals)' (Ak 8:312, my emphasis). The analogy between the civil condition and the federation is drawn very tightly here as although the distinct states still exist as separable legal personalities, they are, if bound by a public law moved here beyond the state of nature. The distinction between the civil condition and the federation in this model consists only in the fact that the former has a centralised legal form embodied in the figure of the sovereign whilst the latter is decentralised and hence includes no place for a sovereign. Clearly, with this model Kant has established a framework for something that would transcend the state of nature and allow for a substantial import to be given to the findings of the federation which would therefore be able to enforce its decrees on particular states with a binding mandate drawn from a notion of law that is clearly specified as transcending mere standards of natural justice.

In contrast, in *Perpetual Peace* Kant speaks instead of a 'pacific league' that would seek to end all war but in this work he specifically denies that the league would have the power to subject states to 'public laws' (AK 8:356) thus denying the recourse of this league to the standards of a coercive law that were enunciated clearly in the essay on theory and practice. It is worth pointing out that it is in *Perpetual Peace* that Kant is also at pains to state the necessity of ruling out wars that would attempt to change the government or constitution of other states, as this proviso (built on a strong notion of the legal personality of the state) is clearly connected to the drawing back from the notion that the constitutional solution to the problem of peace is one that should take the form of substantial law. The notion of the pacific league effectively enshrines the state of nature in which states exist with regard to one another allowing only for an organisation that would have as its mandate the orientation of states towards peace rather than effective sanctions being embodied in a law which transcended that of any particular state.

The final instance where Kant discusses this problem is in the conclusion of the Doctrine of Right. Here Kant frankly states that perpetual peace is an unrealisable ideal and that it can only have regulative status as something that we approximate towards. In connection with this claim he now states that the association of states should be termed a 'permanent congress' and he is now at pains to distinguish this from the notion of federation: 'By a *congress* is here understood only a voluntary coalition of different states which can be *dissolved* at any time, not a federation (like that of the American states) which is based on a constitution and can therefore not be dissolved' (AK 6:351). This further weakening of the model of the association is intended to ensure that there is no prospect at all of viewing the association as embodying public law even though Kant clearly states here that the point of it is to give nations a court to which they could appeal for the resolution of disputes. The congress is therefore a court without authority or sanctions and nations are entirely free to fail to recognize or respect the congress. It is thus just a body set up to adjudicate in cases of dispute concerning the private rights claimed by the nations in question and to interpret the standards of natural justice. Thus it effectively institutionalises the state of nature between states rather than transcending it as Kant's original model of a federation did.

Kant hence moves from a positive model for ensuring perpetual peace to a negative one. The most peculiar feature of this model is the suggestion that the congress in question should be permanent, a notion that suggests that a substantial achievement would be made with its establishment but, since Kant also allows for any and, by implication, every state to secede from the congress there are no conditions established for permanence. Thus Habermas sees the later stages of Kant's conception as purely moral in their status and no longer legal. Habermas' argument for Kant's caution with regard to this notion concerns the arrival of constitutional states at the time that Kant was writing and suggests that the attempt to safeguard the legal personality of states from external intervention was motivated by a desire to protect these new types of state from assault by the powers that surrounded them (with republican France here very much in mind).

II. The second stage: political lessons since Kant

Kant's solution as to how to arrive at the differently projected notion of an association concerns his philosophy of history; an account set out in distinct ways in distinct places but always involving a description of rational hope. The guarantee that this rational hope can be realised is also related in the structure of *Perpetual Peace* to a secret article calling for free public exchange between philosophers. Here the philosopher is proposed to stand in for disinterested human reason, and freedom of the pen is presented as a basis for advice to rulers urging them towards conciliation. Whilst the full details of this picture would require a lengthy description of the nature of Kant's treatment of history, what can be said simply is that here Kant reveals the necessity of practical reason becoming public and being allowed the space to articulate proposals for a public that could reflexively modify the practice of its statesmen. It is this conception that is in fact closest to some of the key impulses of Habermas' work with his conception of rational discursive justification.

Although this is a point of proximity between Habermas and Kant, however, the solution offered is one that Habermas tests precisely through the appeal to historical evidence that he had indicated would form the frame for his reflections on the Kantian project. The Kantian proposal conjoins rational publicity with the effect of trade suggesting that wherever the appeal of the former to disinterested grounds does not prevail the disruption of trade that war produces gives a prudential ground for states that allow a public space to be oriented towards pacific tendencies of behaviour. In response to this Habermas points to the growth of a political force that scarcely existed when Kant was writing but has proved of immense importance subsequently: nationalism. Nationalism enabled the call to a public to belligerent behaviour despite the appeals of rational disinterested reason and those of prudential calculation. The possibility of this, however, although referred to by Habermas as indicating a lacuna in Kant's analysis is also quickly passed over in Habermas' own. The importance of the analysis of nationalism in the discussion of cosmopolitan prospects is, however, surely one that requires greater investigation in terms of the historical conditions for its successful mobilisation and the conceptual basis for its description of a public. With regard to the latter what nationalism indicates is that belonging to a public order that a state represents involves an engagement not merely with rational or prudential reasons but with pathological engagements that include attachments to practices, places and persons. The articulation of a supra-national identity would require alternative locales to be provided for such attachments and, in accordance with Kant's notion of anthroponomy, an alternative engagement with feeling to that which is focused only or primarily on a purely pathological conception of emotion. In other words, for practical reason to be politically effective, the engagement with a rational anthropology that would permit supra-national correlates to the pure feeling of respect requires articulation and also the effort at institutional identification. The failure of Habermas to go further here is an indication not merely of his lack of engagement with such a transcendental project but also with the questions necessarily involved in political identification of factors that move to action if these factors have a character that presently has no institutional embodiment. However, in an attempt to partially address this problem Habermas suggests that the motivation of citizens is one that can largely be counted on in democratic societies to favour relations with other democracies at the expense of dictatorships indicating that in his view there is an effective power of human rights motivation in the public sphere that presses towards world-wide results of enlightenment. He also connects this to a notion of 'constitutional patriotism' that is intended to fill the gap left by the ban on nationalist feeling. The nature of the type of feeling that would be involved in this identification is not, however, subjected to any extended analysis and to the extent that it is thematised at all merely appears to be a large projection of findings from empirical psychology.

In connection with the hopes that Habermas therefore has for the expansion of a public sphere that includes pressure for the pacific settling of conflicts through the expansion of the number of democracies is his analysis of the historical movement since Kant. The account adopted by Habermas of the geo-political history since Kant is one whereby, subsequent to the Second World War the internal constitution of states has increasingly been affected by a movement similar to that Kant predicted for the power of trade prematurely. Habermas describes this in two ways, first through the disintegration of the status of distinct states through a co-mingling that is beyond their control: 'globalization puts into question the presuppositions of classical international law, namely, the sovereignty of states and the sharp distinction between domestic and foreign policies' (Habermas 1995, 122). Here Habermas is referring to the way in which the interpenetration of societies has reached a pitch and density that puts into question the view that policies of a purely national kind are any longer possible, and in view of this the distinction between internal and external affairs of the kind that underpins Kant's declaration that interference in the affairs of another state has been rendered anachronistic. The second way in which Habermas describes this indicates some of the forces that lead to this conclusion: 'Non-governmental actors such as multinational corporations and internationally influential private banks render the formal sovereignty of nation states increasingly hollow' (Habermas 1995, 122).

The combination of interdependence of states with para-state actors that are themselves governed by the increasing body of international private law indicates that states today are massively constrained in their actions and are also required to act increasingly in accordance with regulations that emerge from beyond their boundaries and without appeal to their own autonomous bodies of decision. The element in this description that, however, requires some reflection on the part of Habermas here is in terms of the necessity of his appeal to a discursive public space having thereby to be seen as global and this motivates his description of a global civil society populated naturally by global citizens. The place is then created for such global citizens claiming and exercising rights that go beyond those of specific constitutions and require reference to the body of historically accumulated law that is at an extra-national level and has its legitimacy granted to it not merely by agreement between states. However, this also, as Habermas puts it, 'robs the subjects Kant had counted on in his association of free states of the very basis for their independence' (Habermas 1995, 123).

Not only does the analysis of the history from the time of Kant suggests that the appeal to the inviolable status of the sovereignty of states lacks purchase today, but also the appeal to the realm of publicity itself is one that Habermas, from the writing of *The Structural*

Transformation of the Public Sphere onwards, has given reason to mistrust. The arrival of mass techniques of persuasion and trivialisation has ensured that the medium for the exchange of rationally communicable thought has been largely overtaken by the consumptive priorities of leisure pursuits. In such a situation the appeal made by Kant to the enlightened possibilities of public reason appears again to belong to a time that is, to put it politely, not ours. The peculiarity of this point, however, in regard to the Habermasian reformulation of Kant's thinking is that it is also Habermas, more than anyone else today, who refers all the same to the possibility of a communication that would reach beyond that of the massified society towards a possible public reason. The basis of this continued appeal is twofold: in his reflections on *Perpetual Peace* Habermas refers to the possibility of a global public sphere that would realise Kant's demand that a wrong committed anywhere be felt everywhere. This global public sphere indicates a parallel to the corporations in the shape of global campaign groups that constitute the international civil society of global citizens.

The reference to such phenomena appears, however, somewhat gratuitous unless we refer also and more importantly to what Habermas takes to be an integral phenomena of modern institutions, which is their ability to blend together prudential reasons with practical ones. The prime example given of this by Habermas is found in the situation of law to the analysis of which I turn later in my concluding discussion. The key point concerning this analysis is however the suggestion that there are immanent processes that tilt against the globalised rule of the corporate promotion of a restless leisure time and that what motivates this analysis as having any purchase is precisely that it is not purely normative but also descriptive.

From the time of Kant, therefore, two threats have arisen to the sphere of publicity: nationalism and domination of the medium of publicity by discursive forces that represent the opposite of conditions of rationality. In connection with these threats to publicity has come the threat to national sovereignty in the shape of forces of trade that now shape the internal structure of nations, including their laws. However, what Habermas hopes to salvage from this situation is the control now exercised *over* states by laws in the shape of the arrival of war crimes in the shape of crimes *of* war as proclaimed in the Kellogg–Briand Pact and the Nuremberg trials, factors that have ended on his view the presumptions that states exist in a state of nature and ushered them into a decentralised public authority of the sort envisaged in Kant's first proposed federation. Hence, the original impulse of Kant remains active and is connected for Habermas to the immanent possibilities of constitutional law and the shaping of a global public that can challenge the domination of compulsory triviality.

III. The third stage: Habermas' new cosmopolitics

The traversal of Habermas' reconstruction of Kant's thoughts when connected with the description he has of the lessons of political history since Kant gives us access now to the level of analysis that Habermas himself thinks possible in the contemporary conditions of cosmopolitical reflection. The first point, that follows from the response to Kant's shifting descriptions of the association of states, is that Habermas approaches the present conjuncture as one in which the need for the decentralised international law that, on his view, already exists, to be given further representation in international institutions. However, the radical element of Habermas' analysis is not really found in a renewed appeal for the federation that Kant initially indicated as necessary to supersede the state of nature. It is rather that there should be not merely a form in which states are permanently and publicly held to account through a federal structure but that, furthermore, there should, in accordance with Kant's distinction between international and cosmopolitan reflection, be specifically cosmopolitan rights. In *Perpetual Peace* Kant distinguished international right from cosmopolitan right indicating that whereas the former governed nations, the latter allowed rights to persons, which transcended state boundaries. In this work, however, Kant limited cosmopolitan right to conditions only of hospitality indicating thereby a precursor of rights to asylum. In re-treating this question in the Doctrine of Right Kant also there states that cosmopolitan right concerns the right of individuals to visit all places in the world without being treated with hostility, and initimates in addition that such rights control the treatment of maritime traffic.

Habermas' discussion of cosmopolitan right is much more extensive in comparison. According to him individuals have rights with regard to the world, and these rights are not mediated for them through the nation-state to which they belong. Hence there is a right to claim cosmopolitan rights, rights which are not merely defined by conditions of hospitality but human rights as are embodied in the Universal Declaration of Human Rights adopted by the United Nations. The extensive nature of such rights include not merely the generally recognised formal rights, such as the right to life, liberty and the holding of property or merely negative rights, such as the right not to be tortured, but also substantive, material positive rights, such as 'holidays with pay' (Article 24). The worldwide enforcement of such rights against any and all governments would create conditions of a very different kind than those presently observed. In addition to allowing such rights, Habermas' account of cosmopolitan right also includes the consequence that the arrest of persons for crimes committed in the service of a state (even heads of state, as in the case of General Pinochet) follows as a matter not merely of international law but of cosmopolitan law in pursuit of the rights of the citizens against whom crimes were committed.

However, following from these observations is also a drastic limitation of the possibilities of state sovereignty. Habermas is quite clear about this and points to the important precedent of the intervention into the internal affairs of another state that was carried out by the coalition assembled against Iraq in 1991, with the establishment of safe havens for the Kurds. The legal status of such safe havens is one of providing protection for those gathered there, under provisions that on Habermas' construal are cosmopolitan. The violation of internal affairs of a state involved in such an establishment of areas covered by the jurisdiction not of the recognised sovereign government but rather of world officials as mandated by the duly constituted authority are a dramatic example of the interventionist logic of cosmopolitan thought in its Habermasian guise. The analysis that follows for him concerning the present state of the world with regard to the realisation of cosmopolitan law is however ambiguous as he stated in 1995: 'The contemporary world situation can be understood in the best-case scenario as a period of transition from international to cosmopolitan law, but many other indications seem to support a regression to nationalism' (Habermas 1995, 130).

IV. The principles of Kant and Habermas contrasted

The shift that has been accomplished in Habermas' analysis can be summarised in the broadest terms as a shift from a negative role for cosmopolitical reflection to a positive one. What this means in practice is that not only does the analysis thus endorsed include within its purview a recognition of events and tendencies missing in Kant's original diagnosis, but it also builds on them, in the process taking them to incarnate normative tendencies of a sweeping nature. Rather than adopting Kant's cautious response that leaves nation-states as inviolable legal personalities, the new analysis effectively subordinates them to the tendency towards a world rule that Kant often feared would produce despotism. The reason underlying the change in status of reflection from Kant to Habermas, in fact, resides primarily in the basic conceptual resources that underpin their analyses. Kant's account has a two-fold structure: at the most basic level of any normative discussion the appeal to the categorical imperative reveals the means by which any maxim can be comprehended as in accordance with that which is right by stating as a condition that the maxim in question has to be universally applicable. To this is, however, conjoined a principle that specifies the application of the categorical imperative to conditions that we would recognise as political and this is the supreme principle of right, a principle that describes the conditions of external freedom: 'Any action is *right* if it can coexist with everyone's freedom in accordance with a universal law, or if on its maxim the freedom of choice of each can coexist with everyone's freedom in accordance with a universal law' (AK 6:230). This principle is stated in a constitutively negative form and one of the reasons for this is that the condition for the realisation of the principle of freedom is comprehended according to a schema of the law of the categorical imperative and schemas realise by restriction. The form of restriction of freedom is its capacity to describe action that is conformable with the freedom of others. This allows also for coercion, forcible action to prevent conduct that does not comply with equality of respect for the conditions of freedom. However, this entails that for Kant all talk of right is specified as negative in form, not positive. Owing to this analysis of the condition of right, the composition of Kant's thought could not be such that it gave permissive expansion of positive rights in the manner of Habermas.

Habermas' description of cosmopolitan right as having a positive form emerges, by reference, as a very different conception of law to Kant's. Whereas Kant formulates the categorical imperative as emergent from the structure of reason itself, Habermas turns rather to the conditions of communicability of reason as prior to any reflection on the requirements said to be emergent from it. This supplies him, in contrast to the categorical imperative, with the discourse principle. The importance of this principle for all of Habermas' reflections can hardly be overstated though the formulation of it in his work has undergone in recent times a remarkable transformation. In his description of philosophy of law, he turns to what he takes the origin of legal norms in modernity to be, that is, something that he thinks is co-constitutive with moral norms in the shape of this discourse principle. The principle is stated there as: 'Just those action norms are valid to which all possibly affected persons could agree as participants in rational discourses' (Habermas 1992, 107). Although the distinction between this principle and Kant's supreme principle of right may not at first sight appear to accord with a difference between a positive and a negative one, it is immediately apparent that the nature of them as principles is quite distinct. Kant *is* careful to argue that the supreme principle of right applies not to maxims themselves but to behaviour, arguing that there is no basis for forcing adoption of the principle as one to which any should agree but that coercion to ensure actions in accordance with it are performed *is* permissible. In contrast, Habermas' principle, like the categorical imperative, applies to maxims (or 'action norms' as he terms them) themselves. Hence, Habermas' principle is a replacement for the categorical imperative and from it the principles underpinning law are apparently derived. It indicates, like the categorical imperative, a universal procedure of testing of norms and shows that this condition is one of rational discourse as such, and in specifying how it operates Habermas states that it 'explicates the meaning of impartiality in practical judgments'. This description of the normative range of the discourse principle as the description of the impartial basis of legal and moral reasoning imparts, however, a disagreeable tone to Habermas' use of the discourse principle. One of the reasons for the use of this term is apparently to distinguish this principle from moral principles (such as he takes the categorical imperative to be). Matthias Kettner indicates a problem with the notion of impartiality as a standard for moral discernment writing: 'It is a mistake to equate impartiality with justice or fairness. Unjust and just laws can both be administered impartially, and action norms arrived at in impartial deliberations can be outrageous on all counts' (2002, 209). This is precisely the complaint launched against the standard effort to explicate norms by reference to a notion of impartiality: utilitarianism. Habermas in loading his basic principle with the characteristic of a description of impartiality decides in favour not of a process of universalisation that is, as he believes, neutral but rather one that imports into his theory a commitment to a process that will have to aggregate in some sense the goods being described and articulated. With reference to action norms these are further specified to include reference in conditions of political deliberation to involve 'the decisive reasons' that are acceptable to those said to share 'our' traditions. Therefore, in regard to political deliberation the aggregation in question concerns effectively a pre-given tradition within which we sketch an agreeable allowance of goods and since 'our' tradition is one of rights, it is rights that will be so treated.

This helps to clarify the manner of Habermas' positive construal of rights. Rights are not, as they are for Kant, only negative conditions for the possibility of truly ethical conduct and maxim formation. Rather they are simultaneously legally valid and ethically mandated so that the legal order on this analysis is one that effectively incarnates, in an imperfect form, the perfectly conceivable telos of our rational articulation. In other words, we do in fact live in a condition of virtue in possessing modern law, albeit an imperfectly realised one. Thus, whereas Kant's portrayal is one in which the categorical imperative is connected to conditions of action through a negative schema of restriction and realisation, Habermas' description, in contrast, is of an expansive sort that allows for the incarnation by degrees in political form of a perfectible rational process. In conclusion, I indicate the degree to which the Habermasian analysis, therefore, allows for conditions that are not plausible for Kant and to indicate what the problems with this might be.

V. The advantages and disadvantages of Habermas for cosmopolitical thought

Habermas' analysis permits an understanding of the law as the site of immanent development from national to international to cosmopolitan right that progressively expands the range and effective applicability of rights. This has the effect of legitimising the process whereby rights are, as many modern movements have insisted they should be, conceived beyond the narrow formality of classical liberal thought to include goods that are sought by many actors. It also allows for a description of international relations that is not bound by the pessimistic portrayal of them as locked in a state of nature by referring to this immanent movement as something that will enable the eventual subordination of particularistic claims within the eventually commonly recognised goods of rational discursivity. However, Habermas' analysis involves a number of problems, some of which have already been touched on. First, his institutional diagnosis includes recognition of a systematic distortion of communication with no indication of how the elements of distortion can be removed. Second, the tension between the immanent universalisation of the discourse principle and the conceiving of it with regard to political norms as recognising aggregate goods of traditions suggests a failure to overcome the divide between communitarian and liberal pressures that Habermas' theory was precisely intended to overcome. Third, the discourse principle itself, in its apparent status as founder of all normativity does not allow for the protection of moral status that is enshrined in the categorical imperative as a principle of autonomy. Not only does this permit Habermas to disregard national sovereignty as a value in a manner impermissible for Kant, it also provides no basic guarantee that the subject of rights has an inviolable status. The assimilation of a Kantian logic to a quasi-Hegelian conception of the imminent tendencies within institutions tends to display a strange failure to investigate the basic conditions of the operation of such institutions in practice in favour of a good faith in their logic that is at variance with the description of the negative elements of the present conjuncture that are of importance in Habermas' own analysis.

Whilst Kant's picture of the association of states is unsatisfactory due to its persistent tendency to fail to capture conditions of application of the norms specified as requisite, Habermas' account seems by contrast, to enable not merely the material rights of citizens to be given recognition but also to include no point of resistance to the arrival of a centralised world law. Kant's caution here was of a piece with his rationale for having only a negative conception of rights: positive conceptions of them encourage the state to progressively restrict conditions of external freedom. The premium placed on this notion by Kant attaches also to the legal personality of the state, a guarantor of the freedoms won under republican rule. If we are not to see such freedoms agglomerated in a universal welfare system that is immanently despotic we require a decisive check that will restrain the development of it under the pressure of a civil society that should not be merely regarded as concentrating in political groups but also in the conditions of trade. Although the conditions of trivialisation attached to mass media are real enough the suggestion that the consumptive imperative of modern society is one that purely indicates a commitment to such triviality misses the question of how the institutions of self-making operate in today's conditions. The account required of a cosmopolitical reflection that would not merely endorse the tendency to make the cosmos political would surely also have to allow for a logic within the consumptive that might well be, as Marx once put it, also productive. In lieu of an analysis that can draw together the international civil society as one of reshaping of the human through its engagement with consumption as well as through political action, the communicative imperative is likely to remain an abstraction from the real conditions.

The conditions for reflection on cosmopolitics and perpetual peace have been altered in many of the ways specified by Habermas. However, although the alteration of legal status of cosmopolitan citizens is asserted within international law this has not in fact produced the cosmopolitan law that Habermas wishes for. Nor has Habermas indicated the manner in which conditions of communication can overcome the dialectic of their degeneration or the motivation of a public that could incorporate in its affective involvement with its situation a love of the law that would transcend the conditions of the present. In terms of construing the status of cosmopolitan law as including more than hospitality, there is an immanent request in contemporary conditions for recognition of the material forces of oppression. However, when considering the case for such recognition it is also worth paying attention to the premise of Kant's caution in terms of respecting the conditions for autonomy. A development of a normative thought that begins from Kant's premises without losing sight of the realities pointed to by Habermas may also have to articulate principles not incorporated by either and these will have to include a greater recognition of the possibilities of a non-political civil action that may yet prove to be of more cosmic importance than is recognised by Habermas.

References

Habermas, J. (1995) 'Kant's Idea of Perpetual Peace, with the Benefit of Two Hundred Years' Hindsight' in J. Bohman and M. Lutz-Bachmann (eds) (1997), *Perpetual Peace: Essays on Kant's Cosmopolitan Ideal*, MIT Press: Cambridge, MA and London.

Habermas, J. (1992) *Between Facts and Norms: Contributions to A Discourse Theory of Law and Democracy*, 1996, trans. W. Rehg, Cambridge: Polity Press.

Kettner, M. (2002) 'The Disappearance of Discourse Ethics in Habermas' *Between Facts and Norms*' in R. Von Schomberg and K. Baynes (eds), *Discourse and Democracy: Essays on Habermas's* Between Facts and Norms, Albany, NY: State University of New York Press.

3
Imagination and Reason: An Ethics of Interpretation for a Cosmopolitan Age

David Rose

I. Introduction

The realm of cosmopolitics and international relations, like the realms of right and ethics, is viewed by the liberal tradition as a domain of rational law. Kant's aspiration for cosmopolitics was a sphere in which international law, consistent with the dictates of reason, would express the will of every rational being unbiased by geographical and local contingencies and moral irrelevancies.[1] The Enlightenment project, in so many ways bound to the political device of the social contract, still looms large over any attempt to understand and construct institutions and procedures for those issues which affect individuals, as individuals yet require transnational cooperation and enforcement.

Laws, according to Kant, should be universal, reciprocal and public. These three formal requirements of political right act as constraints on the content of laws, that is those that cannot be accepted by individuals as their own laws are those which do not express the subject's own right to self-determination. Coercive political power is only legitimate if it appeals to reasons that any individual member of the state would freely endorse. Publicity, which is the requirement that laws be codified in such a way that all citizens, if inclined, are able to comprehend and endorse them, is, here, the most significant: in order for a law to motivate me, I must be able to act upon its ground as though it were my own motivation. In that way, I remain free. Kant's avowal of rational autonomy sets the stage for the legitimation of political power in the liberal tradition, culminating in Rawls's own principle of legitimacy:

> Our exercise of political power is proper only when we sincerely believe that the reasons we would offer for our political actions – were

we to state them as government officials – are sufficient, and we also reasonably think that other citizens might also reasonably accept those reasons. (Rawls 1999, 578–9)

Publicity establishes, expresses and protects individual autonomy since a legitimate law is grounded in reasons that an individual would, if he or she were to deliberate impartially, acknowledge as his or her own. In other words, I am not coerced by the state into wearing a seat belt as, if I were to reflect, I would freely constrain myself given the rational ground of the dictate. A law is a rational short cut, a reminder or a prompt, but (ideally) not an imposition.

The putative assumption of contemporary political thought is that the above liberal account of legitimacy entails a universal rights-based and state-to-state model of international relations. However, it may well be that this very presupposition is an orthodox dogma which obstructs a more appropriate and uncorrupted cosmopolitan approach to specific global issues. The reason why liberal rights-based approaches are prevalent would seem to be quite straightforward: publicity demands that one must evaluate the legitimacy of obligations and laws and the liberal position seems to be the only political theory that can offer a justification of these evaluations. Liberal accounts of rational legitimation of law are superior to embedded or contextual ones in that they allow a radical critique of existing laws and institutions from a universal point of view. Embedded or culturally sensitive accounts of rational legitimation are ill placed to evaluate other cultures because of their affinity to relativism, and political legitimacy seems to amount to positive law; one is obliged to obey in virtue of being a member of a certain community. At the international level this problem is compounded since only universal values will be effective to motivate the obedience of all the individuals affected. It is widely assumed that embedded values are inadequate for international dialogue and so, on the global level, liberal values best approximate those values that are most widely acceptable and universal; universal rights are supposed to protect that which is valuable to *all* human beings: liberty, welfare, opportunity and so on.

The opposition between universal values and embedded values can, perhaps, best be illustrated by an example. In the first few weeks of March 2001, officials from the Taliban's Ministry for the Prevention of Vice and the Promotion of Virtue successfully fulfilled the task of destroying two giant statues of the Buddha in Bamiyan, 90 miles west of Kabul in Afghanistan. These idols dated from the second and third centuries of the Common Era. A sense of horror and disbelief swept the world, not only in the West and not only in the Buddhist countries; horror and disbelief that turned inevitably to anger and the demand for justification. Justification had, however, already been given before the act was carried out. In the reported words of Mullah Mohammad Omar we were told: 'Because God is one God and these statues are there to be worshipped and that is wrong. They should be destroyed so that they are not worshipped now or in the future' (McCarthy 2001). But Omar's words only appeal to a specific tradition and a limited group of individuals who share certain values and beliefs embedded in that tradition. The liberal principle of legitimacy requires laws that are based on values and principles which, it is supposed, all men share no matter what their background, tradition or culturally contingent beliefs. This requirement will generally entail that all contingent factors – such as culture, identity and tradition – will have to be bracketed off, that is, pushed to one side. One looks at the question not from the point of me as personal identity, but from the view with which all rational beings can agree no matter what their origins (Berlin 1997b, 80–1).

Does the aspiration to universality resolve the problem? On the one hand, the reason offered is that the destruction of false idols is in accordance with God's will. It would seem that Mullah Omar has already committed himself to a relative argument, in the sense that he expects his listener to embrace the fundamental presuppositions of his way of life, that is orthodox Islam. Surely, if one can find a universal, secular argument for the preservation of the statues, Omar's prescription will be trumped and negated. There was almost universal horror at the wanton destruction of these idols, so one would assume that there are universal principles available. One might claim 'respect' or 'tolerance', but Omar may well demand the same for Islam: respect for Islam requires understanding of his actions and tolerance for Islam to carry out the dictates of its religion. Conversely one may claim that the statues are significant for 'humanity's heritage' but such a vacuous appeal, even if a follower of Omar may agree to it, weighs ill against the requirements of divine law. It seems that universal principles do not help (or – worse – are just not available) for this particular problem. Any appeal to the basic needs and rights required by liberty, equality or welfare is similarly unhelpful.

Liberalism's dogmatic assumption of universality relies on a coincidence between, first, the rights generated by universalism and the goods of the individual, an assumption which may be made at the national but not necessarily at the international level, and, second, that not only do all humans want liberty, security, welfare and equality but they also agree on the substantive content and hierarchy of these goods. These assumptions are often hidden at the local or national level since conflict does not normally lead to a revision of basic moral values. The example of the Bamiyan idols, however, illustrates the hollowness of such assumptions in global political conflict. In national political debate, when one invokes values such as 'respect' and 'tolerance', they are supported by a history of meanings that the participants in the dialogue share. Such values appear universal because their intuitive nature unreflectively appeals to the members of such a tradition and such members share a substantive interpretation of what these values require. Yet, in inter-cultural conflicts such as the Bamiyan idols, it is clear to see how such substantive interpretations differ even if formal values seemingly coincide. The two implicit assumptions of liberalism are supported in national political debate by ethical homogeneity between individual and shared values, embodied in political structures and institutions; a shared moral homogeneity which is absent at the international level. The liberal sleight of hand is harder to conceal in the global arena and yet it still obstructs agreement and free thinking since it is assumed that if coincidence is absent, then other participants in the dialogue are irrational, unreasonable or, simply, in error.

Prior to Kant, both the agenda and the failure of any liberal cosmopolitics had been set by Rousseau: he desired to construct the conditions in which freedom and equality were maximised in spite of rather in accordance with the wishes of the citizens themselves (Rousseau 1997, especially 2, iii, iv, vii, 3, iv, 4, viii). Therein lay the origin of the greatest contradiction of modern liberalism and also the fulfilled Enlightenment dream of cosmopolitan moral and political standards: how does one ensure that a strong enough moral homogeneity exists in order to garner agreement on laws between peoples? The answer may well be a communitarian one: through a shared tradition and history of social meaning and values. Before Rawls's own discovery of the tension between free institutions and the burdens of reason and an optimistic hope in the formation of a 'sense of justice', Rousseau sought to impose and support the liberal values of liberty and equality through draconian institutions such as a moral censor and a civil religion (Rawls 1993, lecture 1). It is perhaps the case, contrary to liberalism's universalism, that secular, liberal principles adhere in our society because of the coincidence between these and our shared moral fabric, not vice versa. When raised to the international level, the moral fabric – that is, those beliefs, concepts, values and norms which govern the subject's practical reasoning and derive from his or her membership of a particular culture, history or tradition – which supports the rights-based approach to law is no longer ubiquitous and one is left with the choice: either to abandon cosmopolitan politics or to find an alternative approach. This chapter is a tentative attempt to offer an alternative approach.

II. The misrepresentation at the heart of liberalism

The criticism that liberalism is at heart disingenuous is now well known and established, centring upon the conception of an abstract personality which engages in deliberation (Mulhall and Swift 1996). Liberalism itself is charged with being a conception of the good and not an impartial, universal point of view as it implicitly embodies certain social goods in its accounts of rationality and moral value which are unintelligible or undesirable outside a specific culture. Social goods, critics of liberalism hold, are constitutive of the identity of the person and are dependent upon a tradition or community for their meaning. The abstraction from them in order to posit a universal account of personality is incoherent and leads to subjectivism: the idea that values are akin to mere preferences and tastes. This means that a dialogue, if one accepts the liberal worldview, is not between rational values and principles, but between tastes and preferences and the procedure of resolution will not be rational but owing to the intensity (power) of one's preferences. At the local level, the problem goes unnoticed because there is a general ethical homogeneity between individuals, and a minimal rationality is possible because of a shared moral fabric (we as a group share the meaning of 'tolerance' or 'respect' and can use it both formally and substantively in dialogue); but, at the global level, the state of war between nations for liberals remains and must remain a case of might is right (Hobbes 1991, chapter 17). The communitarian challenge raised to the global level has a weak and a strong form: weakly, liberalism either contributes to a misunderstanding of the interests and values of other cultures by assuming that all human beings are alike in certain significant respects; or strongly, it is a type of cultural imperialism that seeks to impose its own values on other cultures, minorities or individuals. Either the weak form or the strong form is damaging for liberal cosmopolitanism since, at the international level, such a misrepresentation of the participant in dialogue is amplified into an abstraction of an abstraction and agreement between nations is either impossible or improbable since the moral fabric required to give substantive content to the abstract rights and wants of 'universal man' is absent.

Liberalism has always understood the goal of politics, whether at the national or international level, to be the organisation and mediation of conflicting interests between atomistic individuals. This contract model of compromise between wills was extrapolated from the individual-to-individual level to the state-to-state level, using the idea of a state will, or a homogeneous idea of a people or society. Such a contract requires that an agreement be made which is fair and just, that is, is not affected by partisan interests or contingent facts; so agreements must be made as the result of dialogues between abstract personalities and not actual personalities. If one adopts a rights-based contractual model of cosmopolitanism, then it will badly corrupt actual dialogues on matters such as the environment, trade and arms through a misrepresentation of personal or particular preferences and values, making legitimate agreement impossible.

III. Liberalism and the social contract

As Hobbes inaugurated the liberal project, he defined politics as the science of 'men in multitudes' and political power was justified to minimise conflicting interests between individuals in a fixed territory. For Hobbes, the only motivation capable of securing political obligation was the universal, substantive desire for self-preservation (Hobbes 1991, part I). The problem for later liberals was that, in truth, Hobbes spoke of self-interest and justified the existence of political institutions and laws only as a *modus vivendi* which could be destabilised by a single individual. Kant departs from this Hobbesian picture only insofar as laws ought to be based on reason rather than exist as a mere contingent *modus vivendi* derived from basic needs and desires. The rationalist departure from naturalism demanded that the motivation to obey law should not be grounded in universal, substantive desires but in a moral obligation: the formal requirements of right demand that a law or institution is justified if it is acceptable to individuals' reason.

However, what was gained in stability was lost in terms of motivation. The hypothetical nature of the contract was transposed from human nature to universal rationality; from 'if you want x, then you ought to y (and all human beings want x)' to 'if you are rational, then you ought to y (and all human beings are rational)'. Thus, the agenda of liberal politics was fulfilled: only those laws which would be acceptable to the free and rational individual were legitimate and could be sanctioned by the state. The meaning of 'publicity' is that coercive political power is legitimate if it makes appeal to reasons that the individual would freely endorse in an ideal deliberating position: 'All actions affecting the rights of other human beings are wrong if their maxim is not compatible with their being made public' (Kant 1991c, 126).

However, it is this very contractarian tradition which frustrates the political achievements of the cosmopolitan viewpoint. Kant's mistake – and consequentially that error which resides at the heart of most liberal transnational politics – was to raise the same demands of rationality into the international sphere.[2] The social contract model – the conjectural metaphor which Kant inherits from Rousseau – casts nations as persons and demands they act according to the rational will which represents the will of their citizens.[3] International agreements must meet the same demands as contracts reached at the national level: reciprocity, publicity and universality.

Kant's publicity grounds the notion of law and cosmopolitan law as not exempt from this requirement. What distinguishes cosmopolitan law is its subsidiarity or the level at which a conflict must be resolved. Conflicts between individuals have their appropriate level of appeal: an argument between siblings should be resolved within the family, an argument about the use of land should be resolved within the local community, educational policy at the national level and trade restrictions at the international level.[4] Some problems are well suited to a contractual model of international relations, mostly those of trade, when there exists a recognisably national will which a sovereign government can represent (all citizens would desire economic stability and growth, *all things being equal*, if they reasoned impartially). The problem arises concerning issues which are not reflected in any *person* of the nation. Some problems (poverty, environment, the rights of a specific, minority culture) cannot be dealt with by nation-state politics and so necessitate a cosmopolitan viewpoint, that is the viewpoint of communities with shared interests that are transnational. Within a state, there may exist no homogeneous opinion about the environment or arms since these are not subjects which are divided by national identity; what is good for one citizen may not be good for another (the industrialist sees environmentally inspired sanctions as punitive, the resident on the coast of East Anglia sees them as necessary). Poverty, the environment, the arms' trade transcend a strict state-to-state multilateralism and necessitate a transnational, hypercommunal standpoint that will often divide the citizens of nations into different interest groups incapable of representation in the unified *person* of the state. Cosmopolitics, as a model of international relations different from the standard state-to-state model, possesses the advantages of separating the individual's voice from the national voice, undermining non-democratic governments where there is not even the weakest link between individuals and their representative on the international stage and also representing voices from smaller countries or minorities that are drowned out in the cacophony of shrill, international dialogues.

However, the metaphor of the social contract model which views nations as persons continues to obstruct and corrupt the dialogue at the heart of cosmopolitics. It forces individuals to recognise themselves in a national will which is not representative of their own values and preferences. The social contract model rests upon a false analogy: the same procedures involved in intra-state justification are applied to inter-state justification and nations are cast as persons with a unified will in order to agree on laws, conventions and resolutions to conflicts in the role of contracting parties, as though they existed in a Hobbesian state of war. This process rests on a fundamental error of analogy that assumes that the nation corresponds to a person but, as has already been mentioned, cosmopolitan issues are those in which the national will is not a unified will. At the state level, one deals with an abstraction of 'my personality' to generate the agreement (the ideal deliberating position): those factors which are morally irrelevant are dissected from what is 'essential' to rational agreement. However, at the international level, one deals with an abstraction of an abstraction. The question becomes whom the *person* of the nation actually represents. Cosmopolitics will represent 'community interests', but for any international law derived from these interests to be legitimate, it must be public and universal. Whereas an individual within a given state can recognise what is morally relevant in the abstraction of his personality for the purpose of agreement with fellow citizens, such recognition at the international level, when one's will is represented by an abstraction of the government, disappears. The ideological mistake of traditional international politics is the universalisation of social atomism on to a higher level and it attempts to silence the worry that modern states do not properly represent the unified interests of a people.

The contract model of international relations incorporates two anomalies: first, it relies on a coincidence between the political and ethical cultures which is characteristic of a particular ideal of the nation. So, for Western states, the ideas of formal rights are reflected in democratic institutions and policies that embody substantive values familiar and acceptable to us all. In other words, there is an alignment between universal rights dictated by reason rights all men would accept if they were to abstract themselves from the contingencies of their situation and substantive moral evaluations of the Western mind. Our ethical identities ensure political homogeneity; our national identity generates agreement. And, second, it assumes that a nation can adequately represent the unified will of a people on all issues.

IV. The dialectic of rational legitimation

Cosmopolitics, in an attempt to respond to these anomalies, divides itself into two main strategies: the universalist and the particularist (Rengger 2003). The first seeks universal consensus in desires or values that all human beings share. The advantages of such an approach are that it is inclusive as well as being non-perspectival. The disadvantages are, of course, the non-existence or formalism of universal values or desires and the denial of difference to the point of exclusion. The communitarian critiques of liberalism repeatedly assert that formal right is empty and unable to supply positive obligations unless accompanied by a substantive account of the good, or at least a guide to how to interpret the universal rights of liberty, equality, respect and dignity.[5] All agents may agree the world over that respecting one's dead is a social practice which ought to be tolerated and maintained, yet the obligations that such a practice involves may well be abhorrent to a specific culture:

> Darius, after he had got the kingdom, called into his presence certain Greeks who were at hand, and asked – 'What he should pay them to eat the bodies of their fathers when they died?' To which they answered, that there was no sum that would tempt them to do such a thing. He then sent for certain Indians, of the race called Callatians, men who eat their fathers, and asked them, while the Greeks stood by, and knew by the help of an interpreter all that was said – 'What he should give them to burn the bodies of their fathers at their decease?' The Indians exclaimed aloud, and bade him forbear such language. (Herodotus 1936, 160–1)[6]

If at the national level where a shared tradition exists or a dominant one defines the moral fabric which is to serve as a standard and a hierarchy of conceptions of the good, pluralism threatens the universal application of rights, then the problem at the international level can only be amplified, where there is no single, homogenous or historically dominant conception of the good which determines values, positive obligations and substantive norms.

In contrast to this universalism, a second, particularist strategy identifies particular communities as persons with their own specific values, hence it proposes values which will motivate and be substantively efficacious in practical reasoning. But, this celebration of difference and openness to other ways of life is bought at the cost of comprehension and agreement:

> According to all reports, it was Cortés himself, perhaps yielding to a
> subconscious impulse to justify his own deeds, who first attempted to
> convert Moctezuma. The emperor politely heard out the Spaniard's
> harangue. When the great conquistador invidiously compared the pure
> and simple rite of the Catholic Mass with the hideous Aztec practice of
> human sacrifice, however, Moctezuma put in a word. It was much less
> revolting to him, he explained, to sacrifice human beings than it was to
> eat the flesh and blood of God himself. We do not know whether Cortés
> was quite able to counter this dialectic. (Ceram 2001, 337–8)

Rational values dissolve into particular relative expressions of interests
and worldviews incapable of convergence.

For a cosmopolitics to be adequate to its task, it must be articulated in
terms of values which are intelligible and recognised by each community
involved in the dialogue. In other words, these values must be universal
without being empty, substantive without being local. One way values can
meet this requirement is by respecting the difference between traditions
and communities, but these values cannot be purely local or intelligible
only to the specific few because reason cannot be a free and arbitrary play
of concepts: one's values and political judgements must be structured and
intelligible. That is to say, those values and statements which are to play the
role of legitimation must not just be intelligible to all, but must be possible
motivations for all. Reason alone is stuck between the dialectical poles of
the need to respect difference on the one hand and the need to make universal judgements on the other. In legitimating international law, a reliance
on universal good or rights leads to either empty agreement or simple non-
agreement; whereas, a reliance on substantive conceptions of the good
leads to relativism and non-agreement. Unless a universal account of
human nature or interests can be found, one either has to retreat back to
formal right or abandon any hope of a cosmopolitan politics.

The practical problem with rationalist approaches is an overburdening
of reason which either results in vacuous agreement or pure and simple
non-agreement. The appeal to the faculty of reason is one-sided unless one
also makes an appeal to the faculty of imagination: nations, even where
they can be clearly defined and designated, are complex, multifaceted and
plural communities, ruled in part by reason but also the values dictated by
history, tradition and contingency. The reliance on reason alone negates
this fact, abstracts from what is real and makes any agreement alien and

incoherent to the very agents it affects. If it respects this fact, reason makes agreement impossible. It, therefore and in both cases, violates the condition of publicity so central to the notion of a legitimate law. There is a very real need to appeal to actual communities with actual interests, not abstract political entities with supposedly unified interests, in order to generate true agreement. The hermeneutical requirement that an explanation be meaningful rather than causal – that is, a condition that the particular agent represents what the legislator determines him to do as something he himself would want – is another way of understanding the requirement of publicity. Without the faculty of the imagination this is impossible.

V. The faculty of the imagination

If reason is the sole faculty which governs practical wisdom, then one finds oneself caught in a dialectic. On the one hand, if the prescriptions of reason are universal, then normative terms such as 'respect' are formal and empty in that participants in a discourse can agree that respect is a good, but not what such a good should substantively entail, whether it be respecting one's dead or treating men as equal. On the other hand, if one starts from the particular prescription of reason, then agreement is at best improbable and, at worst, impossible. For me, homage to one's gods is paid by sacrificing willing victims, for you it is in metaphorically consuming His body, but one (or both) of us is just wrong. To say one ought to tolerate a repulsive practice because it can be understood in terms commensurable to both practices is to make the terms unintelligible to the participants in the discourse. One will be unable to use prescriptions – because they are to be generated bottom-up – to criticise those practices in other communities that one feels, intuitively and reasonably, to be wrong: the destruction of ancient statues, human sacrifice, cannibalism and also others not discussed here: female circumcision, slavery and child exploitation, for example.

Resolution may well be impossible since such an approach to the understanding of foreign cultures and cosmopolitan prescriptivism is dominated by the Kantian tradition and the faculty of reason. To put it more simply, it seems to ignore – and here it is in no way unique in philosophy – an alternative faculty or a way of knowing, that is the imagination. One could invoke a separate, hermeneutical tradition which represents this way of knowing and its centrality to the human and social sciences which would contain names beginning from the Italian humanists, Vico, Herder, Dilthey, Heidegger, Gadamer, Berlin, Hampshire and Walzer which would represent this way of knowing and its centrality to the human and social sciences.[7] Imagination in its most basic form asks 'what if things were not as they are, if they were different' and 'what if I were you'. Such imagination begins with the conflict of values and does not seek to overcome it in terms applicable to each agent. Instead it is the attempt on the part of a political agent to truly comprehend the force and meaning of an alien obligation. The imagination is the negation of necessary prescriptions of reason, the opening up of possibilities and this is the first step of both understanding and critiqing. Imagination begins with substantive values, not formal requirements.

Beginning from the particular instance of conflict and of injustice and not from the prescriptions of reason, however, seems to encourage relativism and particularism, yet such a claim depends on whether one begins from *reason* in the particular, or from *imagination*; that is, a form of knowing as a way of understanding, of interpreting the different moral fabric of an alien community and coming to see it from inside. To begin from reason is to stay trapped in reason; imagination opens up a dialogue, whereas reason closes it off. Imagination allows the political agent to enter the mind of the other participant in the discourse, to overcome the axiom of practical reason which obstructed Cortés and Moctezuma from understanding the true meaning of each other's ritual. To reveal and interrogate one's own implicit standards of reasoning often requires this step outside oneself into difference rather than into the abstract personality of liberalism, so the aim is two-fold: to understand the other and oneself better through the faculty of the imagination. Only when true comprehension is achieved, only when political agents have overcome those prejudices and ideologies which haunt their view of the world, can reasoning begin. The resolution of conflicts of values and the construction of prescriptions with universal appeal are as concerned with the imagination as they are with reason. The Kantian approach demands publicity, reciprocity and universalism, but reason alone creates a tension between the first and last conditions. The imagination is an attempt to ensure the harmony of all three.

Cosmopolitics understood in this way affirms itself as a fundamental commitment to the interests of humanity: each person is a citizen of the world and this affords him or her respect due to this status. The faculties of imagination and reason in tandem will allow agents to formulate prescriptions and laws which take account of this humanism and, therefore, meet the requirement of publicity. The imagination, though, faces the problem of normativity: can one say 'you ought to imagine thus and so' in the same way that one can say 'you ought to reason thus and so'?

In order for an alternative cosmopolitanism which takes seriously the role of the imagination to be possible, one has to show that the imagination can impose normative constraints on its own production.

VI. Vico and the new science

The nature of the constraints that the imagination imposes on its own production should not be confused with universal ethical norms. If one were to do so, one would fall into the trap of rationalism and be guilty of imposing ethical norms on a discourse which is exempt from such considerations: a sane man can write *American Psycho* or film the *Texas Chain Saw Massacre* and we can imaginatively participate in reading or viewing such works. When one writes a horror, a science fiction or a detective novel, there are structural prescriptions dictated by the genre and these act as constraints on the possible production of imaginative objects.[8] Similarly, and more banally, when one imagines where one wants to go on holiday, there are constraints to the spontaneous formation of judgements concerning possible holidays. So, the object of our judgement is pivotal in the constraints that apply to our production. The mind can imagine any nature of cruelty or immorality and any number of oppressive, inhumane social structures, but the goal of the imagination in political cosmopolitanism is not to imagine a possible way of life, but more pertinently a way of life one would find intelligible and accept. In order to constrain the *political* imagination, one ought to first recognise that it is aimed at a specific production: the production of possible political and social fabrics and their embedded reasons for action. If one imagines a society and says, 'No one in their right mind would want to live there', then, regardless of its possibility to exist, it is not a legitimate society because it does not meet the rational requirement of publicity. However, the faculty of reason *alone* cannot furnish us with prescriptions; neither can the faculty of imagination *alone*. Particularism demands imagination, universalism demands reason. One way forward is to bring together the two aspects of knowing in order to offer an answer to the question: would I accept these policies, institutions or laws if I were any and all of those agents affected by them? The answer requires both the faculties of imagination and reason to work in tandem.

Such a way of knowing, even if it reveals a different faculty at the base of one's practical wisdom, seems to remain trapped in a particularism: I can fully comprehend why you – as a member of such and such a community – do ϕ, but when I step back into my own community with its norms, values of mode of reasoning, I find it wrong to do ϕ. The problem with reason was that prescriptions aim at what is universal, whereas the imagination aims at what is particular, so – in a sense – it openly admits 'each to his own'. To ask what it would be like to be you, however, requires a foundation of commonality: I can – dependent on the development of the faculty of my imagination – imagine what it would be like to be a woman, to be a French revolutionary, to live in Neolithic times only if there is, at base, something significant (whether it be basic needs and desire or a way of structuring of experience, or something else) that I share with the objects of my imagination. So, in the same vein, I perhaps cannot (so easily) imagine what it would be like to be a bat, a cat, a hat or a gas-based life form living in Alpha Centauri. The aim of an ethics of interpretation is to identify what is shared and significant: I may be short-sighted like a bat or share the name 'Sam' with my cat, but these are inconsequential since it does not help me to imagine the bat's or the cat's world.[9] The prescriptions and elements which govern possible objects of imagination and the formation of spontaneous judgements require an ethics of interpretation to meet the need to distinguish between legitimate social orders and illegitimate ones; one needs to ask: can I imagine myself as a political agent bound by laws, values and social goods in this particular society? To illustrate such an ethics of interpretation and to identify what the basis of the commonality between human beings might be, it is pertinent to return to a neglected figure in the history of philosophy, Vico.

Vico's criticism of natural law and social contract theory coincides neatly with comments made above about modern liberal assumptions concerning universal rights and goods. He also criticises the rationalist politics of Plato because this approach imposes philosophical ideas top-down on all civilisations, ignoring the reliance of one's own civilised reason in the arbitrary and contingent primitive myths which form the origin of one's 'sophisticated' reason. Such rational appeals to self-certainty can only be accepted by those who share the same history and tradition as oneself (Vico 1982a, I, sections 3–5). The historicism implicit in his 'new science' offers a hermeneutical account of historical understanding that opens the possibility of a political critique of established practices and institutions and also the possibility to understand alien cultures 'from the inside'.

Prior to the word 'science' being appropriated by the natural and empirical sciences, its meaning was broader, a breadth still implicitly in play in most Latin languages: science was synonymous with the ways of knowing and these were plural, not merely the one sole method which we now nominate when we use the word. Vico's intention was to offer the proper method or mode of knowing for history understood as an anthropological and sociological description of human living. History has no proper method and is littered with errors because men, when in a state of ignorance, have a tendency to judge what is different in terms of what is familiar; to domesticate the alien (Vico 1970, sections 2–4). For Vico, the knowledge applicable to historical understanding is that which is generated by the imagination. Perception is often erroneous, judgements are often immediate and unfounded and reasons offered to support these judgements are often defective. The only certain items of knowledge for Vico are those which the human mind produces (Vico 1982b, sections 7.4–7.5).[10] The faculty which produces knowledge is ingenuity, the imagination, a faculty of the mind which invents in art, synthesises in geometry and perceives similarities between instances in arguments.[11]

With regard to the nature of society, Vico occupies an odd position: like Aristotle and Hegel, Vico does not think human beings can exist independently from a social order, but like Hobbes, Locke and the social contract tradition, he sees society as an artificial and not a natural entity. To put it simply, society is a man-made object, but is necessary for a certain species of animal to become human through the re-channelling and redirection of desires and passions into the creation of a moral, socially adjusted being. Society begins with an imaginative leap and the invention of a religion; the ideas, rituals and practices of which form the basis of social living and the substantive dictates of practical reason. This initial imaginative leap creates the basic axioms ('credible impossibles') of one's practical reason and substantiates them in institutions, a conception of the good and a web of social values and meanings. Society is artificial, in the barest sense of being made by man, but its creation is not motivated by reason but emotion, first amongst all, fear. Any ahistorical account of natural law is in error because there is no one law accessible to all rational beings equally throughout history. Rather reason is dependent on contingent axioms derived form worldviews which are creatively born from the imagination and ingenuity of the first peoples and, most notably, their poets. It is a 'conceit of scholars' to think that the laws of our day are adequate for earlier ages or that their own conceptions of law were either mistaken or inadequate approximations of our own.

Historical science has hitherto failed because it has sought to impose our own concepts and values on to minds which thought and lived differently from ourselves and also assumed that the way in which we understand the world is adequate to understand a former way of life. And, since history is necessary to sociology and political science, these two disciplines are also in error. The appeal to moral intuitions or common sense is valid only within a specific tradition: 'Common sense is a judgement without reflection, shared by an entire class, an entire people, an entire nation, or the entire human race' (Vico 1970, I, paragraph 142). Common sense is the unreflective certainty of a human being based in his customs and traditions and, thus, common sense requires a shared tradition or history and not all humans share the same history. However, as this quotation reveals, Vico admits that there is a form of common sense universal to all humans:

> Now since this world of nations has been made by man, let us see in what institutions all men agree and always have agreed. For these institutions will be able to give us the universal and eternal principles (such as every science must have) on which all nations were founded and still preserve themselves. (Vico 1970, I, paragraph 332)

Although political and moral judgements are expressions of a culture, there are some in which all men will recognise themselves. It is these ideas and obligations which will form the constraint on the imagination when utilised to imagine what possible social and political obligations can exist for the individual. Ideas which are universal amongst all people must have a common ground and so relativism only concerns certain judgements, whereas universalisation consists in the fact that a deep language must be based in naturalism (needs all humans share). These needs will be reflected in the universal institutions shared by all societies:

> This, and no other, is certainly the human nature which, at all times and in all places, has based its practices upon the following three common senses of mankind: first, that providence must exist; second, that men should beget certain children by certain women, with whom they must share at least the rudiments of a civil religion, in order that children be bought up by their fathers and mothers in a spiritual unity in conformity with the laws and religions amongst which they were born; third, that the dead should be buried. (Vico 1982c, I, section 1)

Myths, metaphysics and languages reflect the institutions which gave birth to them ('The order of ideas must follow the order of institutions.')

and institutions reflect the 'mental vocabulary' which is universal (Vico 1970, I, paragraph 238). Vico calls this a common mental language: human nature is a product of society, but for a group or tribe to be a society, it is necessary that they are bound by three necessary institutions: marriage, respect for the dead and religion.

Science must begin from 'philology' or the laying bare (through hermeneutical analysis) of those assumptions implicit in the language, institutions, metaphysics and myths which ground and frame a way of life. Such a science must begin from the faculty of the imagination or ingenuity and not rational argument. So, if one is to imagine what life would be like for a *human* at a specific historical time, then one must first recognise that in order to be a human he or she must be moulded by those primitive institutions necessary for social living, that is marriage, death and religion which reflect the natural conditions of human existence. To imagine outside these is to imagine a being which is not human. And to comprehend the particular nature of a culture, one must look at the actual form of its myths, institutions and language in order to understand its view of the world and the agent's own understanding of his roles, duties and obligations. This ethics of interpretation is an alternative to the top-down approach of rationalism in that it appeals first to comprehension rather than substantive universal reasons.

When employed in history, sociology or political science, the imagination is constrained by the dual axis of philology and philosophy. Philology is the hermeneutic interrogation of the myths, religion and self-understanding of a people. Philosophy is the rational endeavour to divide what are merely contingent manifestations of desires, wants and preferences from the expressions of necessary natural and social needs. What counts as a possible reason for action depends upon the structural fabric of what is a possible human society and Vico's investigation reveals that in order for a human to be a human as opposed to an animal, his mind must be formed and informed by the social and moral fabric constituted by a theology, a metaphysics, the concept of responsibility and the motivation of self-love (Vico 1970, I, paragraphs 339–41).

VII. The philological–philosophical method as a way to formulate universal principles

The commonality of humanity is, then, represented by three universal institutions: religion, marriage and respect for the dead. These in turn represent that the fact that humans qua humans will have a basic web of beliefs about creation, purpose and the intelligibility of the universe (religion, science, metaphysics), they will have basic divisions of roles and rights and an interlaced hierarchy of obligations and duties (family and class structures), and also they will see death as, in some sense, intrinsically significant in the life of the community as a whole and to the individuals who constitute that community (rites of death, sanctity of human life, the intrinsic worth of human life, a system of rights, etc.).

Vico holds that the commonality of humanity is found in his social existence as constrained by a minimal naturalism and, so, he grounds his historical science in the faculty of imagination regulated by basic universal facts about human beings. It seems that, at base, the aspect of universality for political judgements is to be grounded in naturalism, but Hobbes's project, which sought to unite ethics with self-regarding reason to generate political norms, reduced human beings to asocial, atomistic bundles of desires that are too simple to explain the multifaceted variety of social behaviour. For Vico, naturalism constrains the faculty of imagination which produces the foundations for substantive judgements of reason only indirectly. Hobbesian rational naturalism is too restrictive since it begins and ends with reason alone: all men want welfare, that is the maximal satisfaction of desires. However, this underdetermines the possible constitution of welfare and has the consequence of oversimplifying sociology by not supplying the necessary concepts for a full understanding of human behaviour. Humans often sacrifice their own felicity, and that of their families, for other social goods whether significant or trivial, and unless one can understand the nature of these sacrifices, sociology as a science remains incomplete. The basic needs and desires of humans can be satisfied and manifested in a myriad ways depending on one's worldview.

Vico's naturalism does not reduce human beings to bundles of desires, instead holding that the commonality of human nature is the necessary boundedness in structurally universal institutions required for human existence and although these institutions are themselves grounded in desires and needs, it is the *meanings* of the institutions and not the *causal efficacy* of desires which provide the content for obligations, duties and social roles. The philological–philosophical method is indirectly grounded in a minimal naturalism because the faculty of imagination is constrained by these considerations in the production of possible social worlds. A reflective attitude to one's social practices and mores will disclose their contingent grounding in an imaginative creation of a possible way to exist *humanly*. Such a minimal naturalism when applied to the issue of conflict demands that for a social fabric to fulfil its role it must embody the human commitments to the value of life, the significance of death, the goodness of security, the rightness of law, the badness of unnecessary pain, and so on. And, more importantly, the violation, repression or contradiction of any of these requires justification which appeals to central values of the tradition, the grounding myth. Any society which engages in violating practices is either illegitimate or needs to offer a 'bloody good reason' for the violation.

Of course, the burden of the argument rests heavily on that last comment. It is sociologically true that religion, for most cultures, has a monopoly on the storehouse of 'bloody good reasons': Moctezuma, for example, offered an eloquent rejection of the Catholic Mass in favour of a ritual of human sacrifice and Omar offered a more direct, yet coherent, reason for the destruction of the Bamiyan idols. It is here that one must separate the sociological aspirations of the philological–philosophical method from its normative commitments. As a method for sociology, hermeneutics has a definite role to play, but there is little reason to suppose it can provide normative constraints.

Unless, that is, one is involved in conflict between ways of life and each 'agent' in the discourse is committed to peaceful resolution. Once one is disposed to dialogue rather than aggression then certain levels of society are no longer allowed to the negotiating table. Moctezuma's civilisation is an example of the heroic stage of history: a society still bound to inegalitarianism and right is might. The same could be said for fundamentalists as opposed to religious reformers. To complete the picture of Vico's science, one must posit an ethics of interpretation which determines those traditions which are reasonable or responsible and only these can enter into dialogue. Such a move will supply the universal procedural norms of negotiation between substantive accounts of the good. In modern secular societies the situation of pluralism has made it impossible to appeal to metaphysical, theological or comprehensive ethical beliefs in the legitimation of laws. Such a secular society for Vico is characterised by the norm of equality; a norm characteristic of a mature, reflective tradition.

One may well object that it is folly to assume that participants in the international arena are committed to peaceful resolution rather than expressions of latent force. Yet, such an objection misses a point central to cosmopolitanism. Cosmopolitanism, following the picture outlined here, is a commitment to seek a resolution without recourse to violence and is an implicit avowal of the maturity of a tradition. The alternative is war.[12] Vico delineates three social paradigms, the ages of 'gods', 'heroes' and 'men', and it is only in the latter of these that agents are committed to democracy and discursive reason (Vico 1970, I, paragraph 31).[13] Only those cultures which are examples of the 'age of men' will be committed to cosmopolitanism since conflict resolution for the other ages would be violence and might (justified by divine right and natural power respectively) and there is no need to recognise others as humans with equal moral worth, but rather to consider them as barbarians, aliens, strangers and primitives.

By beginning from the faculty of the imagination, normative constraints on what is or is not permissible in all cultures is possible. The imagination can ask the question whether this practice, institution or policy can be made intelligible or whether the agent ought to demand 'bloody good reasons' for obeying it which do not seem to be available. In order to engage in reflection and conversation aimed towards peaceful resolution, one must belong to a mature, democratic tradition or, to use Vico's term, to the 'age of men'. And, in such a tradition, the commitment to equality and understanding (reciprocity) seems to put in question the sincerity and validity of reasons which would justify such practices as the destruction of ancient statues, ritual sacrifice, cannibalism, female infibulation, child exploitation and slavery.

VIII. The proper meaning of political liberalism

One need not endorse Vico's philosophy of history in its entirety, but it may well be an expression of something which has central importance for cosmopolitanism. In the previous section equality as a norm is described as one which is adopted by 'mature' or 'reasonable' traditions and such traditions are characterised by an awareness of the embedded and contextual nature of any seemingly self-evident and intuitive moral values. What appears intuitively to be thus and so to one agent will not appear to another from a different tradition. For Vico, the sovereignty of reason needs to be humbled because the axioms it holds to be self-evident are refined expressions of an arbitrary and arational historical origin. Such a thesis parallels the claim that one's moral values are embedded in metaphysical and comprehensive visions and cannot be otherwise.

The maturity or reasonableness of a tradition is constituted by the awareness of this finitude and the impossibility of universal, substantive justifications of a law. Therefore, the political agent is aware that he or she cannot but speak from a perspective and that this is also true of all participants in the dialogue; neither can claim default privilege. The model of an abstract, individual in an ideal deliberating position is replaced by concrete participants engaged in an ideal dialogical position. Mature traditions, in consequence, must be those which are committed to respecting the finitude of others in order to bring about non-violent resolution and such respect translates into the norm of reciprocity: in the absence of other considerations, each perspective must have equal weight and a law which affects both participants cannot accord with one tradition and not the other. The norm of reciprocity coupled with the faculty of imagination also ensures publicity, for respect demands that one *truly* comprehend the claims of the other. Of course, that leaves but one – and perhaps the most important norm – to be justified, that is universality.

What we saw in the introduction of this chapter was the way in which liberalism required a sympathetic and homogeneous moral fabric in order to be practically efficacious on the individual. One problem we have encountered again and again is that though I may comprehend your reasons for action (philological), I see no reason for them to motivate me when my imaginative identification is over (philosophical). Such an attitude undermines agreement on policies. However, implicit to this is the assumption, given the motivations of your way of life and of mine, since there exists no reason to prefer one or the other, I opt for what is familiar and more immediate. This is once more an error highlighted by Vico. In order to make impartial practical judgements, Rorty assumes that obligations to others must be grounded in some sense of identification or a 'one-of-us-ness' (Rorty 1998). On the national level, the state uses nationalism to foster such a sentiment. On the level of international relations, this requires a commitment to a common humanity which serves to constrain the play of the imagination. Imagination fosters fellow-feeling because it is a faculty which makes identification with others possible on the basis of what we have in common. Vico's science posits as its ground a shared human nature which could form the basis of recognition on certain issues.

Rorty sees the formation of community through dialogue as a way to resolve conflict, as a form of justice. He again sees it as purely determined by reason, but already reason is broader and more in line with what has been described above:

> In this account of rationality, being rational and acquiring a larger loyalty are two descriptions of the same activity. This is because *any* unforced agreement between individuals and groups about what to do creates a form of community, and will, with luck, be the initial stage in expanding the circles of those whom each party to the agreement had previously taken to be 'people like ourselves'. The opposition

between rational argument and fellow feeling thus begins to dissolve, for fellow feeling may, and often does, arise from the realization that the people whom one thought might have to go to war with, use force on, are, in Rawls's sense 'reasonable'. They are, it turns out, enough like us to see the point of compromising differences in order to live in peace, and of abiding by the agreement that has been hammered out. They are, to some degree at least, trustworthy. (Rorty 1998, 54–5)

One could perhaps be more optimistic: we can come to comprehend the values of the other and imagination will constrain our interpretation from partiality through the historical–hermeneutic axes. Consensus requires both reason and imagination. It relies on, first, understanding but also on offering 'reasons' acceptable to all. Cosmopolitanism requires a sophisticated account not just of reason but also of the imagination, each constraining the other – not identification (we are the same) but recognition (I comprehend your difference and what we have in common). We share the same motivations even if expressed differently and our interests coincide more closely than those of national identity; we form a person of 'common interest'. And since we share an interest, if we form an agreement, I am sure you will abide by it and we can enter into the dialogue as a *concrete person* with an interest.

The maturity of a tradition and the subject who is at home in it commits the international sphere to a form of political liberalism, but one capable of avoiding the ambiguity of whether tolerance, respect and equality are substantive or formal values. Hampshire has something similar in mind when he states:

The opposite of monotheism and of this monomoralism is the recognition of polymorphous ideals and of diverse conceptions of the good, tempered by respect for the local conventions and rules of conflict resolution. It is reasonable to be a universalist in the cause of reasonableness in the regulations of conflicts ('hear the other side'), but not a universalist in the defence of particular outcomes of particular conflicts of moral opinion. (Hampshire 1999, 56)

In the procedural sphere, one sees reason as dominant, in the sociological sphere one holds hermeneutics to be dominant. One must respect difference, but simultaneously strive for intelligibility, and also be sincerely committed to the aim of the dialogue, that is resolution or accommodation. Such an attitude characterises a mature tradition. So, reason has two roles: one, the *universalist* demand for 'respecting' difference and others (a necessary presupposition if one wants to overcome conflict rather than repress it); and two, the interrogation of a form of life and its motivations in accordance with basic human needs, wants and desires. Imagination augments this activity by revealing those standards of reasoning in play by both participants in the dialogue, reason *formally* demands that the dialogue be free and public and *substantively* demands that motivations be possible reasons for action for agents. The tandem approach of imagination and reason can be subsumed into one activity, a methodological bottom-up reasoning with the sole project of interpreting the validity of cultural ways of life and the reasons they offer for action, motivating a movement towards an ethics of interpretation: universal norms which constrain the sphere of a dialogue, a hermeneutical commitment to a greater cultural understanding and a different interpretation of the idea of overlapping consensus of political values from the more commonly held liberal one.[14] When one engages in dialogue, the maturity of the tradition commits one to grant equality to all participants and the true meaning of the values of political liberalism is the embodiment of this maturity without replacing the embeddedness of the tradition's values. There are political values which determine the formal nature of conflict (tolerance, respect, etc.) which are pre-conditions for the resolution of conflict without the recourse to violence (rationalism); there are substantive values that rule what constitutes possible motivations for all human beings (rational naturalism); and finally, there are comprehensive values belonging to agents due to their tradition and social fabric that ought to be heard and comprehended (imagination).

More importantly, such an ethics of interpretation will shatter the tenuous relationship between an individual and his or her state. International issues that cannot be handled through the representation of the person of the state will demand a different, cosmopolitan, approach. What motivates my and the other's reasoned prescriptions? If it is simple self-interest, then agreement will be impossible and compromise unstable since it relies on trust and there is no guarantor at the international level. If it relies on national interest, then the issue is one where I am properly represented in state-to-state international relations. If it relies on obligations from my way of life, are these and the presuppositions that ground them explicable and sanctionable by the other with whom I am in dialogue? And ways of life here refers to one's social roles, interests as part of a larger group separate from the nation and perhaps in contradiction of it (extending as far as a virtual world community in matters such as the environment). These three examples do not exhaust the list of possible motivations but they serve to illustrate one sphere of cosmopolitan action within current political structures.

I stated earlier that for a cosmopolitics to be adequate to its task, it must be articulated in terms of values which are intelligible and recognised by each community whom the ruling affects. The hope is that the through the reciprocal regulation of reason by imagination and imagination by reason, values will neither be forced on nor unintelligible to individuals.

Notes

1. The clearest exposition of Kant's moral philosophy underpinning his position is (Kant 2004). His discussions of cosmopolitanism are best approached through 'Idea for a Universal History with a Cosmopolitan Purpose', 'On the common saying: "This may be true in theory, but it does not apply in practice" ' and 'Perpetual Peace: a philosophical sketch' all in (Kant 1991b) and also (Kant 1996, part 2, iii).
2. According to Wood's interpretation, Kant is aware of the problems with the 'one law fits all' approach, see Wood, 'Kant's project for perpetual peace' in (Cheah and Robbins 1998). Evidence for his interpretation can be found in the opening pages of (Kant 1974) and also in (Nussbaum 1997).
3. 'While the purposeless state of savagery did hold up the development of all the natural capacities of human beings, it nonetheless finally forced them, through the evils in which it involved them, to leave this state and enter into a civil constitution in which all their dormant capacities could be developed. The same applies to the barbarous freedom of established states' (Kant 1991a, 49).
4. There may also be conflicts within persons on one reading of Kant: the rationality of wearing a seatbelt (if purely hypothetical and not categorical) may conflict with my preference to be comfortable and not having it bite into my shoulder. Law is a reminder of the dictates of reason. However, such a discussion belongs properly to moral and not political philosophy and lies beyond this chapter. In the political state, there are three 'persons': the legislator, the executor and the judge. See 'Perpetual Peace' (Kant 1991b) I thank Diane Morgan for reminding me of this point.
5. A critique which repeats the Hegelian critique of Kant's moral philosophy.
6. This point is made clear by Hampshire: 'It is necessary to turn toward the particular case and also toward the negative case, and only then one has sufficient grounds for political action. Arguing for general principles of social justice against traditionalists and conservatives, liberals and reformers had always seemed trapped in circularity, because the conclusions derived from their own arguments supplied the only criterion of rationality and acceptability that they were prepared to accept' (1999, 8).

7. This is a list if names which may well be objectionable to some. I believe I have it correct otherwise I would not have listed them, but I do not intend to justify particular thinkers' inclusion. Neither is the list exhaustive, more names could be added. As a brief guide, see Berlin (1997a), Herder (1968), Dilthey (1961), Gadamer (2004), Hampshire (1999), Heidegger (1993), Vico (1970) and Walzer (1987). The Italian humanists I have in mind include Mussato, Boccaccio and Salutati. A useful discussion of many of these thinkers and their connections is in Grassi (1990). It is interesting to note that Hampshire thinks the Kant of the third critique also might be worth a mention, see (Hampshire 1999, 8), but that would be too contentious to include in a brief footnote and I personally remain undecided on this issue. Of course, this list discloses the problem with this alternative tradition: it has always been highly influential in the descriptive social sciences, but not so much in the normative philosophical sciences, which still rely heavily on the natural sciences for their model. This is a discussion in itself. The one exception is perhaps phenomenology which sought to use the imaginative faculty in order to both disclose truth and also, in its later manifestations, critique.

8. Of course in artistic production, these constraints are not immutable: the production itself is a challenge to, a playing with or a conversation with expectations.

9. Once again, my gratitude to Diane Morgan who helped me clarify this.

10. Vico believes the only response to traditional, pyrrhonistic scepticism is a faculty of imagination which produces knowledge and it forms the foundation for his verum/factum principle.

11. Note that this is not so radical as one thinks: Kant believes the faculty of imagination synthesised our concepts into judgments. See (Kant 1993).

12. War is still a possibility between reflective and non-reflective traditions, that is between those prepared to enter into dialogue and those that are evangelical about the truth. Kant thought war directed the development of mankind towards international law, see (Kant 1991a, 7th proposition). Note that Vico does not accept the Enlightenment account of linear progress, see (Vico 1970, bks 4 and 5).

13. Vico does not make any explicit normative claims about which is better, and he criticises the last due to a dissolution of the social bond and the rise of anarchy. Here, I am making a normative claim on his behalf.

14. 'The two elements in procedural justice – a universal rational requirement of two-sidedness and respect for locally established and familiar rules of procedure – are linked as two natural needs in our minds in their practical and political workings. If either the rational requirement or the respect for custom breaks down and ceases to operate, we should expect catastrophe. Conflict will then no longer be resolved within the political domain but will be resolved by violence or the threat of violence, and life will become nasty, brutish, and short. Whatever one's conception of the good, such anarchy will generally be reckoned a great evil, alongside starvation and near-starvation, disease, imprisonment, slavery, and humiliation' (Hampshire 1999, 91–2).

References

Berlin, I. (1997a) *Against the Current: Essays in the History of Ideas*, London: Pimlico.

Berlin, I. (1997b) 'The Divorce between the Sciences and the Humanities' in (ed.), *Against the Current: Essays in the History of Ideas*, London: Pimlico.

Ceram, C. (2001) *Gods, Graves and Scholars: The Story of Archaeology*, London: Phoenix Books.

Cheah, P. and Robbins, B. (eds) (1998) *Cosmopolitics*, London: University of Minnesota Press.

Dilthey, W. (1961) *Meaning in History; W. Dilthey's Thoughts on History and Society*, London: Allen and Unwin.

Gadamer, H. G. (2004) *Truth and Method*, London: Continuum.

Grassi, E. (1990) *Vico and Humanism: Essays on Vico, Heidegger, and Rhetoric*, New York: Peter Lang.

Hampshire, S. (1999) *Justice is Conflict*, London: Duckworth.

Heidegger, M. (1993) 'Letter on Humanism' in Martin Heidegger, Farrell Krell, D. (eds), *Basic Writings*, London: Routledge.

Herder, J. G. (1968) *Reflections on the Philosophy of the History of Mankind*, Chicago, IL: University of Chicago Press.

Herodotus (1936) *The History of Herodotus*, New York: Tudor Publishing Company.

Hobbes, T. (1991) *Leviathan*, Cambridge: Cambridge University Press.

Kant, I. (2004) *Groundwork of the Metaphysics of Morals*, Cambridge: Cambridge University Press.

Kant, I. (1996) *The Metaphysics of Morals*, Cambridge: Cambridge University Press.

Kant, I. (1993) *Critique of Pure Reason: A Revised and Expanded Translation based on Meiklejohn*, London: J.M. Dent.

Kant, I. (1991a) 'Idea for a Universal History with a Cosmopolitan Purpose' in H. S. Reiss (ed.), *Kant: Political Writings*, Cambridge: Cambridge University Press.

Kant, I. (1991b) *Kant: Political Writings*, Cambridge: Cambridge University Press.

Kant, I. (1991c) 'On the Agreement between Politics and Morality under the Transcendental Concept of Public Right' in H. S. Reiss (ed.), *Kant: Political Writings*, Cambridge: Cambridge University Press.

Kant, I. (1974) *Anthropology from a Pragmatic Point of View*, The Hague: Nijhoff.

McCarthy, R. (2001) 'Taliban Order all Statues Destroyed', *The Guardian* 27 February.

Mulhall, S. and Swift, A. (1996) *Liberals and Communitarians*, Oxford: Blackwell.

Nussbaum, M. (1997) *The Journal of Political Philosophy*, Vol. 5, 1–25.

Rawls, J. (1999) 'The Idea of Public Reason Revisited' in J. Rawls (ed.), *Collected Papers*, Cambridge, MA and London: Harvard University Press.

Rawls, J. (1993) *Political Liberalism*, New York: Columbia University Press.

Rengger, N. (2003) 'Cosmopolitanism' in R. Axtmann (ed.), *Understanding Democratic Politics*, London: Sage.

Rorty, R. (1998) 'Justice as a Larger Loyalty' in P. R. B. Cheah (ed.), *Cosmopolitics*, London: University of Minnesota Press.

Rousseau, J.-J. (1997) *The Social Contract and Other Later Political Writings*, Cambridge: Cambridge University Press.

Vico, G. (1982a) 'The First New Science' in L. Pompa (ed.), *Vico: Selected Writings*, Cambridge: Cambridge University Press.

Vico, G. (1982b) 'On the Ancient Wisdom of the Italians Taken from the Origins of the Latin Language' in L. Pompa (ed.), *Vico: Selected Writings*, Cambridge: Cambridge University Press.

Vico, G. (1982c) *Vico: Selected Writings*, Cambridge: Cambridge University Press.

Vico, G. (1970) *The New Science of Giambattista Vico*, Ithaca and London: Cornell University Press.

Walzer, M. (1987) *Interpretation and Social Criticism*, Cambridge, MA: Harvard University Press.

Part II
Other Varieties of Cosmopolitics

4
Cosmopolitics and Its Sadian Discontents

Meredith Evans

I. Introduction

'In the course of my life I have seen Frenchmen, Italians, Russians etc.; I even know, thanks to Montesquieu, that one can be Persian; but as for *man*, I declare I have never met one in my life'. In part, because of its pithy dismissal of abstract universalism, several theorists of cosmopolitanism have resuscitated Joseph de Maistre's quip.[1] Those theorists who take their cue from de Maistre elaborate their cosmopolitan visions in the perceived absence of a transcendental principle that would apply equally to everyone – to 'man' – and legitimate moral and/or political action. Consequently, they seek a more variable and unexportable guide for action, one contingent upon those local mores, customs, histories and so on, that determine particular communities. When too unreflectively celebrated or too rigidly pressed into the service of politics, however, such contingencies can have unfortunate consequences for the way in which community is delineated. If 'community' is understood in narrowly cultural terms, for example, it sacrifices specific political definition to an etiolated, aestheticised definition, while if understood in narrowly ethno-regional terms, it becomes vulnerable to the exclusionary, potentially incendiary ideology of *Volksgeist*. In either case, the difficult question arises of what can motivate and legitimate moral and/or political action, for when universalism is traded for a more particularist principle of affiliation, such action can no longer be legitimated – or contested – with reference to norms upon which 'we' can all agree.

In light of this problem, an alternate cosmopolitical vision seems necessary. This alternate vision would retain the 'human' as a recognisable if polyvalenced and densely articulated entity, and posit it as the ultimate source and object of moral obligation. The most promising strand of this alternate vision attempts to navigate the fissure between abstract universalism and particularist affiliation without doing violence to either. It retains a strong normativity and, without cancelling the demands that national or cultural identifications make on us, argues for a form of affiliation more capacious than that of cohesive nationalism. By extension, it confronts, if not resolves, the relationship between the unconditional demands of morality and those more particular demands that arise in the contested field of politics. With Kant's seminal 'To Perpetual Peace: A Philosophical Sketch' and Derrida's 'On Cosmopolitanism' serving as the lenses through which this alternate vision can be sharpened, I examine the theoretical contours and coherence of the uneasy reconciliations it reaches towards, and upon which the viability of a cosmopolitics that is both politically motivated and morally grounded rests. I begin, however, by presenting the Marquis de Sade as a vital if largely unacknowledged part of the genealogy of cosmopolitanism.

II. Politics in the bedroom

That cosmopolitanism, however variously defined, cannot easily do without normative legitimation is suggested by the fact that some of its advocates[2] have returned to the Marquis de Sade (besides Nietzsche, the perennially challenging anatomist of ersatz noumena) as an occasion for negative self-definition. To say that Sade provides cosmopolitanism with an occasion for negative self-definition is not to say that he is the 'other' of cosmopolitanism in any simple sense. Rather, by mapping at least part of the theoretical terrain that cosmopolitanism occupies, Sade presents an instructive challenge for its slanted and compromised, but not abandoned, Enlightenment ideals. The issues that crystallise around Sade – and in particular his pamphlet 'Yet Another Effort, Frenchmen, if You Would Become Republicans', published the same year as 'Perpetual Peace' (1795) – make him an important touchstone for cosmopolitanism. As an anti-Enlightenment Enlightenment thinker, Sade embodies the contradictions and complexities that attach to the tensions between particularist affiliation and normative legitimation as they surface in cosmopolitan discourses.

De Maistre learned from Montesquieu, but Sade might have too. In place of universalism, Montesquieu attends to place or context as that which determines who we are. By extension, for Montesquieu law cannot arise except in *places*. Far from being something that exists independently of its subjects and their contingent characteristics, able to

gather them into a universal order, law is more like an indigenous plant
that expresses the natural conditions that nurtured it. As Montesquieu
puts it in 'The General Idea' of his *Spirit of the Laws*: 'If it is true that the
character of the spirit and the passions of the heart are extremely different in the various climates, *laws* should be relative to the differences in
these passions and to the differences in these characters' (1989, 231). In
effect, Montesquieu proposes law as a *naturalised* principle of legitimation. Similarly, Sade attends to the importance of place as that which
informs value, thus making value resistant to the sort of transplantation
that a universalist conception of value demands. As a character in Sade's
Justine expresses it: '... virtue is not some kind of mode whose value is
incontestable, it is simply a scheme of conduct, a way of getting along,
which varies according to accidents of geography and climate and
which, consequently, has no reality. ... there is not, upon the entire
globe, two races which are virtuous in the same manner' (Sade 1965,
544).[3] For Sade, particular values are neither grounded nor defended by
a normative principle; they are simply 'a way of getting along', determined by the natural accidents of place. And insofar as affiliation is
formed around shared values, they are drawn contingently for Sade; no
normative principle exerts a centrifugal force on them.

That said, Sade is interested in the *collision* of restricted or particularist
affiliation and normative legitimation, and not merely in the cancella-
tion of one by the other. While the general tendency of the book is to
ridicule it, the eponymous heroine of *Justine* maintains a transcendental, universalisable conception of value. As she travels throughout the
land, discovering that what she took to be places of refuge are in fact
places whose non-negotiable rules of social and sexual transaction
('ways of getting along') are applied to her with relentless consistency,
she becomes a sort of cultural tourist whose supposedly universal values
are confronted with culturally specific life-forms. In the course of this
confrontation, Justine's abstract principles are not only reduced to the
morally inconsequential specificity of the body ('How can a girl be so
dull-witted as to believe that virtue may depend upon the somewhat
greater or lesser diameter of one of her physical parts?' [Sade 1965, 487]),
but also confronted with exigencies of that more concrete topos of
affiliation: the state.

The state does not function here as a normative, if lesser, abstraction,[4]
but as an extension of Sade's natural principle of affiliation. As she
protests against what she perceives to be murderously sensual and mer-
cenary principles, Justine is told: '... the virtue whereof you make such a
conspicuous display is worthless in this world. ... Does it matter [if you

perish]? We have more subjects in France than are needed; given the mechanism's elastic capacities for production, the State can easily afford to be burdened by fewer people' (470). As some political theorists have less dramatically argued, universal principles like the 'right to life', some version of which Justine implicitly adopts as she pleads for her life, are not supported by the more immediate context of the state, but are, rather, deeply problematised when annunciated within it (cf. Geuss 2001, 147). Nevertheless, Justine's insistence upon her repeatedly violated virtue serves not so much to keep the bathetic, pornographic fantasy of the ever-virginal, eminently corruptible body intact, as to betray a conservative belief in the ability of value to transcend material context, and hence in a normativity that remains uncompromised by its *de facto* breaches.

At this point, we can begin to see why cosmopolitanism might fruitfully use Sade as an occasion for negative self-definition, especially insofar as cosmopolitanism is concerned to locate some principle of affiliation – something that can unite a multitude of differences that are preserved as such – without abandoning the universalist project of legitimation. Importantly, this concern arises in a context in which transcendental principles are not obviously available as the source of a moral and political jurisdiction that could further the realisation of emancipatory ideals. As Sade puts it in 'Yet Another Effort': 'Is it thought that this goal [the progress of our age] will be attained when at last we have been given laws? Abandon the notion; for what should we, who have no religion, do with laws?' (1965, 296). But the absence of a transcendental framework also poses a problem for affiliation. What, if not a transcendental principle, will bind the members of even a delimited community together? Sade's naturalisation of the state-form provides one possible answer to this question. As an entity equipped with 'elastic capacities for production' that help it manage overabundance and scarcity, the state is less like a 'mechanism', as Sade says (470), than a self-regulating organism. As such, it provides its members with a unifying scheme of conduct in much the same way as climate and geography do.

Supplemental to this naturalisation of the state is a hollowing out of its members' supra-natural convictions: 'It would ... not be merely to tolerate indifferently each of the cults that I should like to see us limit ourselves; I should like there to be perfect freedom to deride them all' (Sade 1965, 308). Sade aims not only to secure the freedom of derision but, more positively, to avoid the divisive, violent dispute of post-revolutionary society: 'Regarded in any other light, religions become serious, and then important once again; they will soon stir up and patronize opinions, and no sooner will people fall to disputing over religions than some will be beaten into favoring religions' (308). Thus what in a multicultural society, where citizens' different beliefs demand recognition and respect, might pose a problem for social cohesion, is in Sade's world set at naught. But even if the sort of belief that drives ideological conflict has been weakened with derision, the question of what best serves to harmonise disparate peoples who have different convictions remains. As Sade's naturalisation of the state leads us to expect, natural law steps in to serve this purpose. 'Natural law', for Sade, is the law that appeals to 'Nature' as a legislating principle and a final source of moral sanction, and according to which whatever *is* is good: 'only that is really criminal which rejects [this] law', and while Nature can help us discriminate between vices and virtues, it has need of both (307). The law that is to govern the subjects of the new republic, then, must not so much sublate naturally arising 'manners' as incorporate them: 'the laws to be promulgated will issue from manners, and will mirror them' (307).

If anything, law, as a formal expression of the particular variables of a society (mores, customs and so on), would only constitute another source of division. But if those variables – what Sade laconically calls 'manners' – can be revamped to suit the new republican government, then it is indeed to law, as expressive of these manners, that we must look for stability.[5] Crucially, the relevant context here is not international but national, since nothing so place- and culturally specific as manners could foster transnational solidarity. Thus naturally derived laws foster national cohesion and stability: '... it is purely a question of giving an indestructible quality to the laws we employ, of seeing to it that the laws we promulgate have, as ends, nothing but the citizen's tranquility, his happiness, and the glory of the republic' (Sade 1965, 338). This means, moreover, that 'Frenchmen' must be concerned only with themselves: 'a model to every race, there will not be a single government which will not strive to imitate you ... but if, for the vainglory of establishing your principles outside your country, you neglect to care for your own felicity at home, despotism, which is no more than asleep, will awake, you will be rent by intestine disorder ...' (339).

About his nationalist principle of affiliation, Sade is rigorous. By 'Frenchmen' he means not those near 'us' who happen to be French, but Frenchmen *per se*; other, more narrowly circumscribed objects of loyalty are excluded. Thus Sade argues, for example, that separating (French) children from their (French) families will not only provide for a more politically efficacious distribution of 'the portion of affection they ought [otherwise] to distribute amongst their brothers' (321), but will also allow them to become 'purely *les enfants de la patrie*' (322). If affective identification is understood not only pathologically but also, as Sade seems to understand it, quantitatively (i.e. as an individual's *limited* capacity, such that I am capable of being loyal to *x*, but not to *x and y*), then it must be given clear parameters. These parameters are the theoretically arbitrary but pragmatically exigent ones of the nation-state. After the death of God and King and the normative legitimation they provide, it is not just Nature that takes their place and serves to affiliate people, but Nature – or the laws derived from it – *as incorporated in the nation-state*. In this way, 'man' and 'citizen' are brought into line under laws that both mirror and constitute them.

Sade's understanding of 'community' thus expresses itself as a fantasy of self-containment, such that affiliation transpires within a circumscribed domain of self-sameness and indeed, self-interest. It's logic does not dictate a conflict of co-constitutive forces that expands the domain of a political culture; rather, it only allows for but the possibility of a foreign culture looking in from the outside and replicating what it sees there. Thus, he urges Frenchmen, 'Invincible within, and by your administration and your laws a model to every race', not to sacrifice 'your own felicity at home' 'for the vainglory of establishing your principles outside your country' (339). For all his apparent normative modesty, however, Sade implicitly maintains the exemplarity and universal rightness of the French form of government and political culture. Hence, he condemns their active promulgation, not as impossible – for that would too obviously compromise the implicit claim to universality and rightness – but merely as 'vainglorious'. In other words, embedded in Sadian nationalism is a crypto-normative imperative to extend French political culture beyond France's borders, even though this imperative is not sponsored by a transcendental framework, and even though Sade's 'natural' model of political culture argues for its inherent non-transferrability. While strong intervention on the international stage is disqualified, this imperative appears in the imitative model of political culture's dissemination that Sade offers: '... let other people observe you happy, and they will rush to happiness by the same road you have traced for them' (339).

Generally speaking, cosmopolitanism is not as sanguine as Sade about considering the nation-state in isolation, and where Sade brings 'man' and 'citizen' into line rather seamlessly, the disarticulation of these entities persists as a problematic in and for cosmopolitanism. Nevertheless, the crypto-normativity implicated in the Sadian political community betrays a peculiarly cosmopolitan tension between abstract universalism and particularist affiliation. And while cosmopolitanism refuses Sade's strong nationalism, it grapples with the same question Sade does; namely, what, if not transcendental norms, will motivate and legitimate moral and/or political action? Especially if Sade's insulated nationalism and crypto-normativity seem politically or theoretically unsatisfying, his example motivates a re-examination of a cosmopolitanism that retains a strong normative framework. In any case, it remains to consider what relationship between politics and morality is entailed by a cosmopolitical vision that adheres to universal norms.

III. Cosmopolitanism, bestiality?

In 'Perpetual Peace', Kant sketches the principles of a 'universal nation of men' (*ius cosmopoliticum*) founded on a universal right of humanity as the basis for perpetual peace. Kant's *ius cosmopoliticum* is not dismissive of a Hobbesian conception of the political, but takes it as its *raison d'être*: 'the natural state' of 'men living in close proximity' 'is a one of war. ... The state of peace must therefore be *established*, for the suspension of hostilities does not provide the security of peace, and unless this security is pledged by one neighbor to another (which can happen only in a state of *lawfulness*), the latter, from whom such security has been requested, can treat the former as an enemy' (349).[6] Nor does Kant's cosmopolitanism dispense with the nation-state. Developed partly as 'an expression of support for the [French] Republic', which, according to Kant, monarchical states should view 'as the potential leader of a peaceful cosmopolitan federation' (Wood 1998, 59), it retains state sovereignty as a necessary element of that federation. In the 'Preliminary Articles for Perpetual Peace Among Nations', Kant lists as the fifth article, 'No nation shall forcibly interfere with the constitution and government of another'; such interference, he argues, 'would violate the rights of an independent people struggling with its internal ills' (Kant 1983, 346). In Kant's cosmopolitical order, the constitution that presides over international relations conforms to the civil rights of national citizens and the rights of nations in relation to one another; it respects rather than homogenises transnational differences. But, importantly, this constitution must also conform 'to the *rights of world citizenship*' (1983, 350). Again, this is not opposed to a politics of natural enmity but follows from it: 'if even one of these [nations] had only physical influence on one another, they would be in a state of nature, and consequently they would be bound in a state of war' (350). For Kant, a state of lawfulness in which rights are protected is the necessary condition for perpetual peace; as the guarantor of peace, able to mediate political conflict as it were from above, it is transcendent and prior to the political. Thus, abstract principles of legitimation have priority over concrete principles of affiliation, even as the former contribute to a (normatively grounded) expanded affiliation (i.e. world citizenship); justice, that is, trumps loyalty.

Given that Kant's cosmopolitanism adheres to the right of nations, Kant does not call for a world-state: 'in place of the positive idea of a *world republic* [is] put only the *negative* surrogate of an enduring, ever expanding *federation* that prevents war and curbs the tendency of that hostile inclination to defy the law' (1983, 357). Because of its negative status, however, this federation is potentially crippled: how can a surrogate, negatively defined institution command the loyalty necessary to secure perpetual peace, and how can such broad political affiliation be motivated morally? What principle of legitimation will provide the kind of 'motivational anchoring' (to borrow Habermas's term) capable of solidifying a large association of citizens? These are questions about the 'disagreement between morals and politics in relation to perpetual peace', the subject of Appendix I to 'Perpetual Peace' (370). For Kant, this disagreement is resolved not by political expediency but by principles of right (cf. Wood 1998, 61); while political realities may indeed cast doubt on them (cf. Kant 1963, 355), such principles must serve as 'a limiting condition of politics', and not *vice versa* (372). What Kant is rejecting here is, of course, a prudential or eudaemonistic management of the contingent realm of politics. A prudential morality that subordinates the principle of right to desired political ends, as the so-called political moralist does, defeats 'the purpose of effecting an agreement between politics and morals' (376). It does not so much resolve as dissolve the conflict between politics and morality within the immediate demands of political expedience.

Thus, for prudential morality Kant substitutes morality as an unconditional law under which politics must be subsumed. By privileging a transcendentally grounded morality, Kant effects an agreement between politics and morality. As 'the totality of unconditionally binding laws according to which we *ought* to act', practical morality is, in Kant's schema, necessary and *therefore* possible. Proceeding from a transcendental 'ought' in this way, Kant is able to argue that 'consequently, there can be no conflict between politics as an applied doctrine of right and morals as a theoretical doctrine of right (thus no conflict between practice and theory)' (370). For, were there to be such a conflict (i.e. were it impossible to translate theory into practice or morality into politics), then morality as such would disappear as prudential considerations come to govern it (370). Unlike the 'political moralist', the 'moral politician' – whom Kant links with 'true republicanism' – conceives of perpetual peace as a *moral*, not a *technical*, task. That is, in problems of practical reason he begins from *formal* principles in accordance with the principle of right as unconditionally necessary (377). In this way, conduct, whether individual, civic or international, can harmonise with morality rather than capitulating to the pull of material principles (cf. 377), just as any fault discovered 'in a nation's constitution or in its relations with other nations' must be corrected in a way that conforms to 'natural right' as 'a model presented by an idea of reason' (372). Moreover, the form of this agreement supplies a moral motivation for broad political affiliation: conduct that harmonises with morality 'derives directly from the general will that is given *a priori* ... which alone determines what is right among men' (378). With the harmonisation of morality and politics, then, comes the seamless convergence of the principles of legitimation and affiliation, both of which depend on presuming the priority of transcendental right.

But does the moral politician, whose actions are guided by a transcendental notion of 'natural right', moralise politics? Is the specifically cos*mopolitical* purchase of Kant's 'Perpetual Peace' compromised by its universalist framework? With Hegel's criticism of Kant in mind, Carl Schmitt (1996) proffered an anti-universalist slogan that sounds like an abbreviated and radicalised version of de Maistre's quip on 'man': 'Humanity, Bestiality' (cf. Habermas 1999, 198). For Schmitt, a nationalist defence of sovereignty, which acts as a bulwark against intervention conducted under the aegis of a universalist rhetoric of human rights, delimits conflict within a political context. By 'political context' we must understand not only sovereign statehood but also Schmitt's roughly Hobbesian, friend–enemy conception of the political – a conception that cannot be sustained within a universalist framework insofar as the 'concept of humanity excludes the concept of the enemy' (Schmitt 1996, 54). Conversely, the universalism of Kantian morality invites an unlimited war against war: by acknowledging but ultimately overriding the claims of sovereign states in the name of humanity, it justifies the expansion of what would otherwise be a contained military struggle. Even if a universalist morality pays lip service to the right of sovereign states, Schmitt argues, its enemy becomes one 'who no longer must be compelled to retreat into his borders only' (36). By the same token, a war conducted in the name of humanity will be especially intense, for 'by transcending the limits of the political framework, it simultaneously degrades the enemy into moral ... categories and is forced to make of him a monster that that must not only be defeated but also utterly destroyed' (Schmitt 36). Thus universalism, according to Schmitt, moralises politics, and in doing so it mystifies and disables real political struggle, even as it releases that struggle in all its fury. Humanity is converted into inhumanity.

As Schmitt's critique of abstract universalism leads us to expect, Kant, displaying what one theorist has called an 'ontotheology' oriented towards a 'dogmatic' teleology (cf. Cheah 1998, 307), evinces a moralisation of politics. For example, Kant maintains the 'sacred' quality of rights 'however great the cost of sacrifice may be to those in power' (1983, 380). Similarly, the nature of the beast that Kant's cosmopolitical order opposes is unleashed from concrete political definition and 'degraded' into a moral category: he describes the 'intrinsic characteristic of moral evil' as having aims that 'are self-contradictory and self-destructive, thus '[making] way for the (moral) principle of goodness ... ' (379). By pushing the actual achievement of peace to some distant future (progress towards 'the ... principle of goodness', Kant admits, 'is slow' [379]), he allows for a protracted present of anarchic and interminable struggles against an abstract conception of 'evil'. Alternatively, if the 'intrinsic character of moral evil' dictates that it will fall not in an unlimited paramilitary war (as Schmitt would have it) but by its own *incoherence*, the peace of a global political order, buttressed by a general will given *a priori* and a transcendental principle of right, remains theoretical. In other words, Kant resolves the conflict between morality and politics only on the level of theory.

As we shall see, Kant himself is aware of the potential limitations of such a resolution, and Derrida's cosmopolitical vision, which retains Kant as an important discursive partner, reproduces this anxious awareness. This awareness can only be heightened by the fact that by surrendering the abstract universalism that Schmitt criticises, the moralisation of politics is not thereby *necessarily* avoided. Recall, for example, Sade's imitative model of the dissemination of political culture. Though it dispenses with a transcendentally sponsored universalism, this model is not obviously separable from moral claims about the exemplarity of a nation's political culture, and hence from the imperative to disseminate it. (Recall, also, Sade's distinctly moral condemnation of more bellicose mechanisms of dissemination, which he deems 'vainglorious'.) Similarly, those who want to see 'human rights' respected worldwide, but who feel uncomfortable about the universalism from which the notion of human rights is inextricable, might hope that rights-respecting states will teach others by example; rather than treating rights as a political issue, they treat them as a moral issue that cannot be enforced politically (Rorty in Cheah and Robbins, 45–58). Since dispensing with universal morality does not guarantee the purity of the political, even those cosmopolitan discourses that temper Kant's stringent universalism continue to worry about the abandonment of politics.[7] Derrida's 'On Cosmopolitanism', which takes conditional, historical politics and unconditional, quasi-transcendental ethics as the two necessary but non-coincident terms of cosmopolitanism, marks an attempt to avoid abandoning the political without falling back onto the kind of 'natural' political order espoused by both Schmitt and Sade.

IV. Derrida's manners

Whether we think of its head as a transcendental principle or a king, despotism, writes Sade, 'depraved our manners', and he calls for new manners – and laws built up from them – more suited to republican citizens (1965, 338). As we have seen, for Sade these 'manners' find a new source of legitimation in a determinate and largely 'natural' context. What might be called Derrida's 'manners' – namely, those dispensations that structure our relations with others – are the opposite of determinate: they evolve within a context of undecidability and are bound to the absolute imperatives of the unconditional, quasi-transcendental realm of ethics. Though refractory to natural conditioning, however, they do not disregard the conditional, whether by 'conditional' we mean the domain of politics or of codified law more specifically. The question I would now like to address is how Derrida's cosmopolitical vision navigates the fissure between politics and morality – ultimately privileging it as a 'both/and' that holds off reification and closure – and how it distributes responsibility between those. Importantly, Derrida's vision draws on the Enlightenment ideals promulgated by Kant. As he remarked in a speech given on the occasion of *Le Monde diplomatique*'s fiftieth anniversary, counter-globalisation efforts to reform post-cold war institutions like the IMF and WTO might best be furthered by recognising Europe's 'unique responsibility', a responsibility derived from Europe's status 'as a proud descendant of the Enlightenment past and a harbinger of the new Enlightenment to come'. At the same time, the close formal relationship of familiar Derridian *aporias* to cosmopolitanism's post-Enlightenment impasse lends Derrida's cosmopolitical vision a particular freshness and persuasiveness.

In *On Cosmopolitanism and Forgiveness*, Derrida considers how to conceive of a cosmopolitical order without abandoning the political, but also while retaining ethical force. In other words, justice, or the conceptually similar (because similarly absolute and undeconstructable) 'unconditional hospitality' that structures Derrida's cosmopolitan order, cannot be reduced to a principle at the service of political exigencies, yet the conditional, determinate realm of politics is retained as the necessary field of cosmopolitanism. By attending to both political and ethical imperatives, Derrida's cosmopolitanism avoids the moralisation of politics entailed, according to Schmitt, by a reliance on the abstract principle of human rights as natural law. While Derrida is concerned to redefine and develop the right to asylum, natural law, which is one possible source of this right, does not figure in his cosmopolitical order in any clear way. In fact, Derrida criticises natural law as it appears in Kant's 'Perpetual Peace' (cf. 1983, 20–1). Nevertheless, in Derrida's vision there is something sufficiently similar to human rights – something as inalienable and unconditional – to make Schmitt's argument speak of it in an illuminating way.

Part of the pointedness of Derrida's titular allusion to Sade's (1965) 'Yet Another Effort, Frenchmen, if You Would Become Republicans!', which in his text becomes 'Cosmopolites de Touts les Pays, Encore un Effort!', concerns the role of the nation-state. Derrida departs from both Sade and Kant, united as they are by their common commitment to the republican nation-state, by relocating cosmopolitics to the *city*:[8] 'At a time when the "end of the city" resonates as though it were a verdict ... how can we still dream of a novel status for the city, and thus for the "cities of refuge?" (Derrida 2001, 3). The task is not only to imagine this 'novel status for ..."cities of refuge" ', but to have these cities 'reorient the politics of the state' (4), and hence the laws that govern them. This shift to the city is a response to what Hannah Arendt (1975) calls 'The Decline of the Nation-State and the End of the Rights of Man' in her text of that name. Derrida writes: 'Whenever the State is neither the foremost author of, nor the foremost guarantor against the violence which forces refugees or exiles to flee, it is often powerless to ensure the protection and the liberty of its own citizens before a terrorist menace, whether or not it has a religious or nationalist alibi' (6). The shift from the nation to the city, then, is in part a response to the failure of the monopolisation of violence that Norbert Elias – writing as Arendt was under the shadow of National Socialism – hoped would one day restrain the genocidal horrors that marked the twentieth century. Furthermore, these cities, 'as independent from each other and from the state as possible', must be 'allied to each other in forms of solidarity yet to be invented' (4). What principle of affiliation might consolidate this alliance is, Derrida suggests, an open question, but it is 'our task' to address it, and it must be addressed, as Kant also says, in relation to continually evolving political realities: 'the theoretical or critical reflection it involves is indissociable from the practical initiatives we have already, out of a sense of urgency, initiated and implemented' (Kant 1983, 4). Thus his is 'a theoretical task indissociable from its implementation' (9). In Kant's words, it is both a moral and a technical task.

Despite his insistence upon implementation, Derrida gives primacy to ethics as a principle of legitimation possessed of normative force. He preserves the priority of (what Kant would call) morality, but unlike Kant, he shies away from stating it as universal in a clean, unambiguous way. For Derrida, this principle is quasi-transcendental; while from an ethical point of view it must necessarily be stipulated, it is impossible, *in the meantime*, to realise politically. And though he is concerned to see rights registered in (a transformed) international law, he offers no mediating mechanism for ethics and politics. Like Kant, he conceives of a cosmopolitical order in terms of rights (the right to asylum) and duties (the duty to hospitality) that are absolute and unconditional, even though they have a history and even though there exists 'an always possible perversion of *the* law of hospitality' (17).[9] Thus Derrida writes: '... one cannot speak of cultivating an ethic of hospitality. Hospitality is culture itself and not simply one ethic amongst others' (16).[10]

The status and purchase of 'culture' here is unclear. By evoking it Derrida means to lift the 'ethic of hospitality' above those who 'cultivate' it, but how can culture be separated from cultivation, and why would Derrida want to absolutise it in this way? Perhaps Derrida's question, '[how] can the right to asylum be redefined and developed without repatriation and *without naturalisation?*' can shed light on his use of the term 'culture' (7; emphasis added). 'Naturalisation' is offered here as an alternative to repatriation: a means of enfolding the naked moral person, or the stateless refugee, within the mantle reserved for the legal person or citizen and bestowed upon her by the adoptive nation-state. Because the protective nation-state is by no means definitive for Derrida, his cosmopolitical vision cancels naturalisation as an option. Moreover, Derrida would clearly reject a naturalisation according to which those who have the right to asylum need to be sufficiently 'like us', whether linguistically, culturally or otherwise. But the 'naturalisation' that Derrida rejects also includes the Sadian principle of affiliation, which gathers disparate individuals into a republican state whose laws take their orientation not only from a loyalty to that state form, but also from 'Nature' itself. Thus Derrida's opposition to Sade, conjured by the title of his text, consists not only in his privileging of cosmopolitanism over republicanism, but also of 'culture' over 'Nature'. What 'culture' must refer to here, though, is neither a denaturalised national identity, nor a 'given', 'the material conditions of [culture's] effectivity as a historical force' (Cheah 1998, 299). 'Hospitality,' 'culture,' 'ethics': all these are, at least initially, offered as equivalent terms (cf. Derrida 2004, 16–17); they all name an unconditional, limitless, quasi-transcendental law, our duty to which is likewise unconditional, and likewise limitless.

Yet, if Derrida's rejection of 'natural', Sadian law in favour of something more like a moral law situates his cosmopolitanism in close proximity to Kant, he also critiques natural law as it functions in 'Perpetual Peace'. There, cosmopolitan law, which is 'to encompass universal hospitality *without* limit', is determined as natural law, and therefore as 'imprescriptible and inalienable' (Derrida 2001, 20). Thus, the right to universal hospitality 'belongs to all men by virtue of their common ownership of the earth's surface' (Kant 1983, 358). In Kant's peculiarly literal understanding of globalisation, people cannot scatter themselves infinitely but must 'tolerate living in close proximity, because originally no one had a greater right to any region of the earth than anyone else'; thus 'the right to the *earth's surface* ... belongs in common to the totality of all men' and constitutes the basis of the right to hospitality (358). According to Derrida, this appeal to natural right as a right to inhabit the surface area of the globe functions not simply to render the right to hospitality limitless (i.e. to render it applicable to all parts of the globe), but 'above all to expel from [this common place] what is *erected, constructed, or what sets itself up above* the soil: habitat, culture, institution, State, etc.' (21).[11] Thus, Derrida's definition of the right to hospitality as 'culture itself' is not so much a de-transcendentalising move as a de-naturalising move that aims to make the globe, including the artificial institutions erected upon it, *unconditionally* accessible, and hence to surpass Kant's exclusionary 'institution of limit as a border, nation, State, public or political space' (Derrida 2001, 21).

Derrida's expanded cosmopolitical territory, which pertains not only to unconditioned moral law but also to conditioned, 'artificial' political institutions, is one way in which the indissociability of the ethical and the political manifests itself. Beyond requiring this particular expansiveness, Derrida attends, if fleetingly, to the need to translate the right to hospitality into concrete historico-political terms. He wants not merely 'to keep the gap between empty form and concrete content *visible*' (Glynos 2000, 7), but to bring form and content (or theory and practice) together. So, for instance, Derrida asks how we can conceive of 'a novel status for ... the "cities of refuge" *through a renewal of international law'* (2001, 3). In advocating such a renewal, Derrida gestures towards the juridification of rights, and imagines 'the experience of cities of refuge as giving rise to a place (*lieu*) for ... a new order of law' (23). Indeed, for Derrida the ethical must be moved towards the political even if its absolute status will thereby be compromised. To some extent, the way for this development is already paved by the specificity of 'hospitality' as ethics. For unlike the abstract ideal of 'justice' it is otherwise so similar to, hospitality names the particular, concrete object of it: the stranger who, to receive hospitality, must in some sense remain strange. 'Hospitality' provides for universal affiliation while also militating against the homogenisation of differences dictated, for example, by 'naturalisation'.

Though Derrida's gesture towards the juridification of rights indicates a readiness to compromise (though not necessarily to corrupt) the unconditional, specifically ethical nature of hospitality, hospitality's naturalisation – or politicisation, in Schmitt's sense – is averted insofar as the fissure between ethics and politics is not sealed, but held open as the site of legal and political improvement. For Derrida (2001), cosmopolitanism is 'a question ... of knowing if this improvement is possible within an historical space which takes place *between* the Law of an unconditional hospitality, offered *a priori* to every other, to all newcomers ... and *the* conditional laws of a right to hospitality' (22–3). The association of law or politics on the one hand and morality on the other is thus a cleavage, both a splitting and an adherence. This basis of cosmopolitical association is not secured by a Sadean crypto-normativity, but by the openly ambivalent normativity of the ethical affirmed as a quasi-transcendental principle (i.e. as a condition of possibility *and* impossibility). As the impossibility of fully realising ethics in the conditional realm of politics, this principle guards against the moralisation of politics that stems from positing transcendental, 'natural' rights as the foundation for cosmopolitanism. As the possibility of realising ethics in politics, it ensures that ethics, as the demand of hospitality, is not surrendered to politics.

V. Good bad infinity

For Kant, 'true politics' – and cosmopolitics *a fortiori* – 'cannot progress without paying homage to morality' (1983, 380), but can the relationship between politics and morality progress beyond one in which each merely pays homage to the other? Both Kant and Derrida's answers to this question remain ambivalent, even though – or perhaps because – the question goes to the heart of cosmopolitanism's highest aspirations as well as its most enduring challenges. Indeed, this ambivalence is an important characteristic of their cosmopolitical visions, particularly as it gets thematised as a necessary rift that keeps both morality and politics in circulation, and which allows for an expanded affiliation that neither homogenises national differences nor surrenders normative force.

Kant ultimately resolves the conflict between politics and rights-based morality in favour of the latter: 'Here we cannot go halfway, cooking up hybrid, pragmatically-conditioned rights (which are somewhere between the right and the expedient); instead, politics must bend its knee before morality, and by so doing it can hope to reach, though but gradually, the stage where it will shine in light perpetual' (1983, 380). By paying homage to the transcendental principle of morality, *objectively* (i.e., in theory) the conflict between politics and morality will be resolved. Subjectively, things look rather different: '... subjectively (in the self-seeking inclinations of men, which, because they are not based on maxims of reason, must not be called the [sphere of] practice [*Praxis*]) this conflict will always remain ...' (379). But, Kant continues, 'as well it should; for it serves as the whetstone of virtue, whose true courage ... consists ... in detecting, squarely facing, and conquering the deceit of the evil principle in ourselves, which is more dangerously devious and treacherous because it excuses all our transgressions with an appeal to human nature's frailty' (379). Valorisation of the rift between politics and morality along these ontotheological lines, however, is open only to a cosmopolitanism that takes for granted an autonomous individual who must try to conquer the 'lower' principles of her nature. For this individual, importantly, the quest for self-mastery is infinite. Her 'virtue' consists in the insurmountable difference between her natural, human frailty and her properly 'moral' attempts to overcome this frailty; it consists, that is, in her infinite attempt to bring her phenomenal self into line with apodictic moral law, and not at all in her success at doing so. In short, she can only '*hope* to reach, though but gradually, the stage where' her virtue 'will shine in light perpetual' (380; emphasis added). For Kant, this hope, and the moral agony that attends it, is what morality consists in. To extinguish it in success is to extinguish morality as such.

Sade's naturalism, refracted through the state and its political exigencies, pits itself against this Kantian moral agony. In his attempt to heal the bifurcated subject produced by a law that that subject is constitutively incapable of following, Sade does indeed excuse our 'transgressions with an appeal to human nature's frailty' (Kant 379) – though that 'frailty' is sublimated as 'Nature's' strength and virtue. While the Sadian narrative certainly does not resolve itself in Spirit, this sublimation, which dissolves the slavish self-estrangement produced by positive law in a 'higher' reconciliation, is structurally similar to Hegel's triumph over Kantian 'unhappy consciousness' or 'bad infinity', where the diremption between law (or politics) and ethics (or morality), and consciousness' restless return to the divisiveness of incomplete negations, are solved: consciousness in its concrete presentness (in, for example, the form of affiliation designated by *Sittlichkeit*) no longer has to bend its knee to law projected as an asymptotic 'beyond'. In this way, the Hegelian critique of the Kantian moral agent offers cosmopolitanism a blueprint for healing the rift between politics and morality.[12] However, a cosmopolitanism which, while elaborating the sort of concrete affiliation that *Sittlichkeit* affords, wants to retain normativity *without* grounding those in Nature or Spirit, must stop just short of the final consummation of Hegelian *Aufhebung*. Thus, where affiliation is concerned, cosmopolitanism's relationship to Hegel looks necessary and productive, but as cosmopolitanism retains and even affirms the 'bad infinity' Hegel sought to overcome, it also comes to look deeply conflicted.

Rather than looking to 'hybrid, pragmatically-conditioned rights' that combine Kantian and Sadian attitudes to normativity as the guarantor of (for example) hospitality, cosmopolitanism might stay within the rift between morality and politics, as if to say, with Kant, as well this conflict *should* remain. This is, in effect, the course Derrida charts. Though he valorises the rift between politics and morality in structural rather than moral terms, the ambivalence between politics and morality persists. As Critchley remarks: 'On the one hand, ethics is left defined as the infinite responsibility of unconditional hospitality. Whilst, on the other hand, the political can be defined as the taking of a decision without any determinate transcendental guarantees' (quoted in Glynos 2000, 6). With morality and politics associated as what I have called a cleavage, the ethic of hospitality is a quasi-transcendental ideal that remains unconditional and absolute even while it is brought to bear on the conditional, contingent realm of politics and law. However, this phrase, 'being brought to bear', hedges the issue somewhat. Certainly, it does *not* suggest the mutual activation of politics and morality. Nor does it suggest their easy coalescence. Indeed, such scenarios of reconciliation are in Derrida's account not only impossible but undesirable, insofar as they would compromise the force of the ethical and our infinite responsibility to it. If the concrete reconciliation of ethics and politics must therefore be endlessly deferred, and if, moreover, this deferral is a specifically *ethical* imperative, does Derrida merely pay homage to politics in the end?

An affirmative answer to this question is suggested by Derrida's admission of irresolution. Towards the end of *On Cosmopolitanism and Forgiveness*, he writes: 'All these questions [e.g. whether, and what it means, to make hospitality dependent on state or city sovereignty] remain obscure and difficult and we must neither conceal them from ourselves nor ... imagine ourselves to have mastered them' (22). Here Derrida seems to collapse the systematic and ethical necessity of irresolution with irresolution as both an unavoidable shortcoming of his analysis, and as a product of the historical condition in which we now find ourselves. For instance, if 'the experience of cities of refuge' will '[give] rise to a place (*lieu*) for reflection – for reflection on the questions of asylum and hospitality – and for a new order of law' (23), what exactly is the connection between ethical reflection and this new order of law? Derrida's admission of recalcitrant obscurity is admirably honest and attentive to political realities. Nevertheless, the confounding of theoretical, systematic irresolution and practical, historical irresolution invites further consideration of the nature of Derrida's valorisation of the rift between politics and morality.

Despite his adherence to the ineliminable irreconcilability of politics and morality, Derrida does designate a topos for their resolution. This topos, or u-topos, is the space '*between* the Law of an unconditional hospitality ... and *the* conditional laws of a right to hospitality' (2001, 22) (similarly, 'a novel status for ... the 'cities of refuge'' is to be conceived of 'through a *renewal* of international law' [3]). The 'thresholdism' of this proposed resolution – where politics and morality are always just about to convergence, and where morality only prefigures its legal and political instantiation – is a product not only of Derrida's theoretical insistence upon the necessary cleavage of politics and morality, but also, and perhaps primarily, of the need to bring politics and morality together *in actuality*. That is, the political demand that an ethics of hospitality should govern the contemporary problems posed by the increasingly heavy presence of the refugee puts pressure on Derrida's valorisation of the distance separating concrete political demands and quasi-transcendental moral imperatives (a pressure, it must be said, that Derrida heartily acknowledges as a call 'for an urgent response, a just response' [23]).

Since hospitality pertains to 'the residence, one's home, the familiar place of dwelling, inasmuch as it is ... the manner in which we relate to ourselves and others' (16–17), thresholdism is an apposite way of conceiving of the Derridian cleavage. For it is precisely the threshold, and the crossing of it, that is at issue, whether that threshold marks the permeable division between oneself and others, between one nation and another, or between the private and the public. But, like a bifurcated theoretical orientation that straddles the divide between morality and politics without affording their mediation, Derrida's quasi-transcendental principle straddles the threshold as the contested site of hospitality. If his designation of the site of resolution as 'an historical space' (22) does not necessarily cancel the theoretical cleavage he maintains, or if it does not obviously crowd out the 'place ... for reflection' he wants to hold open, it might well provoke us to ask what exactly this deferred historicity consists in. In the good 'bad infinity' of Derrida's cosmopolitical vision, then, open doors leave questions open.

VI. The perpetual promise of cosmopolitanism

That Kant and Derrida, in their different ways, privilege the rift between politics and morality as necessary and productive does not prevent the inconclusiveness of their cosmopolitical ideals from recurring as a problem for them. As they oscillate between the already established and some normatively sponsored 'beyond' of futurity, the fear that the ideals they articulate are empty and naïve – that, in the end, we are just paying empty homage to morality – surfaces again and again. For instance, with what Wood nicely describes as 'a mixture of dignified self-assertion and self-deprecating good-humor' (1998, 61), Kant offers a 'Secret Article for Perpetual Peace' according to which '*The maxims of philosophers concerning the conditions under which public peace is possible shall be consulted by nations armed for war*' (Kant 1983, 369), even as 'he is concerned to rebut any accusation that he is naive or excessively optimistic' (Wood 1998, 61). Thus Kant asserts: '... the idea of cosmopolitan right is not fantastic or exaggerated, but rather an amendment to the unwritten code of national and international rights. ... Only such an amendment allows us to flatter ourselves with the thought that we are making continual progress towards perpetual peace' (360). Similarly, Derrida acknowledges that his '[dream] of another concept, of another set of rights for the city' 'might appear utopian for a thousand reasons' (2001, 8), and, as if in response to this symptomatic juxtaposition of 'reasons' and 'dreams', he stresses his concern to keep the law of hospitality from 'remaining a pious and irresponsible desire, without form and without potency' (23).

This law could be given form and potency through its juridification; positive law, in other words, could carry us over the threshold separating politics and morality. But if the juridification of moral (or, let us say, human) rights is to provide the basis for Derrida's cosmopolitical order, then, it seems, a double entry orientation must be adopted for these rights. To remain *moral* rights, they must be suprapositive rights pertaining not to the *citoyen* but to *l'homme*, but at the same time function as constitutional norms with positive validity. When human or moral rights are understood as rights that exist independently of their instantiation in actual political or legal orders, and which can be appealed to whether or not they exist *de facto*, but also when they lack absolute, transcendental legitimation, then when we argue for their juridification what we are really saying is only that 'we think it would (morally) be a good idea if they were enforced' (Geuss 2001, 144). Their juridification would then beg the question of where this moral belief originally came from, and since moral beliefs might not be shared universally, it would be hard to justify their universal imposition. Thus, arguably, the juridification of rights would only reinscribe the conflict between politics and morality within law itself, and both rights and the institutions that express and protect them would be in danger of losing their particularly moral force.

Such impasses demonstrate the theoretical consistency of Kant's insistence upon the absolute primacy of morality. If consistency is unsatisfying from a cosmo*political* point of view, they also heighten the appeal of Derrida's insistence upon a fundamental separation of politics and morality. These impasses might not be insoluble. Certainly, they invite further reflection. But whatever the particular contributions of various cosmopolitical visions, the value of cosmopolitical thinking in general inheres in its uncompromising refusal to sacrifice the variables of a given geopolitical order to the ideal of a universalisable principle of legitimation. Or vice versa. Such an uncompromising stance has a price. This price is most apparent in the infinite deferral of Derrida's cosmopolitical order – the sense of which is only sharpened by the ever-growing need to realise that order. As Derrida writes in his *Le Monde* speech, the expansive solidarity of those anti-globalisation movements that refuse automatically to convert (for example) pro-Palistinianism into anti-Americanism helps him 'not only to dream … that another world is possible, but to muster the strength to do all that is needed to make it possible'. But to make this world possible is not (yet) to make it actual. So as cosmopolitanism proffers a specifically *political* vision mounted on promises of a peace to come, it shows itself to be strongly invested in futurity, even as it construes the emergence of a future – and, more particularly, the historical and philosophical conditions of that emergence – to be inherently *vexed desiderata*.

Acknowledgement

I would like to thank Amanda Anderson and William Connolly for their comments on earlier versions of this chapter.

Notes

1. See, for example, Robbins (1999, 148) and Appiah (1998, 111), whose translation I quote.
2. Derrida, for instance; see below. See also Kristeva (1993, 74).
3. This leaves open the possibility that there may be some value besides virtue that *is* incontestable. This value, though, turns out to be 'Nature' itself. See text below.
4. As some theorists of cosmopolitanism view it; cf. Robbins (1999, 156).
5. Cf. Montesquieu (1989): 'It is a maxim of capital importance that the mores and manners of a despotic state must never be changed; nothing would be more promptly followed by a revolution. For, in these states, there are no laws, so to speak; there are only mores and manners, and if you overturn them, you overturn everything' (314).
6. Page numbers refer to those of *Kant's Gesammelte Schriften*, which Humphrey gives in his translation (Derrida 2004).
7. See, for example, Bruce Robbins, Pheng Cheah, and Julia Kristeva.
8. Here Derrida, following Arendt, draws on medieval tradition and the principle of *quid est in territorio est de territorio* (cf. 7, 18).
9. It is precisely *as* hospitality that ethics has this history – one that includes force and violence – and this potential to be perverted.
10. Compare Kant on universal hospitality: '... our concern here is not with philanthropy, but with *right*' (358).
11. Derrida makes this claim despite Kant's insistence that the 'state of peace must ... be *established*' (349).
12. For examples of how the Hegelian critique is taken up by cosmopolitical discourses, cf. Rorty (1998, 49) and Robbins (1998, 156). Kristeva (1993, 28–9) acknowledges the critique but opts to celebrate a 'torn consciousness'.

References

Appiah, K. A. (1998) 'Cosmopolitan Patriots', in Pheng Cheah and Bruce Robbins (eds), *Cosmopolitics*, Minneapolis, MN: University of Minnesota Press, pp. 91–114.
Arendt, H. (1975) 'The Decline of the Nation-State and the End of the Rights of Man', in *The Origins of Totalitarianism*, Florida: Harcourt & Brace, pp. 267–302.

90   *Meredith Evans*

Cheah, Pheng. (1998) 'Given Culture: Rethinking Cosmopolitical Freedom in Transnationalism', in Pheng Cheah and Bruce Robbins (eds), *Cosmopolitics*, Minneapolis, MN: University of Minnesota Press, pp. 290–328.

Critchley, S. (1997) 'Deconstruction and Pragmatism – Is Derrida a Private Ironist or a Public Liberal?' in Chantal Mouffe (ed.), *Deconstruction and Pragmatism*, New York: Routledge, pp. 19–40.

Derrida, J. (2004) 'Enlightenment Past and to Come'. 06 November. <http://mondediplo.com/2004/11/06derrida>.

Derrida, J. (2001) *On Cosmopolitanism and Forgiveness* trans. Mark Dooley. New York: Routledge.

Geuss, R. (2001) *History and Illusion in Politics*, Cambridge: Cambridge University Press.

Glynos, J. (2000) 'Thinking the Ethics of the Political in the Context of a Postfoundational World: From an Ethics of Desire to an Ethics of the Drive'. *Theory and Event*, Vol. 4, No. 4, 1–16. <http://muse.jhu.edu/journals/theory_and_event/v004/4.4glynos.html>.

Habermas, J. (1999) *The Inclusion of the Other* ed. Ciaran Cronin and Pablo De Greiff, Cambridge: The MIT Press.

Kant, I. (1983) *Perpetual Peace and Other Essays* trans. Ted Humphrey Indianapolis: Hackett Publishing Company.

Kristeva, J. (1993) *Nations Without Nationalism* trans. Leon S. Roudiez, New York: Columbia University Press,.

Montesquieu, C. (1989) *The Spirit of the Laws* trans. Anne M. Cohler, Basia Carolyn Miller et al., Cambridge: Cambridge University Press,

Robbins, B. (1999) *Feeling Global: Internationalism in Distress*, New York: New York University Press,

Rorty, R. (1998) 'Justice as a Larger Loyalty' in Pheng Cheah and Bruce Robbins (eds), *Cosmopolitics*, Minneapolis, MN: University of Minnesota Press, pp. 45–58.

Sade, M. de (1965) *Justine, Philosophy in the Bedroom, and Other Writings* trans. Richard Seaver and Austryn Wainhouse, New York: Grove Press.

Schmitt, C. (1996) *The Concept of the Political* trans. George Schwab, Chicago, IL: University of Chicago Press.

Wood, A. W. (1998) 'Kant's Project for Perpetual Peace', in Pheng Cheah and Bruce Robbins (eds), *Cosmopolitics*, Minneapolis, MN: University of Minnesota Press, pp. 59–76.

5

'ConcateNations': Globalisation in a Spinozist Context

Yves Citton

In little more than a decade, everybody in the Western world has become remarkably fluent in the 'global talk'. Although few among us could precisely define the words we use so commonly, we all see ourselves as living in a 'global' (globalised, globalising) world. Even if we usually shy away from the implications of this obvious reality, we are all aware of the inter-connectedness that is the fabric of our everyday life, from wearing clothes 'made in Indonesia' to seeing our pension funds divest from Brazil or Argentina.

A number of questions can be raised regarding this by-now trivial awareness of being a planetary consumer: is it as new as we believe it is? If it does indeed have older roots, how far back do they go, and where do they come from? The word and the notion of *concatenation* provide, as I hope to show in this chapter, a remarkable vantage point to address such questions. What is at stake here is both the *archaeology* and the *imaginary* of globalisation – two dimensions which have been ignored by the doubly naive assumption that we are witnessing something in rupture with the past, and that the current process is driven first and foremost by the hard facts of political economy.

Against such naiveté, it is important first to relocate 'globalisation' within its long-term history. Although most publications devoted to this best-selling issue limit their historical scope to opposing the bi-polar, military-led, ideologically structured world of the Cold War to the multi-centred, economically driven and value-free process of globalisation, we must clearly state that the 'new' geopolitical order is little more than colonisation by other means – along the good old core/periphery model developed by Wallerstein and Braudel thirty years ago. It is only insofar as we frame globalisation within the past five centuries of Western expansion over the planet that we have a chance to understand what is currently happening: a mere *retour de manivelle* – which may indeed lead to a major and dramatic inversion of movements and flows, but which may equally well remain a minor bump in the long road of Western hegemony. In any case, the true questions linked with globalisation emerge only once we look beyond the horizon of the Cold War, and place it instead against its *archaeological background* made up of the past five hundred years of Western expansion.

It is equally important to move away from a narrow definition of globalisation in mainly economic or political terms. My point here is less to develop our sensitivity to the cultural stakes of globalisation – since countless studies already flourish on this issue – than to invite us to question the *imaginary dimension* of our reference to globalisation. What are the images, anxieties, dreams, visions, utopias, which haunt our minds when we use this word? In this regard, it seems fruitful to consider globalisation under the Lyotardian category of a *master-narrative* – a legitimising myth centred on a universal protagonist and whose power of legitimisation comes from a promise for the future. Right after Lyotard had made us 'post-modern' in view of our incredulity towards any meta-narrative, we all fell prey to the (not so) new *grand récit* of globalisation. Exploring the imaginary dimension of this master-narrative can thus bring a much needed critical distance towards a constellation of signifiers, clichés, assumptions, confusions, beliefs, values, which currently thwart the public debate about the meaning, threats and promises of globalisation.

Thus framed, the notion of *ConcateNations* appears both as the keystone and as the weaker link of the globalisation meta-narrative. By going back to some of its roots in the seventeenth-century philosophy and in the eighteenth-century political economy, I hope to show that the *chain* which ties *nations* together is a bond of servitude only insofar as we ignore the analysis of 'freedom' developed by determinist thinkers such as Hobbes and Spinoza, and that it can instead become a tool of liberation once we follow the chain of consequences implied in their conception. As I hope we will see better by the end of my presentation, what our age of globalisation needs first and foremost is a new (Spinozist and counter-intuitive) definition of 'freedom'.

I. Chayns, chaine, chains: three quotations from Hobbes

Concatenatio: well before the seventeenth century, the Latin word had been used to express the idea of a chain (*catena*) tying together (*con-*) various events in a sequence of causes and effects. In his classic study, Arthur O. Lovejoy has well shown the permanence of the theme of *The*

Great Chain of Being, from Plato and Plotinus to the French Enlightenment and German Romanticism. The two main dimensions of this topos, the *inter-connectedness* and continuous *hierarchy* of all things, appear clearly in Macrobius' *Commenarius in somnium Scipionis,* a text which informed much of the later tradition:

> since all things follow in a continuous succession, degenerating in sequence to the very bottom of the series, the attentive observer will discover a connection of parts [*una connexio*] from the Supreme God down to the last dregs of things, mutually linked together [*mutuis se vinculis religans*] and without a break [*nusquam interrupta*]; and this is Homer's golden chain [*catena*], which God, he says, bade hang down from heaven to earth. (Macrobius in Lovejoy 1976, 63)

From Neoplatonism to Christian theology, this chain almost always pointed towards God, both as its first and most noble link, and as its overall author/maker. From the seventeenth century on, in close parallel with the development of 'scientific' inquiry, an increasing number of philosophers attempt to conceive of this *catena* without attributing it to any Great Concatenator. A rich display of the political as well as of the ontological implications of this attempt is offered by the famous chapter XXI 'Of the Liberty of Subjects' of *Leviathan.*

In three occurrences of the word *chain,* Thomas Hobbes sets in place the main coordinates of the Modern take on the concatenation issue. It all starts with his (in)famous definition of freedom in purely mechanical terms:

> LIBERTY, or FREEDOM, signifieth (properly) the absence of Opposition; (by Opposition, I mean externall Impediments of motion;) and may be applyed no less to Irrationall, and Inanimate creatures, than to Rationall. For whatsoever is so *tyed,* or environed, as it cannot move, but within a certain space, which space is determined by the opposition of some externall body, we say it hath not Liberty to go further. And so of all living creatures, whilest they are imprisoned, or *restrained* with walls, or *chayns* [...] But when the impediment of motion is in the constitution of the thing it selfe, we use not to say, it wants the Liberty; but the Power to move; as when a stone lyeth still, or a man is *fastened to* his bed by sicknesse. (Hobbes 1988, 261–2, emphasis mine)

From the onset, Freedom is defined in relation to Power. They both refer to the limits of our actual capacity to do something: *literal chains* in the first case (of an external impediment), *metaphorical chains* in the second case (of an internal impediment, like a sickness 'fastening' a man to his bed). The vocabulary of liberty externalises the obstacle, whereas that of power internalises it, but both are defined in a manner that erases all boundaries between rational (human) beings, irrational (animal) creatures, inanimate things (stone) and unindividualised entities (water).

The question of the concatenation of the parts of the universe appears a page later :

> *Liberty* and *Necessity* are Consistant: As in the water, that hath not only *liberty*, but a *necessity* of descending by a Channel: so likewise in the Actions which men voluntarily doe; which (because they proceed from their will) proceed from *liberty*; and yet because every act of man's will, and every desire, and inclination, proceedeth from some cause, and that from another cause, which causes in a continuall chaine (whose first link in the hand of God the first of all causes) proceed from *necessity*. So that to him that could see the connexion of those causes, the *necessity* of all men's voluntary actions would appeare manifest. (p. 263)

In spite of the parenthetical, and conventional, reference to God as *causa prima*, we are here at the core of the scandalous new worldview which later Christian writers denounce indifferently as 'atheism', 'materialism', 'fatalism', or 'Spinozism'. If all events and all actions – including those that human beings 'freely' (i.e. voluntarily) 'choose' to do – are only necessary links within a deterministic universal concatenation ('*a continuall chaine*') of causes and effects, if even my desires, inclinations and choices are themselves mere effects of pre-existing (exterior) causes, then the very foundations of our moral universe seem to be cut at their roots: without freedom of the will, no 'responsibility', and without responsibility, no possibility of accounting for the Good or Evil nature of our (neighbour's) actions. As, over the following four centuries, scientific discourse (from biology to psychology and sociology) has increasingly made us '*see the connexion of those causes*', 'the necessity of men's voluntary actions' has appeared increasingly 'manifest', and it has become increasingly difficult for the free-will advocates to locate exactly where that 'continuall chaine' could be satisfactorily broken. Apart from Descartes' pineal gland or various short-lived redefinitions of the 'soul' (as distinct from the 'mind'), a common solution has consisted in making the chain more complex (rather than attempting to break it): along the lines suggested by Hobbes himself in his controversy with Bramhall on free will, one has tended to see in 'the concourse of all causes' not 'one simple chain or concatenation, but an innumerable number of chains joined together, not in all parts, but in their first link' (Hobbes 1654, 20) – our practical sentiment of freedom finding its last refuge in our impossibility ever to see 'the whole cause' of our inclinations in such a hyper-complex maze of cross-determinations.

To prevent the string of anti-social consequences that seems to flow from his deterministic denial of the freedom of the will and from its undermining of the notion of responsibility, Hobbes brings a third reference to chains in the same chapter on liberty:

> But as men, for the atteyning of peace, and conservation of themselves thereby, have made an Artificiall Man, which we call a Common-wealth; so also have they made Artificiall Chains, called *Civill Lawes*, which they themselves by mutuall covenants, have fastened at one end, to the lips of that Man, or Assembly, to whom they have given the Soveraigne Power; and at the other end to their own Ears. These bonds in their own nature but weak, may nevertheless be made to hold, by the danger, though not by the difficulty of breaking them. (pp. 263–4)

As they constitute political societies, human beings only add more chains to the concatenation of causes constitutive of natural necessity. Laws are metaphorical-internalised chains: their efficacy relies on 'the danger' of bringing upon oneself the real (literal) chains which are used to restrain law-breakers; when I refrain from stealing an old man's wallet, the impediment to motion is – like in the sick man's case – in the constitution of the thing itself (my will), that is, it pertains to a question of power rather than to a question of (corporal) liberty. The counter-intuitive result of the institution and internalisation of this artificial impediment is, however, that, as a citizen living in a reasonably well-ordered society, I am incomparably more powerful and free than I could ever be in any pre-political state (of nature, isolation, lawlessness and war). To summarise Hobbes' argument: chains emancipate us. Or more precisely: emancipation relies on a good use of chains.

II. Spinoza's emancipatory concatenations

In spite of its intimidating abstraction, all of Spinoza's philosophy has a very practical purpose, which is precisely to define and teach us what could be a good use of chains (causal and otherwise). It is therefore no coincidence if the word *concatenatio* appears in crucial moments of his writings, and offers us a striking vista on the overall movement of his thought. At first sight, Spinoza seems only to refine and further develop insights inherited from Hobbes, as well as from the earlier stock of images concerning the 'great chain of being'. One can still hear echoes of Macrobius' turns of phrases when an early work such as the *Treatise on the Reformation of the Intellect* evokes the 'unbreakable concatenation [*irrefragabili concatenatione*]' through which causes produce their effects, or when the same text invites us to investigate such causal links 'without breaking the concatenation of things [*nulla interrupta concatenatione rerum*]'. Along the same lines, he defines (what we would call) 'scientific explanation' as 'a concatenation of [ideas in] the intellect which must reproduce the concatenation of [things in] nature [*concatenatio intellectus, quae Naturae concatenationem referre debet*]' (Spinoza 1661, 23, 30 and 35, sections 61 n80 and n95 in Bruder's numbering),[1] and denounces 'prejudices [*praejudicia*]' as that which 'prevents men from embracing the concatenation of things [*rerum concatenationem amplecti*]' (Spinoza 1677, part I, appendix).

Although this 'concatenation of all natural things [*rerum naturalium concatenatio*]', synonym with the 'immutable order of nature [*fixum et immutabilem naturae ordinem*]', constitutes the ultimate horizon of human knowledge, its infinite complexity puts it well out of reach of our limited intellect. We must acknowledge that 'we flatly ignore how things have been ordered and concatenated in reality' and that general 'considerations about fate and the concatenation of causes can only help us very little in forming and arranging our ideas towards particular things'. Our incapacity to embrace the whole and the infinite details of the causal chains that constitute our world makes it therefore necessary 'to explain things by their proximate causes' (rather than by their first or ultimate causes) and 'to consider things as possible' (i.e. contingent, even if they are in fact fully determined) (Spinoza 1670, chapter IV, section 10).

Even though the Great Chain of Causes remains out of our reach, a clear understanding of its overall nature is a necessary pre-condition to the proper orientation of our thoughts and actions. Two scandalous guiding principles made Spinoza's metaphysics an object of abomination for the readers of his time. The first one is his (in)famous assimilation of God with Nature (*Deus sive Natura*) which leads to the denial of Creation, of a Creator, of Providence, that is, of any traditional idea of the Judeo-Christian God. In terms of chains: the world is a concatenation, but there is no Master-Concatenator; the world is a process of auto-production, of auto-organisation, in the absence of any master plan to guide its evolution, to give it an ultimate purpose, meaning, and so on.

The second guiding principle of Spinoza's philosophy asserts that 'only *one substance* can be granted in nature' (Spinoza 1677, chapter I, proposition 14, corollary 1). In opposition to most other philosophers, Spinoza denies that matter and thought (the body and the soul) belong to two radically different spheres or make up two heterogeneous substances: what he calls God, or Nature (which we would call, using a symptomatic definite article, '*the* universe') has to be conceived *as One*. Translated into the vocabulary of chains, to say that there can be only one substance means that there can be only 'one order, or concatenation of things' (no matter how infinitely complex, multi-layered and intricate it actually is) (Spinoza 1677, chapter III, proposition 2, scholium). Three implications of this call to conceive of our world as One made it particularly scandalous. The first is that it denies any essential specificity to the human world. Spinoza tirelessly reasserts that we humans are no more than 'a part of nature', and that most philosophies and religions mislead us when they portray mankind (or the mind within the human body) as 'an empire within an empire' (Spinoza 1677, chapter III, Praefatio): the same necessity and the same natural laws apply to everything (including our will).

The second implication gives us a first glimpse into the relevance of Spinoza's thought to generate a fruitful understanding of globalisation. One of the ideas that the readers of the time found the most outrageous in his system is that, according to its logic, Plato and a worm, the idea of God and the droppings of a pigeon, Spinoza's bed and the Emperor of China are ultimately one and the same, insofar as they are mere 'modifications' of one and the same substance. Such 'monstrous absurdities' led Pierre Bayle to point out that a common war-report such as *The Germans killed ten thousand Turks*, once translated into Spinozese, would read *God modified in Germans killed God modified in ten thousand Turks* (Bayle 1696, 69). Although such a view looked utterly 'extravagant', 'abominable' and 'ridiculous' to Bayle and to most of his contemporaries, it sets a frame of analysis which proves more adequate everyday at the dawn of our third millennium. In the *trans-individual theory of bodies* sketched in the *Ethics*, Spinoza invites us to 'conceive the whole of Nature as one individual [*totam Naturam unum esse Individuum*], whose parts, that is all bodies, vary in infinite ways, without any change to the individual as a whole' (Spinoza 1677 , chapter II, proposition 13, lemma 7, scholium). From this perspective, it is equally justifiable and necessary to consider as an 'individual' a person, a part within that person (her stomach), a part within that part (a group of bacteria), or, in the other direction, the team with which this person works on a daily basis, the city in which she lives, the nation of which she is a citizen, the world region within which this nation's economy is heavily integrated, the planet earth (the 'globe' at the horizon of our globalisation) and so on to the most composed individual, *Facies Totius Universi*. Building on the multi-layered network of causal chains described by Hobbes, Spinoza offers a worldview in which the One (infinitely complex) concatenation of causes making up the universe keeps in ultimate solidarity all the 'individuals' which our limited understanding arbitrarily isolates in it for the practical purpose of fulfilling our various needs. Far from being 'extravagant', this approach brings us closer to the practical truth of phenomena such as wars (human bodies modified in US soldiers killing, human bodies modified in Taliban oppressors) or environmental threats (life on earth reaching the stage where its highest developments undermine its own survival).

In order to better understand our position as humans within this concatenation of universal solidarity, we can now turn to a third implication of the One-Substance principle, that of a *parallelism* between the attribute of Extension (material things, the body) and the attribute of Thought (ideas, the mind). For Spinoza, the cognitive world is in strict parallel with the material world: 'the order and connection of ideas is the same as the order and connection of things' (Spinoza 1677, chapter II, proposition 7). Nothing can affect an idea without something equivalent affecting a body, and conversely. As in the case of a transparent sheet of plastic, nothing can be printed on one side which would not be seen from the other: whatever is perceptible on one has to be equally perceptible on the other. The scandal (and the puzzling elegance) of this solution to the old mind–body question consists in that it precludes any 'influence' of the body on the mind or of the mind on the body. None can influence (or determine, or condition) the other, since there is *only one and the same concatenation of causes* conceived by us under two different attributes.

With this reconfiguration of the mind–body problem, Spinoza displaces the traditional questions: the issue is no longer to decide which one comes first, or how one can influence the other; the main (and new) issue becomes to determine *the logic according to which things get concatenated*. And although this may look frighteningly technical for a chapter devoted to globalisation, we need to follow the details of Spinoza's demonstration on this point, which is crucial to the efficacy of his thought. What is at stake here is the distinction between two registers of functioning of the human mind, the imaginary and the rational.

The logic of *the imaginary* register is that of the impressions made by external objects on our senses and on our memory. Sensory impressions are the result of an interaction between our own body (our sensory organs) and the external bodies that affect them. The order and concatenation of these impressions depend upon the largely *aleatory encounters* between the two. As I walk in the street to come to campus, I pass by a stranger who holds a bunch of roses, and I enjoy their smell: as we have seen, even for a deterministic philosophy such as Spinoza's, this encounter has to be considered as contingent, because the two causal chains (of my going to the university and of the stranger offering flowers) are independent within the limited scope of the proximate causes to which we must limit ourselves. Virtually all of the ideas that I may have during the day are brought about by such aleatory encounters between my sensory organs and the objects that affect them. Virtually all of the ideas that I have stored in my memory are therefore ruled by chance encounters between my body and external bodies. The principle of concatenation between ideas in the imaginary register is that of association by contiguity and resemblance: to take an example given by Spinoza, if a soldier sees traces of horseshoes, he will think of cavalry and battles, whereas a peasant will think of plows and fields. Even if many individuals can find themselves in similar situations, and can therefore end up developing similar ideas, this type of associations is by definition idiosyncratic, since it is tied to the objects that *my* body happens to encounter.

In contrast, the principle of concatenation between ideas in *the rational* register is that of *causality*. As our knowledge develops, we come to understand [*intelligere*] that certain types of conditions systematically produce certain types of effects. Reason, for Spinoza, consists in understanding an event by its causes. When ideas are (properly) concatenated by the intellect [*intellectus*, another name for reason], this concatenation of ideas espouses the concatenation of causes which determines the workings of the universe. Although the imaginary is idiosyncratic (as well as family- and culture-specific), rational intellection can claim universal validity. The difference between the two registers is summarised in a scholium devoted to the definition of the memory:

> I say that this concatenation [of the imaginary register] takes place according to the order and concatenation of the affections of the human body [*secundum ordinem et concatenationem affectionum Corporis humani*] so as to differentiate it from the concatenation of ideas which takes place according to the order of the intellect [*secundum ordinem intellectus*], by which the mind perceives things through

their first causes and which is the same in all human beings. (Spinoza 1677 , chapter II, proposition 18, scholium)

Apart from its consequences on the question of universalism, this distinction is crucial since it holds the key to the foundation of a new ethics, to a (re)definition of the Good and of what we 'ought to' do – a definition fully compatible with its deterministic premises. What we, as humans, 'ought to' do is to develop our rational intellection of the world as far as we can. This development of our intellect ultimately hinges on *our power to concatenate*. And this is the point where Spinoza's philosophy overcomes the passive and reactive connotations usually attached to the image of concatenation and chains, to open a wide perspective of activity, emancipation and invention. Yes, we are inescapably linked to the great chain of causes which constitutes the universe, but, by the very fact that we are a part of nature, we can actively participate in its constant process of causation and creation. We can be concatenaters, as much as we are links: the fact that we are passively *concatenated* with the overall and inescapable order of the universe does not prevent us from actively *concatenating* – within the modest scope of our local environment – our affections and ideas.

This starts with a proper hygiene of life, which takes the form of a certain amount of control that our mind and body can acquire over what affects them. 'As long as we don't run against affects which are contrary to our nature, we have the power to arrange and concatenate [*potestatem habemus ordinandi et concatenandi*] the affections of our body according to the order of the intellect [*secundum ordinem ad intellectum*]', that is, 'so that we will not easily be affected by bad affects' (Spinoza 1677, chapter V, proposition 10, scholium). Practically, this means that not only can we avoid the contact with nefarious external bodies (poisons), but we also have a certain power 'to separate our affects from the thought of an external cause', and re-link our ideas in a different order (Spinoza 1677, chapter V, proposition 20, scholium): instead of becoming angry, violent and revengeful when someone harms us, a proper understanding of the necessary concatenation of things will lead us to master our aggressive affects, and see instead what can be done most effectively to prevent a repetition of similar harm.

As 'intellectuals' – to be understood not merely as specialised workers of the intellect, but rather as (co-)producers of intellection in cooperation and solidarity with *all* other human beings – we also have the power 'to direct and concatenate our clear and distinct perceptions' [*nostras claras et distinctas perceptiones dirigere et concatenare*] (Spinoza 1666), so that more causal links can come to light and be put to use towards improving our prospects of life. The power [*potentia*] specific to these particular things which we identify as human beings (an inseparable coalescence of mind and body) resides in their *power to invent*:[2] their power to discover new (unsuspected) causal links, their power to create new technological devices, new forms of social cooperation, new political institutions, new aesthetic experiences. If the *Ethics* carries an imperative as its final lesson, it clearly is: 'Develop your intellect as much as you can, in order to be as inventive as you can!'

From the starting point of a deterministic concatenation of causes which debunked our claim to free-will, until this final perspective of a proper human freedom relying on our power to concatenate according to the order of the intellect – *De potentia intellectus seu de libertate humana* is the title of the fifth and last part of the *Ethics* –, Spinoza offers a philosophy of emancipation.[3] But a very peculiar and original one, which only a few later thinkers have fully grasped and pursued (Diderot, Nietzsche and Deleuze obviously come to mind.) Within this unorthodox framework, liberty is not defined in relation to a stable state, which one would enjoy or be deprived of, but as an endless process of liberation: one can always become more free (i.e. more rational, more powerful) than one currently is. More originally still, in contrast to most other political theories, liberty is not conceived in terms of *contractual rights*, but purely in terms of *actual power*: I am only as free as what I do. Along with Hobbes' intuitions, I can never be free alone: I need social institutions (and their artificial chains of civil laws), and, more fundamentally, I need the cooperation of *all* my fellow humans in order to be as free (and inventive) as I can. For once we peel off the elitist tone of certain quotes, the logic of Spinoza's thought leads to *the most radical form of democracy* because: (1) the supreme good is the development of the general intellect; (2) this development requires the cooperation of the highest number of well-instructed brains (and therefore of well-fed and well-maintained bodies); (3) the most powerful mode of cooperation translates in the form of its institutions the fact that all power comes from the multitude of bodies which make up the collectivity; and (4) it is in the nature of any stable institution to betray and constrain the power of auto-production through constant (re)invention and adaptation which is the true essence of politics – Spinoza, as early as 1677, paved the way for a conception of democracy-as-process which should inspire us, today more than ever, to look far beyond the traps and limitations of our current parliamentary systems of representation.

More to the point of globalisation, Spinoza's democracy is deeply pluralistic. Against most of our modern tradition inspired by both Christianity and Kant, Spinoza emphatically denies that there would be *one* 'essence of man' to which every individual should conform (to be endowed with a soul, with free will, to have access to a moral realm). Not only are we parts of nature (and nothing else or nothing more), but also each human being (as well as each cat or each pebble) constitutes 'a singular essence'. And although social cooperation requires a certain amount of conformity among the agents, so that they can fit [*convenire*] within a collective scheme, its power of (re)invention and ultimate strength will depend upon the capacity for each participant to express his/her (personal or cultural) singularity and difference – as it is the case with (modernist) artistic creation, which provides a good model to understand Spinoza's political ideal. Consensus and homogeneity are a threat as much as they are a requirement: here again, the yardstick that enables us to draw the line between the good and the bad is provided by the question: *do they increase or constrain our power to invent?* On top of offering an already globalising vision of mankind in its inextricable concatenation with nature (including human nature, its affects and other limitations), Spinoza provides us with a political blueprint for globalisation conceived as a universalistic process of democratisation (empowerment of the multitudes) and as an enrichment of our powers of (self-)invention through the confrontation with difference – that is, as a renewed way to concatenate our civil laws and our ideas.

III. Concatenations in early economic liberalism

The true impact of Spinoza's writings on eighteenth-century thought remains a contested issue. Although I tend to favour the type of views illustrated by Jonathan Israel's recent study, which places Spinoza at the centre of a vast network of influences permeating virtually through all spheres of the Enlightenment movement (Israel 2001),[4] it seems to me equally probable that the inner logic of European development, between 1650 and 1800, would lead several authors, more or less independently, to (re)invent a similar view of human nature and of human societies. The fact is that from Fontenelle, Boulainviller, Fréret or Vauvenargues to Voltaire, Montesquieu, Helvetius, Du Pont de Nemours, Diderot, Bonnet, Du Laurens, d'Holbach, and countless others, the concatenation motif (*l'enchaînement nécessaire des causes et des parties de l'univers*) – and more specifically the question of the (in)existence of a master plan guiding the concatenation – plays a crucial role in the development of the *Philosophes* movement.

To focus on the early perception of globalisation, it is obviously more than a coincidence if the writers mentioned above lived in Holland, Great Britain and France, since these countries were at the core of the international division of labour structuring the world system of the period. The Enlightenment corresponded to the most intense period of activity of the transatlantic slave trade, which quadrupled from the seventeenth to the eighteenth century – mostly in order to provide French and English palates with cheap sugar, 'a truly international crop combining an Asian plant, European capital, African labor, and American soil' (Pomeranz and Topik 1999, 95). As Voltaire vividly pictured in the Surinam episode of *Candide*, the concatenated global markets of the time made extensive use of very literal chains on non-European human bodies.

From a diffuse guilt towards the distant sufferings generated by the Western lifestyles to anxieties about a hegemonic global language (French at the time), from the first comprehensive international conferences (Münster 1648; Utrecht 1713) to the development of a reliable postal system linking the most important cities in Western Europe, from the increasing curiosity towards Chinese philosophy to the profits brought home (to Spinoza's father or to Voltaire's portfolio) by transnational merchant capitalism, the supra-national stakes of the project of modernity became apparent very early on – and their theorisation was *contemporary* to the development of the nation-state system (far from being a sudden discovery of our 'post-modern' era). I mention only two quotes as symptomatic of this early awareness of globalisation. The first one is taken from a work by a physiocratic author Nicolas Baudeau, who repeats as a commonplace in 1770 something Voltaire had already written in his *Défense du Mondain* thirty years earlier:

> You see reunited under your eyes and hands, on your breakfast table, the productions from all climates and both hemispheres. China oversaw the production of these cups and plates; this coffee grew in Arabia; the sugar you put in it was cultivated in America by unfortunate Africans; the metal of your coffee maker comes from Potosi; this linen, brought from Riga, was crafted by the industry of the Dutch; and our countryside provided the bread and the cream. (Baudeau 1770, 846)

The second quote, written by Louis Antoine de Caraccioli in 1776 in his *Europe française*, extends to the sphere of culture this perception of living in a globalised and shrinking world:

> Nothing is more advantageous than having overcome, thanks to public roads and posts, the immense interval which kept Europeans away from each other. It seems as if there were no longer any distance between them. Paris touches Petersburg, Rome touches Constantinople, & it is now only one and the same family which inhabits various regions. (Caraccioli 1776, 351)

But beyond such symptomatic statements, what matters more are the explanatory models which were already elaborated to account for the inner mechanisms of such supra-national phenomena – and/or to provide a 'scientific' caution to the globalisation meta-narrative. Between 1750 and 1775, the founding fathers of political economy (Hume, the Physiocrats, Turgot and Smith) jointly developed a doctrine (economic liberalism) which, for our current purpose, could be summarised in four main points.

(a) *The economic order should espouse as closely as possible the concatenation of causes which make up the order of Nature.* From the very project of the 'physio-cratic' school (to give power back to Nature) to Turgot claiming that 'the course of commerce is no less necessary, no less irresistible, than the course of nature' (Turgot 1773, 382), political economy implemented the Spinozian call to treat man as a 'part of nature', rather than as an (autonomous) 'empire within an empire'.

(b) *Everything is interconnected in the human world (as it is in Nature).* Du Pont de Nemours summarises well the mantra of early political economy when he states that '[e]verything is interrelated [*Tout est lié*], everything holds to everything on earth [*tout se tient sur la terre*], everything is tied by secret chains [*tout a des chaînes secrètes*]' (Du Pont de Nemours 1764, 50). The lexicon of 'chains' is ubiquitous in these early statements in favour of the 'free' market: 'commercial enterprises are made to be chained [*enchaînées*] to each other' (in the productive cycle as a whole, as well as by the pressure of competition) (Le Mercier de la Rivière 1770, 153); society as a whole appears as 'a chain of reciprocal dependencies' (Le Mercier de la Rivière 1767, 17); the newborn science of economics itself is here to make sure that 'consequences are so well chained [*enchaînées*] to each other' that its conclusions will be inescapable (38).

(c) *The economic order transcends political boundaries, and the various national markets are bound to integrate within a single global market.* In 1776, Condillac already described Europe as 'one single common market' [*un seul marché commun*], insofar as easily transportable items (e.g. precious metals) were concerned (Condillac 1776, 128). As the means of transportation improve, this single market is bound to cover more goods and more territories. According to Le Mercier de la Rivière, a global society should not be the object of utopian dreams, for it already is a *fait accompli*:

> [Cosmopolitan philosophers] failed to see that this general society, which they longed to establish, already existed; that it was the result of nature itself; that it was not a question of forming it, but of maintaining it, of not disturbing it, of knowing *clearly* the laws which constitute its essential order, so that we can subject ourselves to it through the only force of the clear advantages which we find in adopting it. (Le Mercier de la Rivière 1767, 245)

(d) *Laissez faire, laissez passer!* Since the 'natural and essential order of political societies' is the one which *naturally*, that is, spontaneously, establishes itself when the course of commerce is left 'undisturbed', Gournay's motto summarises the best possible policy that a government can follow for its own good: *let* the traders *do* their business, *let* the flow of goods *pass* through transparent borders. It is no coincidence if Smith's famous image of the 'invisible hand' appears in a chapter devoted to promoting the free circulation of goods across borders, and to fighting against trade barriers and tariffs (Smith 1776, book IV, chapter II). The free-trade vulgate which came out of (the simplification of) these writers' ideas present a double side of determinism and liberty with which we are by now familiar: it is precisely the *freedom* granted to traders in the global market which puts national governments under the *chains* of a superior necessity.

The concatenation motif plays therefore a central role in the foundations of economic liberalism. The free-trade argument rests on the statement *everything is concatenated*: it presents the great chain of nations as an ineluctable fact, which *already* imposes its pre-determined logic, to which we must necessarily and passively submit (if we do not want foolishly to go against our own interests). Given such 'fatalism', given the strong reference to natural determinations, given a parallel trust in auto-organisation, given an equal faith in scientific Reason, given also more anecdotal features (in appearance) such as a common reference to China – we should not be surprised to see the doctrine of the Physiocrats denounced by defenders of Christianity in terms strikingly similar to those used to discredit Spinozism. In his own early Critique of (physiocratic) Political Economy, the abbé Legros is for instance led to develop attacks which could equally well apply to Spinoza, Helvetius, Diderot or d'Holbach:

> if this grand order, this concatenation [*cet enchaînement*], this general law of movement are eternal […] if they are necessary, then they exist by themselves, by the necessity of their nature; they therefore replace the Divinity, they take its place; if the grand order is one and the only one, then there no longer is any moral order, any meta-physical order, any supernatural order. (Legros 1787, pp. 142–3)

Spinozist or not, the meta-narrative of free-trade globalisation, along with its promise of rivers of prosperity flowing over the entire planet – a promise repeated most of all in the face of dramatic inequalities, eco-nomic downturns and delocalisation of production – was ready as early as the 1770s, as this summary by Condillac should suffice to suggest:

> [once complete and permanent freedom has been granted to trade] if the circulation of wealth takes place with some inequality, one should not fear that this inequality could ever lead to setting extreme poverty [*la misère*] in opposition to opulence. All nations [*tous les peu-ples*] will work following each other's example, because they will all want to benefit from the same advantage; in this competition [*concurrence*], manufactures will close little by little in the provinces which they have made richer, and where the price of labor will have increased, while they will open in other provinces which they must make wealthier, and where labor is cheaper; they will go from province to province; everywhere, they will deposit a part of the wealth of the [global] nation, and trade will be like a long river which distributes its flows into a multitude of channels in order to irrigate, one after the other, all the lands. This revolution will cease only to start again. (Condillac 1776, 253)

If the main articulations of the globalisation meta-narrative were already well in place by the 1770s, so also were the strongest arguments for its refutation. After acknowledging the elegance of the liberal theory, Morelly – the author of the scandalous *Code de la Nature* often attributed to Diderot –anticipated in 1753 what remains today more than ever its main blind spot:

> What!, you will say, isn't trade [*le commerce*] – which binds together fellow-citizens and nations [*les Peuples*] of the earth, with its foundations in self-interests – a rich spring of conveniences, of delights, of wealth, of magnificence, of industry, of good taste, of politeness, etc.? It certainly is; but less than a third of mankind actually benefits from it; the others inherit the work and the worries, with barely enough to avoid starvation. (Morelly 1753, 74)

IV. Thinkers of the world, re-concatenate!

Was Morelly the first 'anti-globalisation' writer? Were Diderot, Raynal and Galiani, in their early denunciations of colonial exploitation and of the delusions of liberal economics, the direct ancestors of today's anti-globalisation demonstrators? Thinking in terms of concatenations helps us see why such questions are much more deeply flawed than their mere anachronism suggests. Even as they fight to emancipate us from the 'iron laws' of economic neo-liberalism, even as they rebel against what Thomas Friedmann suggestively called the 'Golden Straight Jacket' (i.e. the neo-liberal policies imposed on national governments by the international herd of investors), what do these 'opponents' do in fact but form (metaphorical and literal) *human chains* in the streets of Seattle or Genova, as well as on the back streets of the Information Super Highways? It is symptomatic that they increasingly reject the label anti-globalisation.[5] The point is not to deny the reality of the interconnectedness waved by the neo-liberals: let's welcome the slogan *everything is concatenated*. But let's supplement it with the other side of the same coin: *We can re-concatenate things differently*.

The Spinozist tradition allows us not only to catch simultaneously both sides of the coin, but – more importantly – it helps us figure out the real nature of the ethical imperative expressed by this 'should'. In this view, the increasingly dense and intensive concatenation which characterises globalisation is *simultaneously* a source of increasing constraints for every agent (body parts, individuals, families, neighbourhoods and nations) and a potential source of new forms of emancipation. In Spinozese, the principle at stake is that (a) it requires a certain power *to be affected by other bodies* as well as to affect them, and (b) the power to affect always *varies in proportion* with the power to be affected. The power of a stone does not go much beyond being able to crush whatever finds itself caught under it because it is in strict proportion to its power of being affected (a power limited to the laws of gravity). What differentiates our human bodies from a stone is a parallel increase in our power to affect other bodies and in our power to be affected by them.

The more intimately we are concatenated with the rest of the world, the more sensitive we are to its variations, the more we can affect it in return. Not to deny that there are dramatic inequalities and differentials in power between individual agents, of course: the point is to understand [*intelligere*, and this might be an appropriate definition of *intelligence*] what specific and always-limited power comes with every nexus in the concatenation of causes. The practical problem then becomes (and this might be the only appropriate *ethical* question): what helps me *actualise* this power (we'll call that 'Good') and what keeps me *separated from* this power (we'll call it 'Bad').

To label such an approach 'Spinozist' is obviously an over-simplification. What we are dealing with is rather a whole, rich and diverse tradition of thought which keeps (re)inventing itself from Lucretius and the Stoics to Machiavelli, Hobbes, Spinoza, Diderot, Nietzsche, Tarde, and all the way to Deleuze, Negri or a publication such as *Multitudes*.[6] To illustrate this tradition, I sample four sets of eighteenth-century (re-)concatenaters; four links arbitrarily isolated in this long chain of intellectual, political and cultural activists. Their only common point is that they all challenged the borders of the nation-states, at the very moment when these institutions were only taking shape.

Cosmopolitics. Between 1650 and 1815, a number of writer-activists promoted various projects of political unification in Europe. Although their motivations vary widely, from nationalistic hidden agendas to Christian pacifism, and from Crusade projects to proto-socialist internationalism, they all wanted to bring to a higher level the lessons of Hobbes' political theory: human happiness requires the chaining of the individual agents (nations) under the fear of a common power (a federation). Such projects of European Union not only theorised the actual practice of international conferences but also opened up new paths for a reflection that took two centuries to materialise. In all their diversity, and with all their ambiguities, figures such as the abbé de Saint-Pierre, Anacharsis Cloots or Claude-Henri de Saint-Simon were good examples of these active concatenaters in early cosmopolitics.

Political Economy. The trendy windmill of neo-liberalism often prevents us from seeing the obvious: those fathers of modern economics, who claimed the loudest that everything is (already) concatenated, were also very actively involved in re-concatenating the ideas and the institutions of their time. Not only did they establish strong transnational links – Hume, Smith, Turgot and the Physiocrats all met and/or exchanged letters; the main experiments in applied physiocracy took place in Germany; Turgot wrote his main theoretical treatise to convert China to the beauties of the free market – but the Physiocrats as a group were the first ones to constitute this highly efficient form of agency known today as a 'think-tank': from highly theoretical articles in the first specialised publications devoted to the 'new science', to 'economic catechisms' in the form of plays to be performed in villages so as to reach the illiterate masses, and from networking activities among the intelligentsia of the times to infiltration of the royal administration, they did manage to push reforms through the implementation phase (even if such implementation eventually backfired). Quesnay, Baudeau, Du Pont de Nemours, Turgot, Le Mercier de la Rivière were the living proofs that even the 'spontaneous logic of the market' requires a lot of political activism to (re)concatenate our economic interactions.

The Encyclopaedist Movement. The purpose (and the recurrent underlying image) of the *Encyclopédie* was not only to 'express, as much as it is possible, the order and concatenation of human ideas [*exposer autant qu'il est possible, l'ordre et l'enchaînement des connoissances humaines*]', but also to contribute to the 'chain [*la chaîne*]' which unites the sciences and the arts by intensifying 'the inter-connections between discoveries' [*la liaison que les découvertes ont entre elles*] (d'Alembert 1751, tome I, 76). The whole project of (the Radical) Enlightenment is a vast enterprise of re-concatenation: when d'Holbach translates Hobbes or when he spread Spinozism in the *Système de la Nature*, when Diderot directs the *Encyclopédie* or composes the *Voyage de Bougainville*, they both mobilise a wide and international network of connections (travellers, colporteurs of forbidden books, scientific correspondents, readers of the *Correspondance Littéraire*, Tahitian characters, funds from the Russian court) in order to 'transform our common ways of thinking', that is, in order to make us re-concatenate our ideas, our affects, our values along newly invented lines.

Multitudes. All these intellectual endeavours developed in interaction with social movements, to which they reacted (usually led by the dominant affect of fear) and which they sometimes fed in return (boosting affects of hope). The new historical scholarship helps us conceive such movements (slave rebellions, peasant resistance, proto-proletarian organisations), beyond the category of 'the people' (permeated by connotations of race and nation), through the Spinozist notion of *multitude*: when 'crowds' determine the course of the National Assembly by burning castles, or impose the 'just price' of bread on their local baker under the threat of their sheer number (Gauthier and Ikni 1988; Markoff 1996); when the flows of goods carried by colonial trade drag behind them workers constituting multi-ethnic communities on ships or in ports (Rediker 1987; Rediker and Linebaugh 2000); when the workers' capacity to flee (escape, migrate, change jobs) appears as the *primum mobile* in the development of labour relations over the past 500 years (Boutang 1998); in all such cases, it is the very *fluidity* of the multitudes which enables them to exploit and subvert the channels of their exploitation. Their re-concatenation through trade unions, political parties or social safety nets appears in this perspective both as a conquest and as a danger: like all chains, these new bonds are at the same time a form of empowerment and a constraint.

Cloots, Hume, Du Pont, d'Holbach, Diderot, and probably a good number of the obscure agitators who carved new paths of emancipation of the multitudes, have all been labelled – depending on the period and the milieu – 'Spinozist', 'determinist', 'materialist', 'atheist', 'fatalist', 'communist'. To conclude, let's attempt to summarise what their long tradition of reflection and work on the Great Chain of Nations can teach us today about globalisation.

1. *Chains of Command.* Whenever we think in terms of concatenations, the first challenge consists in broadening our view from noticing the obvious *chains of enslavement* to mapping the more elusive *chains of 'command'* which structure our planet – in the specific sense given to this word by Adam Smith when he quotes Hobbes' equation between wealth and power, measuring them by 'the quantity of labour which [the rich person] can *command*' (Smith 1776, book I, chapter V, 34–5). We are in a 'post'-colonial age only insofar as inter-continental chains have refashioned their appearance. A change for the better, obviously, and certainly not an insignificant one. But a change in surface more than in structure, since it is still the economic-political chains of Western capital which 'command' the (under)development of four-fifths of mankind.

2. *The Nation.* Within these chains of command, the status of the nation(-state) cannot be decided in the realm of abstract theory, but depends upon the singularity of each historical situation. In the rich Western world, national borders, passports and immigration laws tend to produce the highly oppressive chains of a new form of apartheid,[7] which exposes (much needed and abundantly used) 'illegal' workers to the harshest forms of exploitation and abuse. In other parts of the world, or on specific issues like the protection of local cultures, an appeal to the nation-state may still be a powerful tool of self-defence, an emancipating chain likely to 'command' a significant quantity of political

labour in order to curb and resist the Americanisation of the world. To evaluate the merits and demerits of a reference to the 'nation', we should consider the etymology of the term, which evokes the 'birthing' process [*natus*]: each individual's 'extraction' (out of the material world, out of a family, a social group, a geographical area) is necessarily unique, and yet it is also, and no less necessarily, the result of a process involving a whole network of participants. Each individual is defined by the singular *catena* of causes which, together [*con-*], produced its singular *natio*. An appeal to the *nation* is justifiable only within a promotion of this double singularity – which involves the promotion of the other singularities participating in the *concatena*.

3. *Power* versus *Rights*. Beyond such trivial observations, a Spinozist view of concatenations allows us to redefine the basic principles on which a truly cosmopolitan and constructive work towards building a Great Chain of Nations could be grounded. In contrast with the neo-Kantian obsession with Human Rights which has bogged down political rhetoric over the past thirty years,[8] Spinoza (along with Hobbes) leads us systematically to reduce considerations of the *right* to measurements of *power*. Nothing can protect us from chains of enslavement except other chains (of command). Human reality is not based on the inner virtue of contracts, but on the underlying relations of force which structure them. In the field of local politics as well as on the geopolitical stage, emancipation cannot be conceived merely as the acquisition of formal rights, but is achieved only through the actual use of actual powers. When Spinoza writes that 'the true aim of government is liberty', it does not simply mean that everybody is *allowed* to be informed, to vote and to speak out, but it means that 'the human mind and body actually and safely fulfill their functions' to the maximum extent of their power [*mens et corpus tuto suis functionibus fungantur*], which implies that people 'make actual use of their free Reason [*libera Ratione utantur*]', and therefore actually participate in the political process (Spinoza 1670, chapter XX, sections 19–20). In the Great Chain of Nations, it means that our efforts in re-concatenation should aim at helping the dominated multitudes (wherever they are) to acquire the practical means (whatever they are) to make actual use of their free reason.

4. *Liberty and Fear*. It is obvious that the Spinozist approach leads to a drastic redefinition of the notion of liberty. In contrast to most common views, liberty does not consist in being 'free from someone else's command'. An awareness of our concatenated fates reveals that we are inextricably bound to countless chains of commands (through the division

of labour, the participation we have in each other's fate, the knowledge we share, the love we inspire in each other, etc.) If, as we have seen, institutions concatenate us more rather than less, there is one thing from which their chains can emancipate us: 'the ultimate aim of government is [...] to free every man from fear [*unumquemque metu liberare*], so that he may live as safely as it is possible' (Spinoza 1670, chapter XX, sections 19–20). Beyond its commonplace (Hobbesian) implications at the domestic level, this emphasis on the relation between freedom and fear anticipates many current (i.e. post-9/11) reflections on geopolitics. On the one hand, the concatenation of technological processes (air traffic, skyscrapers, nuclear power plants, ozone layer depletion, CO_2 emissions, etc.) has generated global fears which tie all humans together, *volens nolens*, in a deepening 'community of fate'[9] – of which the current boogie man of 'terror-ism' is only a very superficial and highly misleading figure. On the other hand, the use of fear is a good indicator of the nature of the political regime in place: 'for a free multitude is guided more by hope than fear [*libera multitudo majori spe quam metu ducitur*]; a conquered one, more by fear than hope; inasmuch as the former aims at cultivating life [*vitam colere*], the latter but at escaping death'(Spinoza 1677, chapter V, section 6). In other words: distrust governments that constantly play on reactive affects of fear and revenge by putting crime or terror at the top of their agenda, for such rhetoric is a symptom of a deficit of freedom in the multitude. True liberty calls for constructive projects driven by hopes rather than repressive measures feeding off the anxieties they fuel in return. 'Well-ordered societies' do not so much need to be 'defended', as they need to be 'cultivated', constantly re-invented.

5. *Liberty and Reason.* More radically even, Spinoza's overall determinism allows us to disconnect true liberty from its traditional anchorage in the individual's will, preferences and choices. The fact that a majority of citizens wholeheartedly support their government's decisions is no ultimate proof of a well-functioning democracy: for 'spirits [*animi*] are to a certain point under the domination of the sovereign [*sub imperio summae potestatis*], who can in many ways bring about that the greatest parts of the people, believe, love, hate whatever the sovereign wants'. The strongest and most invisible of chains are the ones consented upon by those who bear them: 'he is most under the dominion of another who with his whole heart determines to obey another's command [*qui alteri integro animo ad omnia ejus mandata obtemperare deliberat*]' (Spinoza 1670 , chapter XVII, sections 11–12). The tripartition offered by

Spinoza somewhere else in the *Theologico-Political Treatise* encapsulates neatly what is at stake with his notion of freedom:

> A slave [*servus*] is one who is bound to obey his master's orders, though they are given solely in his master's interests [*utilitatem imperantis tantum spectant*]; a son [*filius*] is one who obeys his father's orders, given in his own interests [*quod sibi utile est*]; a subject [*subditus*] obeys the orders of the sovereign power, given for the common interest, wherein he is included [*quod communi et consequenter quoque sibi utile est*]
>
> The true slave is he who is led away by his pleasures [*a sua voluptate ita trahitur*] and can neither see what is good for him nor act accordingly [*nihil quod sibi utile est videre necque agere potest*]; he alone is free who lives with his whole spirit under the sole guidance of reason [*qui integro animo ex solo ductu Rationis vivit*] (Spinoza 1670 , chapter XVI, sections 61 and 55)

Nobody is nor can be (absolutely) free in this sense. We can only become more free, more emancipated from our parents', priests', teachers', lawmakers', advertisers' orders, as well as from our various addictions, shopping urges, cinephilic drives and other book-worming obsessions. On this continuum of emancipation, the litmus-test of liberty (and of its opposite, slavery) is *not* to be located in the voluntary or involuntary nature of the action, *nor* in the fact that one obeys someone else's command or not (we all bear the chains of concatenations); it is to be found in whether our actions help us to act in closer conformity with our (common) interest, that is, ultimately, whether our actions help us (individually and collectively) to become more rational, more intelligent. Our emancipation not only depends upon but consists in improving our capacity better to re-concatenate ideas, so that we (individually and collectively) avoid the 'bad encounters' of poisonous foods, destructive floods, clashes of passions, clan rivalries and world wars.

6. *Inventing Multitudes.* 'Reason' does not *exist*. Not only because men are, and will always be, subjected to (irrational) affects. But, more fundamentally, because the Spinozist *Ratio* is not something to conform to, but something to *invent*, to create, to *constitute* – and it is something that can only be invented *in common*, through the cooperation and communication of a multitude of human brains. To adapt Laurent Bove's suggestive formula, for Spinoza, *there is reason in number* ('*du nombre naît la raison*') (Bove 1996, 254),[10]– and, through reason, strength. Here again,

in this most fundamental and most radical affirmation of the democratic principle, the notion of concatenation is indirectly present. In a sentence that could be used to denounce 'totalitarian' tendencies in Spinoza's political thought, the *Political Treatise* draws consequences from the fact that men do not spontaneously behave rationally:

> if human nature were so constituted, that men most desired what is most useful, no art would be needed to produce unity and confidence. But, as it is admittedly far otherwise with human nature, a dominion must of necessity be so ordered [*imperium necessario ita instituendum est*], that all, governing and governed alike, whether they will or no, shall do what makes for the general welfare; that is, that all, whether of their own impulse, or by force or necessity, shall be compelled to live according to the dictate of reason [*ut omnes sponte, vel vi, vel necessitate coacti sint ex rationis praescripto vivere*]. (Spinoza 1677, chapter VI, section 3)

Both aspects of the concatenation motive coincide in the use of the word *coacti*. The always-daunting danger of oppressive chains: all must be compelled to follow the dictates of reason (according to the most common meaning of *cogere*: 'to constrain, to force, to compel'). But also the fundamentally demo-cratic, autonomous and communal nature of this rational necessity: in its root, *co-acti* expresses the cooperation which constitutes this compulsion (according to the original meaning of *cum-agere*: 'to lead together, to reunite, to tighten up, to condense').

This is the horizon opened by the Spinozist view on globalisation and the Great Chain of Nations. We humans must constitute a common reality, we must invent institutions which will compel (*compellere*: 'to push together') us to live according to the dictates of reason. Such 'chains' cannot be imposed from above: ultimately, they will necessarily rely on the power of the multitudes, which will either accept them, or destroy them when they generate too much 'indignation'. As re-concatenators of ideas, we are all co-actors, compulsors in this movement of auto-constitution of a human world. When faced with specific choices – should I activate this link? Should I attempt to break this linkage? – we can look towards the Spinozist tradition for a general rule of thumb: does this connection tend to empower the inventive capacities of the multitudes by helping its individuals (brains, families, social groups, nations, etc.) most uniquely to express their singularity?

Our only wish, here and now, is that this conference on *ConcateNations* can provide a structure of communication good enough to pass this test.

Notes

1. English translations of Spinoza's works are available on the web at http://books.mirror.org/gb.spinoza.html accessed 2/12/2006. All Spinoza references unless otherwise indicated refer to the texts found on the website.
2. To paraphrase the title of a recent book by Lazzarato (2002). Although no apparent relation links Tarde's work to Spinoza's, his reflection is essential for whoever attempts to develop a theory of our human power of invention (in the cognitive, political or aesthetical realm). See for instance Tarde (1893).
3. A number of epoch-making studies have totally renewed our reading of Spinoza's political philosophy over the past thirty years. The most important ones include: Matheron (1969), Negri (1981), Balibar (1985) and more recently the remarkably insightful book by Bove (1996). This renewal has been carried in the United States by Montag and Stolze (1997) and Montag (1999).
4. The classical reference for the French domain remains Vernière, (1954) to be completed with Bloch (1990).
5. See for instance the body of thinking generated by and around Negri and Hardt (2000).
6. Published four times a year in Paris by Exils. Website: http://www.samizdat.net/multitudes. Subscription info available through: http://www.difpop.com under the heading 'Multitudes'.
7. For the use of this term, see Balibar (2001), in particular pp. 190–2.
8. For a good critique of the shortcomings and delusions of this Human Rights ideology, see Badiou (1993).
9. On this notion, see van Gunsteren (1998).
10. To support his formula, Bove mentions Spinoza 1670, chapter VII: section 4; chapter VIII, sections 6–7; chapter IX section 14; and chapter XI section 1.

References

d'Alembert, J. (1751) *Discours préliminaire* de l'*Encyclopédie*, 1986, *Encyclopédie*, Tome I, Paris: Garnier-Flammarion, Collection.
Badiou, A. (1993) *L'éthique. Essai sur la conscience du mal*, Paris: Hatier, [2000, English translation, New York: Verso).
Balibar, E. (1985) *Spinoza et la politique*, Paris: PUF.
Balibar, E. (2001) *Nous, citoyens d'Europe? Les frontières, l'Etat, le peuple*, Paris: La Découverte.
Baudeau, N. (1770) 'Explication du Tableau Économique à Madame de ***', in Eugène Daire (ed.) (1846), *Physiocrates*, Paris: Guillaumin.
Bayle, P. (1696) 'Spinoza', *Dictionnaire historique et critique*, in *Ecrits sur Spinoza*, 1983, Paris: Berg.
Bloch, O. (ed.) (1990) *Spinoza au XVIIIe siècle*, Paris: Klincksieck.

Boutang, Y. M. (1998) *De l'esclavage au salariat. Economie politique du salariat bridé*, Paris: PUF.

Bove, L. (1996) *La stratégie du conatus. Affirmation et résistance chez Spinoza*, Paris: Vrin.

Caraccioli, L. A. (1776) *L'Europe française. Paris modèle des nations*, Turin: Duchesne.

Condillac, E. B. (1776), *Le commerce et le gouvernement, considérés l'un par rapport à l'autre*, 1980, Genève: Slatkine.

Du Pont de Nemours, P. S. (1764) *De l'exportation et de l'importation des grains* in *Oeuvres politiques et économiques*, Vol. I, 1979, The Netherland: KTO Press.

Gauthier, F. and Ikni, G. R. (ed.) (1988) *La guerre du blé au XVIIIe siècle*, Paris: Editions de la Passion.

van Gunsteren, H. (1998) *A Theory of Citizenship. Organizing Plurality in Contemporary Democracies*, New York: Westview Press.

Hobbes, T. (1654) *Of Liberty and Necessity*, in Vere Chappell (ed.) (1999), *Hobbes and Bramhall on Liberty and Necessity*, Cambridge: Cambridge University Press.

Hobbes, T. (1988) *Leviathan*, London: Penguin Classics.

Israel, J. (2001) *Radical Enlightenment. Philosophy and the Making of Modernity 1650–1750*, Oxford: Oxford University Press.

Lazzarato, M. (2002) *Les puissances de l'invention: la psycholgie économique de Gabriel Tarde contre l'économie politique*, Paris: Editions des Empêcheurs de penser en rond.

Le Mercier de la Rivière, P. F. J. H. (1770) *L'intérêt général de l'Etat ou la liberté du commerce des blés*, Amsterdam.

Le Mercier de la Rivière, P. F. J. H. (1767), *L'ordre naturel et essentiel des sociétés politiques*, 1910, Paris: Geuthner.

Legros, J. C. F. (1787) *Examen et analyse du système des philosophes économistes par un solitaire*, Genève, Bardes.

Lovejoy, A. (1976) *The Great Chain of Being*, Harvard, MA: Harvard University Press.

Markoff, J. (1996) *The Abolition of Feudalism. Peasants, Lords and Legislators in the French Revolution*, Pennsylvania: Pennsylvania State University Press.

Matheron, A. (1969) *Individu et communauté chez Spinoza*, Paris: Minuit.

Montag, W. (1999) *Bodies, Masses, Power. Spinoza and His Contemporaries*, New York: Verso.

Montag, W. and Stolze, T. (eds.) (1997) *The New Spinoza*, Minneapolis, MN: Minnesota University Press.

Morelly (1753) *La Basiliade, ou naufrage des isles flottantes*, Vol. I, 1753, Paris: Messine.

Negri, A. (1981) *L'anomalia selvaggia. Saggio su potere e potenza in Baruch Spinoza*, Milan: Feltrinelli.

Negri, A. and Hardt, M. (2000) *Empire*, Cambridge, MA: Harvard University Press.

Pomeranz, K. and Topik, S. (1999) *The World That Trade Created. Society, Culture and the World Economy, 1400–the Present*. New York: Sharpe.

Rediker, M. (1987) *Between the Devil and the Deep Blue Sea. Merchant Seamen, Pirates and the Anglo-American Maritime World, 1700–1750*, Cambridge: Cambridge University Press

Rediker, M. and Linebaugh, P. (2000) *The Many-Headed Hydra*, Cambridge: Cambridge University Press.

Smith, A. (1776) 'Of Restraints upon the Importation from Foreign Countries of Such Goods as Can Be Produced at Home', *An Inquiry into the Nature and Causes of the Wealth of Nations*, Book IV, 1976, Chicago, IL: University of Chicago Press, chapter II.

Spinoza, B. (1677), *Ethics*, Part I

Spinoza, B. (1670) *Tractatus Theologico-Politicus.*

Spinoza, B. (1666) 'Letter to Bouwmeester', June 10, (*Ep.* XXXVII).

Spinoza, B. (1661) *Tractatus de Intellectus Emendatione*,1924–6, ed. Carl Gebhardt, *Opera*, Vol. II.

Tarde, G. (1893) *La logique sociale*, 1999, Paris: Les empêcheurs de penser en rond.

Turgot, A. J. R. (1773) 'Letter to the Abbe Terray on the Marque des Fers', 1895, *The Life and Writings of Turgot*, New York: Franklin.

Vernière, P. (1954) *Spinoza et la pensée française avant la Révolution*, Paris: PUF

6
The Cosmo-Body-Politic

Jill Marsden

> I realize that such a conception, according to which one must think of my body on our earth as connected to other stars by stretched out nerves, is almost incomprehensible to other people considering the immense distances involved; for me however as a result of my daily experiences over the last six years there can be no doubt as to the objective reality of this relation.
>
> (Daniel Paul Schreber (1903),
> *Memoirs of my Nervous Illness*, pp. 118–19)

The year 1903 saw the publication of one of the most extraordinary discussions of corporeality and cosmic connection ever to impact on occidental history. The work, entitled *Memoirs of My Nervous Illness* was written by Daniel Paul Schreber, presiding judge of the Court of Appeal at Dresden and subsequent subject of Freud's well-known case study of psychosis. The *Memoirs* constitute a fascinating record of the illness for which Schreber was hospitalised, an account which elaborates unprecedented possibilities for bodily reconfiguration via a unique technology of transhuman contact. A work of such labyrinthine complexity defies any easy summary, yet there is an important sense in which Schreber achieves what very few thinkers in the Western tradition have managed: namely, a sustained meditation on the integration of human life with extra-human systems – a genuinely exploratory rather than a merely reflective philosophy.

Undoubtedly, Schreber is correct in his assertion that to be connected to the stars by a vastly attenuated nervous system is a scarcely comprehensible prospect. However, as Nietzsche argues in *The Will to Power*, if we analysed our body in terms of spatial conditions we would gain precisely the same image of it as we have of the stellar system and the distinction between the organic and the inorganic would cease to be noticeable (Nietzsche 1968, 676). From the perspective of forces of attraction and repulsion, action at a distance, wave movement and other environmental dynamics, the limit of a human body is as arbitrary a concept as the limit of a sidereal body: the energies of Sirius and the shoulder of Orion are with us now, here. Indeed, for Nietzsche the normative notion of a discrete, functional body is a *political* prejudice of one part of the said body, an enduring legacy of Enlightenment consciousness, which equates human essence with organic unity, individual freedom and rational agency. The illusion that intentionality characterises human thought and action as such persists both philosophically and politically, despite the oft-repeated acknowledgement that by far the greater number of somatic movements has nothing to do with consciousness or sensation, indeed that the processes governing the multiple, minute patterns and rhythms of human physiology are beyond our understanding (Nietzsche 1968, 676). One may have long since abandoned the view that the motions of the stars are produced by entities conscious of a purpose but Nietzsche questions whether this belief has yet to be abandoned in regard to bodily motions and changes (676).

On both counts, Schreber's 'paranoiac' conviction of cosmic persecution is clearly contrary to the letter of Nietzsche's philosophy but in its super-systemic understanding of the fluid boundaries of the body it is profoundly sympathetic to its spirit. By virtue of his nervous illness, Schreber is able to supply unparalleled field notes from a cosmo-body-politic beyond the modernist presupposition of essential identity, biological destiny and species divides. It may seem perverse to look to 'pathological' examples of human experience to explore the cosmopolitical but it is in its aberrant formations and deviant pathways that the *fundamental capacity of life to improvise* is most acutely delineated. Indeed, Schreber's intriguing accounts of unique modes of connection and cross-fertilisation between deregulated organs and discordant senses afford us the ideal opportunity to revisit the body-politic of current philosophical thought. For Nietzsche the philosophical challenge is not necessarily to circumvent the 'despotic' perspective of consciousness (for it may prove to be 'life-preserving') but to examine whether it is possible to 'enter into communication' with the muted 'inferior parts' (Nietzsche 1968, 492). To this end, Schreber's tantalising accounts of cosmic creativity enable us to 'flesh out' Nietzsche's project of regarding the body as a set of power relations within a manifold environment. As will be argued in what follows, this endeavour will also show how habitual assumptions about the relevant categories and tools of current philosophical practice will have to be revised in light of new cosmopolitical horizons.

I. The philosophical body-politic

In its classical formulation the concept of a 'body-politic' denotes a set of significant correspondences between the organisation of the *polis* and the individual human body. Historically, the analogy has been employed to support a variety of different political agendas, most typically to bolster the claim that a 'natural' social order is one which functions in a comparable manner to that of the human organism. Central to the notion of the body-politic is the idea that organisms are structured beings in which the parts function reciprocally as ends and means in the service of the whole. Although this view was eclipsed by social contract theory in the seventeenth century, recent developments in the study of biology have sparked renewed interest in the logics of micro- and macro-cosmic order. The contemporary manifestation of this concern is to be found in neo-Darwinist molecular biology that focuses on nucleic DNA as the intrinsic self-propagating force of the whole. The autonomy of the genetic unit is apparently confirmed by heredity patterns, the potential for variation putatively contained within the germ-plasm and independent of the soma-plasm or environment. Arguably such a view retains the prejudice that the growth and development of the body can be explained teleologically in terms of the survival of the 'whole'. To the extent that this model of evolution takes already individuated organisms as its focus for explaining the self-organisation and reproduction of life it reinforces an anthropomorphic politics of the body. It also reflects a dominant tendency in much of our thinking in general, namely the abstraction of a model or principle of identity from the productive process and its retrospective reinsertion at the 'origin'. Knowledge accordingly becomes a process of *re*-cognition, the assimilation of difference to the same.

In his assorted reflections on the political organisation of our physiology, Nietzsche makes repeated reference to the metaphor of the body-politic. Contending that 'our body is only a social structure made up of many souls' (Nietzsche 1973, 19), he rejects the functionalist view that the 'components' of the body work together as a self-sufficient entity. On the contrary, Nietzsche regards this community of 'souls' as a multiplicity of forces which from a certain perspective share a common holding pattern (Nietzsche 1968, 641). Moreover, he insists that in the 'tremendous multiplicity of events within an organism, the part which becomes conscious to us is a mere means' rather than finality or purpose (Nietzsche 1968, 674). This is because the logic of our conscious thinking is only a *'crude and facilitated form of the thinking needed by our organism, indeed by the particular organs of our organism'* (Nietzsche 1967–77/ 11/462/34[124]). Thanks to the dominance of our 'coarse organs' of knowing and perceiving, reality is always 'only a *simplification* for practical ends': the *'positing* as the same' presupposes a prior *'making* the same' (Nietzsche 1968, 580, 501).

> The development of consciousness as an *apparatus of government*: only accessible to *generalizations*. Even what the eye shows enters consciousness *generalised* and *pre-adjusted*. (Nietzsche 1967–77/11/ 484/34[187])

In essence, Nietzsche argues that the perceptual capacities of a body are a 'product' of their micro-political environment. To say as much is to recognise that thought is a material process which is both 'conditioned' by the values of the body (its habits, moods, prejudices, appetites) and which conditions it in turn (disposes it to these affective and intellectual states). With the cultivation of an 'invented and rigid world of concepts' and the 'reduction of experiences to *signs*' a magnificent capacity to abbreviate becomes invested in consciousness:

> Just as there are many things a general doesn't want to know, and must not know if he is to not to lose his overall view, so in our conscious mind there must be *above all* a drive *to exclude, to chase away*, a selecting drive – which allows only *certain* [*gewisse*] facts to be presented to it. (Nietzsche 1967–77/11/464/34[131])

By analysing the organisation of the body in this way, we are able to discern how politics functions by enabling pluralities to bear the appearance of unities. Nietzsche claims that we are able to grasp the nature of our subject-unity as 'regents at the head of a polity' [*Gemeinwesen*] by recognising the expedience of filtering out difference (Nietzsche 1968, 492). It is suggested that although the rulers and the ruled are 'of the same kind', and in their 'obeying and commanding' are co-dependent, the relative ignorance in which the regents are kept concerning individual activities and even disturbances within the commonwealth is one of the conditions under which rule is possible (492). As a consequence, 'what happens here is what happens in every well-constructed and happy polity: the ruling class identifies itself with the successes of the polity' (492). Since the 'subject-unity' is only able to maintain its domination by suppressing awareness of its inferiors, it is futile to question the 'subject' about itself. Indeed, to avoid the snares of self-reflection and to appreciate that a 'fluctuating assessment of the limits of power is part of life', ways must be found to facilitate communication with the 'subordinates themselves' (492).

What this amounts to in political terms is a retreat from a philosophical body-politic which privileges representation. The aim is not to jettison concepts such as subjectivity, reflection, identity and intentionality but to cease to regard them as the only axial terms for *thinking*. Although it may no longer be controversial to argue that the concept of the 'organism' is an abstraction from the multiple, fluid economy of nonorganic life, it is less easy to dispense with abstractions when considering political organisation since so much of our political vocabulary is invested in the idea of representation. In this regard, Deleuze's comments on the Nietzschean body-politic are particularly pertinent. Deleuze rejects the idea that bodies are defined by their genus or species, their organs and functions: what matters is what bodies can do, the affects of which they are capable (Deleuze 1987, 60). Inspired by Nietzsche, Deleuze defines the body in terms of the relation between dominant and dominated forces:

> Every relationship of forces constitutes a body – whether it is chemical, biological, social or political. Any two forces, being unequal, constitute a body as soon as they enter into a relationship. (Deleuze 1983, 40)

In this minimal definition, the notion of the body is addressed in terms of power relations without the latter being subordinated to an overarching concept of unity or essence. In redirecting our critical attention away from the ontology of form to the matter of relation, we substitute the notion of a political order for the process of ordering. From this perspective we have 'license to divest politics of its restricted state-orientation' so that the constitution of bodies can be thought micro-politically in terms of their ordering of force relations – whereas macro-political bodies such as the state, the party, the social class can be thought corporeally in terms of the forces involved in their ordering of laws (Protevi 2001, 3).

Within this Deleuzian register, the notion of self-conscious purposivity is replaced by the concept of material self-ordering, which expresses the existence of activity at thresholds that is 'decisive' without being deliberative. It has recently been claimed that in its imposition of order from on high a 'hylomorphic representation of a body-politic ... resonates with fascist desire' as opposed to a 'radically democratic' self-ordered and non-organismic body-politic (Protevi 2001, 9). However, lest it be thought that certain forms of organisation are intrinsically democratic or fascistic it is important to be clear that the Deleuzian distinction between micro- and macro-political is not one of scale but of value:

> What characterizes micropolitics are the three questions that it brings to each situation. What are the forces of life in this situation? What are the forces of negativity in this situation? And how can the forces be released? (May 1991, 31)

Understood energetically as forces of becoming, life has no identity in itself other than being that which perpetually differs from itself. The forces of negativity are not different in kind to the forces of life: the question is how the forces of life become self-repressive (a theme Nietzsche (1989) pursues at length in *On the Genealogy of Morals*). In this context, it is essential to establish which values are 'incorporated' by the body-politic and the degree to which they become 'instinctive'. Liberation of the forces of life then becomes a tactic of value-creation, a cultivation of new relations which is itself the cultivation of new value-terms.

The 'coarseness of our organs' may inhibit us from seeing beyond what we take to be 'given' but may also enable politically useful 'repressions' (as Nietzsche acknowledges with respect to the ignorance [*Unwissenheit*] of the regents at the head of a polity). In each concrete, political context, it is the *values* through which forces come to be ordered that are significant, not the persistence or collapse of 'forms' as such. Beyond the political expedience of *not-knowing* [*Nichtwissen*], Nietzsche is concerned to explore the *positive* possibilities of ignorance – to 'unlearn responsibility for ourselves' (Nietzsche 1968, 676). Since for Nietzsche, deliberative consciousness is only the smallest part of us, systems of thinking that escape capture by established forms of knowledge tend towards expression of the 'active' power of life. Phenomena such as dreams, reflex actions, 'intuitions', psychic connection and clairvoyance – a whole host of compulsive behaviours and psychopathologies reveal the existence of powerful 'unconscious' drives which are all too readily dismissed as deviations from the norm of purposive action. For example, Nietzsche argues that with respect to the subtle world of 'inner phenomena' we may be compared with the deaf and dumb who divine through movements of the lips the words that they do not hear.

From the phenomena of inner sense we conclude the existence of invisible and other phenomena that we would apprehend if our means of observation were adequate and that one calls the nerve current [*Nervenstrom*].'We lack any sensitive organs for this inner world, so we sense a *thousandfold complexity* as a unity' (Nietzsche 1968, 523).

Indeed, if means are to be found to refine our bodily-thinking, it is necessary to abdicate from reflexive consciousness for a while, to indulge patterns of thinking which in no way resemble models of knowledge already embedded in the philosophical body-politic. By diverting attention from what is happening at the level of order (policy, programme, campaign etc.) and reconnecting with the unconscious ordering processes – or what we might term the 'nerve current' – the muted, subordinate parts of the body-politic may begin to enter into communication with us.

II. The fleeting-improvised body

In an early work Nietzsche claims that it is in our insomniac moments that an involuntary sensitivity to different environmental cues is imposed.

> There are spirits all around us [*es geht geisterhaft um uns zu*], each moment of our life wants to say something to us, but we do not want to listen to these spirit voices. We are frightened that when we are alone and quiet something will be whispered in our ear and so we hate quietness and deafen ourselves with sociability. (Nietzsche 1983, 159)

It is scarcely fortuitous that profound encounters with alterity should steal upon us at night when reliance on vision is compromised and our normative sensorium is negotiated anew. It is here that Schreber's experiences as outlined in his *Memoirs* are most richly suggestive for our purposes. Schreber's ruinous hypersensitivity to the subtlest changes in his surroundings is precipitated by acute insomnia. In this twilight world, existence is re-set at a higher pitch, the walls begin to 'crackle', the abyss begins to whisper. Before long, Schreber comes to realise that this constant white noise is the incessant chatter of 'departed souls' in the process of migration to 'Blessedness'. These souls are able to summon his attention through a complex cosmic circuitry composed of what he calls 'nerves' and 'rays' that connect his body to the most proximate and most distant things. As 'nerve souls' in transit utilise this capillary network to intercept and pass comment on his mental processes, Schreber initially experiences this extraordinary state of affairs as an act of aggression against 'man's natural right to be master of his own nerves' (Schreber 1955, 70). However, as his 'illness' progresses he relinquishes this paranoid overdetermination of the value of consciousness and comes to affirm the benefits of his extraordinary 'miraculated' body.

This situation has arisen, Schreber explains, owing to a crisis in the Order of the World, brought about by persecution from forces beyond his control. Speculating that he has become the victim of 'soul murder' initiated by his former physician, Dr Flechsig, and then taken up in turn by God, Schreber depicts a nightmarish world of cosmopolitical intrigue, his body the battleground of forces both ignorant and malign. The nature of the conspiracy remains unclear but it is suggested that Flechsig may have discovered the existence of 'divine rays' during therapeutic 'nerve contact' with his patient (e.g. hypnosis). As a result of this treatment a portion of Flechsig's nerves appear to have become fused with Schreber's prior to breaking off and ascending to heaven as a 'tested soul' where it zealously seeks to retain hold of the potent 'divine rays'. Since this means that Flechsig's plans to destroy Schreber's mental and corporeal identity are unknown to Flechsig himself, the hapless judge is plunged into the darkest recesses of social exile. A puppet of forces with whom he is unable to negotiate there is no solution to his torment through the avenues of reason or justice. Despite being 'wrongly represented' by souls who cruelly taunt him, he has no political voice and is unable to offer any plea in his defence.

Schreber's difficulties are compounded by the fact that the theft by the renegade Flechsig's 'soul' poses a threat to God whose nerves have the capacity to transform themselves into all things of the created world (in this regard they are called 'rays'). We are told that in the normal course of events, God only has contact with human beings after death when he 'draws up' nerves from corpses for cleaning purposes prior to incorporating them into his own state of Blessedness. Spiritual transcendence takes this unusual form because 'the human soul is contained in the nerves of the body' (Schreber 1955, 45) and God 'is only nerve, not body, and akin therefore to the human soul', indeed, is nothing other than their aggregation (46). In this primary role God has no commerce with living human beings, but in special circumstances he engages in 'nerve contact' with highly gifted individuals in something akin to poetic inspiration. However, such 'nerve-contact' is not allowed to become the rule because the nerves of living human beings have such a magnetic power of attraction for God 'particularly when in a state of *high-grade excitation'* that prolonged connection endangers his existence (48). A crisis ensues in the Order of the World when due to both Flechsig's conspiracy and Schreber's morbidly excited nerves, God's nerves become perilously melded with his and the whole system of soul migration short circuits. The consequences of this machinic breakdown are devastating for Schreber because the soul-sifting process rhizomatically re-routes itself through his own nervous system. It is not that Schreber takes the place of God, rather that his body becomes the locus for attaining the state of 'Blessedness' which the migrating nerve-souls seek. Intriguingly, this state of Blessedness is likened to 'female sexual bliss' – which is said to be vastly superior to male sexual pleasure. Accordingly, souls are irresistibly drawn to Schreber's body and, as he puts it, he is obliged to cultivate as much 'feminine voluptuousness' as possible to appease them. To this end he maintains that his body has become filled with masses of 'female nerves' and it is his fate to be feminised and sexually abused.

Initially this prospect – which is described to him by the souls as 'un-manning' – is greeted with horror and Schreber's suffering is acute. Goaded to end it all by a hostile universe (particularly by the souls of the Students Corps Saxonia – 'the so-called Brothers of Cassiopeia') Schreber makes a number of attempts to take his own life. Unfortunately, since God does not *'really understand the living human being'* (Schreber 1955, 75) only seeing it *'from without'* (59) he equates inertia with death and proceeds to 'draw out' Schreber's nerves whenever there is a momentary lull in his mental activity: hence the need to enage in constant and compulsive thinking is just one of the terrible torments which the *Memoirs* so graphically depict.

Freud makes much of the fear of unmanning in his diagnosis of Schreber's illness as a paranoid fear of his unconscious homosexual desires (Freud 1911). Situating his dread and later acceptance of unmanning within the nexus of Oedipal conflict, Freud interprets Schreber's relation to God as 'the unmistakable prototype' of his relationship to his father (188). Although thought-provoking and trenchantly argued, Freud's reading remains a politically conservative one, substituting one set of identity terms for another (male/female). Moreover, by treating the connections that Schreber makes with the cosmos as ideal rather than real, his reading fails to interrogate the extent to which Schreber's text is an object lesson in what it means to *embody thought*. Judging, anticipating, responding and assessing are all processes that the body is able to perform without the aid of ideation. Thinking with and through the body involves a multiplicity of practices which only become com- muted to ideas when they are delivered over to consciousness. It is true that unmanning is described in terms of a retraction of the male sex organ (in addition to the extraction of single facial hairs and a diminu- tion in stature) but Schreber's body is also subject to gruesome divine miracles such as the '*compression-of-the-chest-miracle*' (which leads to severe breathlessness), obstruction of the gullet, putrefaction of the abdomen, the sawing apart of the skull in various directions, the pump- ing out of his spinal cord and the application of the 'head-compressing machine' – to mention but a few of the experiences which he undergoes (Schreber 1955, 132–8). Rather than downplaying these diverse and less obviously gendered accounts of torment as signs of nervous tension (or repressed memories of his father's use of disciplinary harnesses and restraints), they suggest a certain plasticity of the boundaries of the body and the boundaries of thought, a point which becomes much easier to discern when the interpretative focus is shifted from the forces of nega- tivity to the forces of life.

With respect to the former, it is particularly significant that Schreber's God should fail to see that what may be specific to life is its irreducibil- ity to its material components. Within the modern philosophical body- politic it is the theocratic model of organisation ('the judgement of God') that commutes living systems to reproductive organisms. On a political axis this is reflected in biotechnological research programmes that foreground genetics (such as the sequencing of human DNA). However, as Schreber's text amply illustrates, what is most vital about the living being is its capacity for disassembling and disorganising that which is most ordered and unified. Indeed, as Schreber comes to recog- nise, his destiny is not to defend the integrity of his individual being but to acknowledge his vital role in maintaining a complex ecology of inter- acting elements.

Schreber's transition from persecuted subject to willing mediator reflects a subtle but significant shift in his view of the body. No longer does he see himself as a victim under attack from without but a vital conduit in the responsive network of nerve souls. In effect, Schreber engages in a micro-political analysis of the forces of life and the forces of negativity in his situation. His painful victimisation by hostile souls aside, he comes to acquire new and intense feelings of pleasure via his burgeoning 'female nerves', prompting the deduction that it may be his spiritual destiny to be transformed into a woman in order regenerate the Order of the World through union with God. Contra Freud, this is not to submit to a passive (castrated) subject position but is to explore 'feminisation' as a vector of escape from the restrictive biologism of sexed being. In any event, it should be noted that divine fertilisation of his female nerves is partial and periodic and never stabilises into a subject position that would allow the redemption hypothesis to be vindicated.[1]

Rather than trading one model of identity for another, Schreber's text tells a number of alternative stories about the possibility of interfacing with extra-human systems. Owing to his 'increased voluptuousness' souls are attracted to Schreber's body and on certain nights thousands of souls 'drip' down from the stars to which they are connected and dissolve into his flesh. His body becomes a cosmic 'nerve centre' for communication through a hundred speech media. As his connections to the environment grow, *that environment becomes his body*. The 'departed souls' in transition between human life and participation in the states of Blessedness are constantly involved in mutating relationships with Schreber's nervous system. Ontologically, these nerve-souls defy easy categorisation in terms of the living and the non-living, the spiritual and the material and the one and the many. Like viruses they are 'virtually real' and may both attack and protect their host. In direct challenge to the dominant model of evolution, these souls demonstrate how the merging of living beings into new collectives disrupts classification in terms of discrete lineages.[2] Indeed, Schreber's text maps the emergence of symbiotic environments without recourse to the standard iconography of closed systems. Moreover, since there is no categorical separation between nerve-souls and their environments, definition of 'identity' becomes a matter of interpretation. This is not to say that there is no recourse to notions of hybridity: for example, there is the kindly intentioned 'little von-W-Schreber' soul who applies balsam to parts of Schreber's head – particularly valuable given the cruelty of 'the scourge of von-W' a soul who moved a scourge around in Schreber's skull causing severe pain (Schreber 1955, 158–9). However, as the latter example indicates, even the elements that combine to make up new souls are themselves implicated in numerous other combinations and incarnations. Take the 'Flechsig-von-W soul' as a case in point. At one stage in the *Memoirs* Flechsig's soul consists of between forty and sixty parts, sometimes in combinations with others, sometimes as the pair the 'posterior Flechsig' and the 'middle "so what party" '. The von-W soul takes yet more exotic forms including the 'mid-day' von-W, the 'O damn' von-W and the 'anyhow' von-W. In short, in its predilection for population thinking rather than typology, for its emphasis on the dynamic production of diversity over the recapitulation of identity and in its appeal to the internal invention of new structures rather than external adaptation to environment, Schreber's body-politic resembles the functioning of *open* systems.

As the *Memoirs* so amply demonstrates, Schreber's nerves are not simply conduits for the transmission of information nor mere receptors of force but are themselves inherently creative. Owing to the intense excitation of his nerves, Schreber attracts the nerves of God and harnesses their generative power. By the same token, the tested souls are able to intercept the divine rays and absorb their miraculous power through the connections forged between the latter and Schreber's body. In effect, this means that every element is both active and acted upon. If we consider this fluctuating set of power relations in terms of the struggle of commanding and obeying 'souls' in Nietzsche's account of the body-politic, Freud's reading of Schreber as a persecuted, impotent and feminised subject looks ever less plausible. The substitution of one sexed position for another maintains an instrumental thinking of the relations of parts to the whole whereas Schreber's burgeoning proliferation of cosmic connections begs the question of who or what is 'in control' as autonomy dissolves into the automatism of the programming loop.

Across searing starscapes far in excess of visual range, Schreber's nerves are brought into contact with other vital systems, prompting us to broaden the parameters of what it means to think. As his psychotic experiences appear to testify, if reconnection with the productive processes of thought is possible, philosophy need no longer circulate within a closed system of re-cognition and re-presentation. In other words, if ontological presuppositions about the real are themselves submitted to critique, philosophy can begin to explore and to create anew.

III. Above and below the suns

To cultivate a philosophical body-politic beyond the requirements of representation entails different tools and tactics of thinking. There is no given 'pattern' of power relations that is inherently life-affirming or life-denying. Nietzsche's infamous admiration for 'aristocratic' political values and concomitant hatred of 'democracy' has frequently been misunderstood on this point. A politics of life is one that focuses on the relations of force in any given circumstance and assesses them from the viewpoint of 'value':

> To affirm is to unburden: not to load life with the weight of higher values, but *to create* new values which are those of life, which make life light and active. There is creation, properly speaking, only insofar as we make use of excess in order to invent new forms of life rather than separating life from what it can do. (Deleuze 1983, 185)

'Value' is essentially the standpoint for the increase or decrease of dominating centres of power and is in no sense a durable unit (Nietzsche 1968, 715). Nietzsche suggests that 'value words are banners raised where a *new bliss* has been found – a new *feeling*' (Nietzsche 1968, 714). Schreber's encounter with a new form of bliss – beyond that prescribed by ingrained prejudices about the biology of the body – constitutes a re-organisation of his affective economy. Having previously never regarded himself as being a particularly creative person, Schreber comes to appreciate the complexities and subtleties of what it *feels like to think*. The constant 'vibration' of his nerves – which occurs when others participate in his thinking – enables him to connect with divine and beatific forces without awaiting the work of the understanding or the imperative of reason. As Nietzsche observes, 'that a multitude of persons seem to participate in all thinking is not particularly easy to "observe" but it is *felt* when every thought first arrives multi-significant and floating' (Nietzsche 1967–77/11/595–6/38[1]).

Schreber's 'commerce' or 'communication' with previously muted forces of the body operates in terms of reflexes rather than reflection, that is, *ideas materialise* without conscious mediation or negotiation with a prior image of what 'thought' is supposed to be. The powers that elude consciousness and purposivity may manifest themselves in ways that are only sensed once the concept of 'connection' is liberated from subordination to pre-given identity terms. For Schreber, mental faculties do not pre-exist the moment at which their relevance emerges. In an encounter with alterity a faculty is produced ('miraculated'). The possibility of a harmony of the faculties does not arise because these forces do not converge on a common object, nor presuppose a unitary subject backlit by the one sun of a coherent world. The body ever more dysfunctional, the faculties ever more discordant, it is through the collapse of meaning that communication is achieved.

Lest it be thought that Schreber's cosmic explorations have little application to those endowed with coarser organs it must be recalled that there is a reflux between the body and its thought. As stated at the outset, for Nietzsche the tendency to assimilate novelty to sameness reflects a stabilised physiology, one which only allows certain facts to be presented to it, lest anarchy reign. Such a physiology is life-negating to the extent that life inevitably seeks *to be more than itself*. Inherently active and self-exceeding, life is 'will to power'.

> The will to power *interprets* (– the formation of an organ is a question of interpretation): it defines limits, determines degrees differences of power. Simple differences of power could not yet feel themselves as such: there must be something that wants to grow, and which interprets the value of other things that want to grow [...] In truth, *interpretation is a means of becoming master over something*. (The organic process presupposes constant interpretation.) (Nietzsche 1968, 643)

The will to power is nothing other than the production of 'values' – the upsurge of energies that intensify feelings, sharpen insights and give birth to new affects. In the formation of an organ it is a question of what can be assimilated to, and what distinguished from, prevailing corporeal thresholds. This delicate feat of organisation is a testament to what is felt at the emerging edge of things, the lapping of a wave against a newly etched shore.

This vital encounter between the body and its alterity – its will to traverse new lineaments of desire – is an outpouring of creative energy beyond the perceptual limits of a pre-constituted consciousness. In light of these reflections it is intriguing to note that recent developments in neuroscience have suggested that reality as we know it 'is largely an internally generated construct of the nervous system' and once constructed it is projected back onto the world through behavioural interactions with objects in our local environment (Finkel 1992, 393). Research in somatosensory physiology has indicated that body maps of the functional domains in the motor cortex are labile at the borders. Rather than static representations of underlying anatomical connections, these body maps are dynamic structures that change over time in response to degrees of stimulation. Given that these maps reflect the interaction of the individual with its tactile environment, they go some way towards explaining anomalous perceptions such as the 'phantom limb': after a limb is lost or amputated, some patients report feeling sensations in the missing body part, an experience which could be accounted for in terms of the subsidence of the cortical maps subserving the limb (Finkel 1992, 399). If we were to think of these maps in terms of the philosophical body-politic, we might justifiably claim that a phantom body persists in our political thinking, a body which represents itself as ordered and self-legislating despite the panoply of ways in which it organises itself otherwise. In this regard it is important to emphasise that the subtly mutable relation between our cortical maps and the environment is not strictly speaking 'purposive'. We do not 'intend' to see reality as we do. It would be more accurate to say that our sensory horizons express the values that we are in the process of embodying. If an economy of self-sustaining values has become deeply incorporated by the philosophical body-politic, we may be unconvinced that novelty is genuinely possible. However, since for Nietzsche values are immanent perspectives on life – its internal differentiations – exploration of alternative ways of thinking gives birth to new affective possibilities. Perhaps increasingly there is a need to represent the parts that we cannot feel because what is missing from our political thinking is an analysis of the affective relations that connect our small sector of quantum-cosmological space to other broader environments.

With this in mind we return to Nietzsche's suggestion that we enter into communication with the subordinate parts of the body (Nietzsche 1968, 492). Nietzsche speculates that thinking has an older ancestry than vision since before we started practicing our understanding of the world as moving shapes, there was a time when the world was grasped as changing sensations of pressure of various degrees. When not supported by the eyes it is possible to 'think in sensations of pressure' (Nietzsche 1968–77/11/643–4/40[28]). If it is the case that 'at every moment' there are countless factors influencing us such as air and electricity which we seldom sense, there may well be forces that continually influence us although we never feel them (Nietzsche 1968, 676). It is uncontroversial that ion storms, X-ray bursts and solar weather can wreak havoc with terrestrial electromagnetic communications systems, of which the human nervous system is but one example. Nietzsche attributed his own chronic migraines and gastric discomfort to meteorological influences, particularly the electrical patterns in the cloud cover and the effects of the winds. There may be many more cosmic maelstroms which we have yet to sense or detect.[3] These are thoughts which escape every mode of knowledge because from the perspective of normative perception they remain undeveloped. As Nietzsche observes, it is improbable that our 'knowing' should extend further than is necessary for the preservation of life (Nietzsche 1968, 494). Our perceptual habits having been formed within a geocentric horizon, it is difficult to expand our sensorium beyond the limits which correspond to the structures of consciousness. However, as we have sought to show, from the perspective of the body the thinkable far exceeds the knowable. What we require are tools of thinking which are generated from the processes of thinking themselves, mobile and fluid principles which do not presuppose being as given.

Schreber frequently describes the people and creatures that he encounters as 'fleeting-improvised' (*flüchtig hingemachten*) on the grounds that he cannot be certain whether they actually exist or have been 'miraculated'. Drawing on this term, we might say that Schreber's cosmos exhibits *fleeting-improvised concepts*. These are not items of knowledge (which frame life in very limited ways) but something akin to dream experience in which a 'felt' identity does not dovetail with anything that is identical conceptually. Scrutiny of the *Memoirs* indicates that Schreber's thought processes do not so much 'progress' as mutually interpenetrate. Indeed, from the perspective of logical relation, Schreber's accounts of the cosmos appear to violate the laws of non-contradiction. However, we might be inclined to say that thanks to the sensitivity of his 'organs', Schreber is able to sense a thousandfold complexity as thousandfold and it is this embodied thinking which provides philosophy with new cosmopolitical horizons.

For example, although some of the manifest contradictions in Schreber's text might seem to be resolved at a later date by his inclusion of postscripts, for example, the sun is initially said to be a 'living being' but later that it is not, relatively little in the text can be clarified at the level of seriality (Schreber 1955, 47, 232). In fact, it would be erroneous to assume that knowledge in the *Memoirs* is achieved cumulatively by successive revisions and additions. For example, God's role and dominion in Schreber's cosmos is constantly re-configured. Initially 'God' is said to consist of anterior and posterior realms, the former referring to the aggregate of departed souls (also known as 'the forecourts of heaven' – above which He dwells) and the latter being further subdivided into a lower God, Ariman, and a higher God, Ormuzd. At times Ariman and Ormuzd appear to be in conflict with one another – since each has his own egoism and instinct for self-preservation – at times they occupy differential relations with Schreber and do not even speak to him in the same way (Schreber 1955, 127, 150–1). Periodically, God takes over the sending of the sun's rays, especially the lower God Ariman who for a while becomes identified with the sun (Schreber 1955, 95). Meanwhile, the upper God (Ormuzd) 'kept himself at a greater, perhaps even still at a colossal distance; I see his picture as a small sun-like disc, so tiny as to be almost a mere point, appear at short intervals on the nerves inside my head' (Schreber 1955, 95). At one stage Schreber witnesses two suns in the same sky, the earthly sun and a second sun said to be made up of the

Cassiopeia group of stars (Schreber 1955, 84). Flechsig's soul is also said to be a leader of two 'suns', with von-W entrusted to lead another disinclined to do so (Schreber 1955,112–13).

In light of such cosmic complexity, Freud's claim that the sun is 'nothing but another sublimated symbol for his father' (Freud 1911, 190) is difficult to sustain. The solar map is constantly rearranged so that what is proximate in one account becomes remote in another.

To complexify matters further, Schreber admits that he is uncertain whether God and the heavenly bodies may be 'one and the same' or whether the totality of God's nerves may be behind the stars – which would then be 'stations' through which his creative power travels to earth and possibly to other planets (Schreber 1955, 46). Every time more detail is given as to the nature of God, the sun or the stars, new relations are posited without the old ones being relinquished. The perhaps inevitable tendency to regard proper names as identity terms encourages the reader to attempt to reconcile incommensurate taxonomies as if there were a univocal syntax that ultimately supervened these incompatible formulations. However, in Schreber's cosmos there is no necessary or direct relation between different bits of 'knowledge'. Some things are more closely connected than others but a concord between all parts is not required in order for the system to function. Something of which one is ignorant shares no common border with other parts of existing knowledge. In fact, we could mark a distinction between systematic non-knowledge – which entails recognition of the lack of knowledge according to bits of knowledge one already has – and non-systematic non-knowledge that describes an inability to assimilate an idea in terms with which the system is already familiar. Such a 'fleeting-improvised' item can only be assimilated by changing the rules for recognition – which would mean that it *is not known on the same plane as existing knowledge*. Here the acquisition of 'knowledge' changes the rules that have gone before. Perhaps what Schreber's cosmos shows us more keenly than anything else is the need to conceive of reality as a continuous upsurge of qualitative changes which coexist with one another without becoming externalised as distinct. No spatial model can do just to this body-politic. This is the cosmos as encountered rather than charted. Just as an anatomical diagram of pleasure zones bears little relation to the oceanic tremoring of the orgasmic body, this is less a cartography than an economy of force, a web of enchantments within which new sensual continents constantly unfold.[4]

Schizophrenia is the possibility of other suns, of multiple points of orientation. The map of Schreber's cosmos is necessarily kaleidoscopic, not simply because of the time-shuffling rhythms that simultaneously connect and dissociate his experiences but because the interpretative component of sensory awareness is intensified in his case. Life's fundamentally inventive and improvisational power is revealed at a tempo otherwise imperceptible to our 'coarse' and 'utile' organs. If the formation of the body is a question of interpretation, Schreber's cosmo-body-politic displays flashpoints for thinking, firestorms that give birth to new solar senses. Panspermic rivers and parthenogenetic rays boil through each other in perpetual motion, burst out of themselves like an offering to unknown and unknowable stars. What we *think of* as the body and what we think of as the cosmos are after-images for contemplation when we have gone beyond the point where we could tolerate perceiving them, let alone perceiving them as co-incidental. *Some ferocious cosmos*, and not an *idea* of it, painted something on the cave walls of a madman's eyes, paining a body with the light of more than one sun.

Notes

1. 'Twice at different times (while I was still in Flechsig's Asylum) I had a female genital organ, although a poorly developed one, and in my body felt quickening like the first signs of life of a human embryo: by a divine miracle God's nerves corresponding to male seed had been thrown into my body; in other words fertilization had occurred' (Schreber 1903,43).
2. It is now accepted that eukaryotic ('animal') cells, in effect all cells with nuclei, 'come from more or less orgiastic encounters (eating, infecting, feeding on, having sex with and so on) among quite different types of bacteria' (Sagan 1992, 366). The technics of incorporation and contagion are the prime means for the development and cultivation of animal bodies. As recent work on endosymbiosis has indicated, an individual bacterial cell is able replicate its components in large numbers, maintaining its own organisation whilst transforming its host. In fact, bacteria are able to trade variable quantities of genes with seemingly no regard for species barriers: 'If eukaryotes could trade genes as fluidly as do bacteria, it would be a small matter for dandelions to sprout butterfly wings, collide with a bee, exchange genes again and soon be seeing with compound insect eyes' (Sagan 1992, 378).
3. Wilhelm Reich believed that he had discovered a cosmic libidinal energy which he called *orgone*, the movements and intensities of which are both constitutive of, and decisive for all life: 'The flickering of the sky, which some physicists ascribe to terrestrial magnetism, and the glimmering of stars on clear dry nights, are direct expressions of the movement of the atmospheric orgone. The "electric storms" of the atmosphere which disturb electrical equipment during intensified sun-spot activity are, as can be experimentally demonstrated, an effect of the atmospheric orgone energy' (Reich 1989, 384).
4. Research into the functional specialisations of the visual cortex obliges us to admit that our sensory experience of the world involves a considerable degree of interpretation. Not only do different areas carry out multiple functions,

connecting up with other areas in complex ways, 'there is no single area that receives connections from every other, or even a majority of other areas' (Finkel 1992, 400). This means that visual information enters the cortex and is split up according to function (shape, colour, motion etc.) but there is no place in which the 'picture' can be reassembled. This suggests that the picture must result from a dynamic process carried out in a distributed fashion over multiple cortical areas: 'In other words, the picture that one "sees" does not exist as a single, complete representation somewhere in the brain, rather it is an emergent property of the system' (401).

References

Crary, J. and Kwinter, S. (eds) (1992) *Incorporations*, New York: Zone.

Deleuze, G. (1987) *Dialogues*, 1977, trans. H. Tomlinson and B. Habberjam, London: Athlone Press.

Deleuze, G. (1983) *Nietzsche and Philosophy*, 1962, trans. H. Tomlinson, London: Athlone Press.

Finkel, L. H. (1992) 'The Construction of Perception', in J. Crary and S. Kwinter (eds), *Incorporations*, New York: Zone, pp.393–495.

Freud, S. (1911) *Psychoanalytic Notes on an Autobiographical Account of a Case of Paranoia (Schreber)* in Pelican Freud Library, Vol. IX, Harmondsworth: Penguin.

May, T. G. (1991) 'The Politics of Life in the Thought of Gilles Deleuze', *Sub-Stance*, Vol. 66, 24–35.

Nietzsche, F. (1989) *On the Genealogy of Morals* ed. and trans. W. Kaufman, New York: Vintage Books.

Nietzsche, F. (1983) *Untimely Meditations*, 1874, trans. R.J. Hollingdale, Cambridge: Cambridge University Press.

Nietzsche, F. (1973) *Beyond Good and Evil*, 1886, trans. R. J. Hollingdale, Harmondsworth: Penguin.

Nietzsche, F. (1968) *The Will to Power*, 1901, trans. Walter Kaufmann, New York: Vintage.

Nietzsche, F. (1967–77) *Kritische* Studienausgabe (KSA), ed. Giorgio Colli and Mazzino Montinari, Berlin: Walter de Gruyter.

Protevi, J. (2001) *Political Physics*, London: Athlone Press.

Reich, W. (1989) *The Function of the Orgasm: Sex-Economic Problems of Biological Energy*, 1942, trans. Vincent R. Carfagno, London: Souvenir Press.

Sagan, D. (1992) 'Metametazoa: Biology and Multiplicity', J. Crary and S. Kwinter (eds), *Incorporations*, New York: Zone, pp. 362–85.

Schreber, D. P. (1955) *Memoirs of My Nervous Illness*, 1903, trans. Ida Macalpine and Richard A. Hunter, London: W.M. Dawson & Sons Ltd.

Part III

Cosmopolitics, Its Boundaries and Limits

7
Nationalist Cosmopolitics in the Nineteenth Century

Daniel S. Malachuk

In recent years, many major philosophers have been eager to demonstrate that national and cosmopolitan allegiances can be reconciled. The pragmatist Richard Rorty has shown how nationalism and cosmopolitanism can be different but overlapping constructions of loyalty (Rorty 1998b). The utilitarian Peter Singer has suggested that nations can be useful tools to the extent that they help us to redress global wrongs (but also that our national allegiance should end when they serve only to exacerbate those wrongs) (Singer 2002, 7). And the Kantian Martha Nussbaum (like nearly all of the many influential contributors to her *For Love of Country?*) offers different approaches to reconciling a love of country with a love of humanity (Nussbaum 2002).

But is the problem of reconciling nationalism and cosmopolitanism as significant as these philosophers' eagerness to solve it would suggest? As Pheng Cheah reminded us in an essay opening the influential 1998 collection *Cosmopolitics: Thinking and Feeling Beyond the Nation*, advocates of Enlightenment cosmopolitanism and of the nationalism that followed generally understood one another to be allies rather than opponents. For example, Immanuel Kant's cosmopolitan ideal was 'not anti- or postnationalist' but rather 'a prenationalist attempt to reform absolutist statism' (Cheah 1998, 24). Early nationalists followed his and other cosmopolitans' footsteps. As Cheah puts it, before these early nationalists found their states, 'the ideals of cosmopolitanism and European nationalism in its early stirrings [were] almost indistinguishable' (25).

In contrast to today, then, attachment to both one's nation and the world was fairly unremarkable during this earlier period, a period that extends, I will emphasise here, further into the nineteenth century than is usually reckoned. Eventually this chapter will evolve into an appreciation of this neglected nineteenth-century nationalist cosmopolitics, but not before pondering what makes the notion of dual attachment such a difficult one for us today. For I believe that when the nature of our own difficulties with dual attachment is properly identified, we can appreciate better the accomplishment of these overlooked nineteenth-century nationalist cosmopolitans.

Contemporary commentators superficially depict the challenge of holding dual attachments as a matter of determining which ones should come first and when new ones should be added. For example, many of the contributors to *For Love of Country?* are drawn to the metaphor of concentric circles of attachment (from family to neighbours to city and so forth), but they debate how quickly new 'outer' attachments should be pursued, or even if attachments should begin at the outside and move inward.[1] A closer examination of the way commentators make these arguments, though, reveals that what is often being debated is not really how to multiply our attachments, but rather whether the various attachments are indeed of equivalent value. This nastier debate usually happens at the level of rhetoric. Consider some examples from this representative volume (the emphases that follow being my addition). Some of the cosmopolitan commentators, like Nussbaum, believe our first attachments must include humanity as a whole, for to begin strictly with just family, friends and neighbours would be to '*stunt* our moral imaginations' (2002, xiv). 'One of the greatest barriers to rational deliberation in politics', Nussbaum adds later, 'is the *unexamined feeling* that one's own preferences and ways are neutral and natural. An education that takes national boundaries as morally salient too often reinforces this kind of *irrationality*' (2002, 11). The nationalist commentators, though, believe our first attachments must be local, for to begin with the global is to begin, in Benjamin Barber's words, with 'the *thin gruel* of contract relations' (2002, 31) or, in Michael W. McConnell's, 'a ... moral education that is too *bloodless* to capture the moral imagination' (2002, 79), an education that will 'likely [be] *destructive of the moral communities* that have managed to persist in the face of Western materialism and cynicism' (81–2).

It would seem, then, that if what today's nationalists and cosmopolitans debate on the surface is the proper order in which to add new attachments, the more coded but more fundamental debate is really about the intrinsic value of these attachments. And, once that more fundamental debate is recognised, one begins to see an important continuity between our contemporary debates about nationalism and cosmopolitanism and the undisguised ideological warfare of the early- and mid-twentieth century. To be sure, today's nationalist theorist does not flippantly toss the adjective 'rootless' around when describing cosmopolitans. Likewise, the contemporary defender of cosmopolitanism does not accuse the nationalist of harbouring a mindless 'oblig[ation] to fight for my nation no matter at what cost to other men', as Isaiah Berlin did in 1959 (Berlin 1990, 177)[2] That said, that a book as otherwise sophisticated as *For Love of Country?* should still resort to phrases like 'bloodless' cosmopolitanism and 'irrational' nationalism should suggest that we have not quite moved beyond this older debate. Nationalism, no matter how sophisticated, seems still to impress many as always threatening to devolve into bloody tribal prejudice, whereas cosmopolitanism for others apparently remains little more than a bloodless, artificial pose.

I recognise that my imputing a deep continuity between Cold War and contemporary theories of nationalism and cosmopolitanism is at odds with the widely held conviction that theorists in the past few decades have indeed advanced the conversation far beyond the cruder debates of the first two-thirds of the twentieth century. It is often contended, for instance, that recent and important theoretical developments now enable us to renounce what is sometimes called 'ethnic nationalism' without abandoning nationalism entirely. A new kind of nationalism, a 'civic nationalism' that is deliberately constructed through an act of 'imaginative ideological labor', 'is probably the most important point to emerge from the more recent literature', as two leading theorists have put it (Eley and Suny 1996, 8). That indispensable move from ethnic essentialism to civic constructivism, it is argued, allows for nationalism and cosmopolitanism to be reconceived as allies rather than implacable foes. But, again, the rhetoric accompanying these reconstructions often seems to betray this admirable project, revealing an abiding fear among cosmopolitans that nationalism inevitably tends towards blood and soil, and among nationalists that cosmopolitanism is simply too contrived to ever win the hearts and minds of the people, no matter how propped up with adjectives such as 'strong' or 'robust'.[3]

The primary interest of nineteenth-century nationalist cosmopolitics, I think, is that the union of affiliations it offers is predicated upon a different kind of essentialism than the essentialism discussed today. If we take essentialism to mean 'a reduction of the diversity in a population to some single criterion held to constitute its defining "essence" and most crucial character', and moreover a criterion 'often coupled with the claim that the "essence" is unavoidable and given by nature' (Özkirimli 2000, qtd 215), then we are certainly right to turn away from this *particularist* understanding of essence. At the beginning of the twenty-first century, we unfortunately do not need more examples (though there are so many still on offer) of the evils that are committed in the name of a particularist essentialism. And, if indeed that is the only kind of essentialism there is, then its implacable foe constructivism – which is the idea that any national identity-formation is 'intersubjective' and thus 'interminably negotiated, revised and refined' (Özkirimli 2000, 217) – would seem to be our only alternative. The equally post-essentialist and constructivist positions of civic nationalism and cosmopolitanism should be (as they generally are among intellectuals at least) the only ones on the table.

However, what the nineteenth-century nationalist cosmopolitans offer is a different kind of essentialism, a universalist essentialism that deserves more careful consideration than it has thus far received. To be clear, there are often repellent ethnic tinges to this nineteenth-century essentialism, but I think we leap to the wrong conclusion when we equate those tinges with the kind of full-blown ethnic essentialism concocted only at the very end of the nineteenth century, once social Darwinist race theory had really poisoned the minds of many nationalists. More often than not, the essentialism that nineteenth-century nationalist cosmopolitans emphasise is universalist in scope. This universal essence of humanity is posited as an objective *telos* for all the world's peoples to realise, rather than the starting (and ending) point of a particular nation's significance. Deep into the nineteenth century, I mean to argue here, nationalism and cosmopolitanism are presented by at least some writers as ultimately allied means to the realisation of our universal human essence. To this end, I offer sketches of four representative nationalist cosmopolitans, all roughly of the generation that dominated the middle decades of the century: the Italian nationalist Giuseppe Mazzini (1805–72), the English novelist George Eliot (1819–80), the American poet Walt Whitman (1819–92) and the French philosopher Ernest Renan (1823–92).[4]

Interpreting Mazzini's nationalist cosmopolitics has its challenges. One is Mazzini's well-known disinclination to schematise his thought, so that his ideas, as his most recent English-language biographer has written, 'must often be pieced together from hastily written articles or letters intended for readers more interested in exhortation and action than logical argument' (Smith 1994, 151). That said, for most if not all of Mazzini's many nineteenth-century admirers his significance lay as much in his deeds as his words, so that many beheld in him (or envied in him, as Malwida von Meysenberg reported of Nietzsche) the 'utter concentration upon a single idea that becomes as it were a flame in which the whole individuality is consumed' (Mazzini 1972, qtd 2).[5]

A second and more significant challenge for modern commentators has been interpreting that 'single idea'. Initially, one may be tempted to read Mazzini as a belated member of the Enlightenment philosophers and revolutionaries who also understood their nationalist programmes to be on behalf of all humanity. When Thomas Jefferson wrote to Joseph Priestly to explain the thinking behind the Declaration of Independence, for example, he claimed, 'we are acting for all mankind'. (Heater 1996, qtd 76). The revolutionary French, too, were engaged in, as Friedrich Meinecke put it in 1906, 'an undertaking beyond national interest [that] helped ignite the national idea in the hearts of men'. '[T]he France of the Revolution', Meinecke wrote, 'burst forth from the womb of the eighteenth century, from a soil imbued with universal and cosmopolitan ideas' (Meinecke 1970, 21). Standing before the Jacobin Club in April 1793, Robespierre announced the new Declaration of Rights, the first article of which was that 'Men of all countries are brothers, and the various nations must assist each other according to their resources, like citizens of the same State' (Heater 1996, qtd 77). These early revolutionary nationalists fully believed that participating in their local polis was continuous with shaping an eventual cosmopolis. And, even as late as the 1830s, these nationalists 'adopt[ed] the role of Messiah for all', in Eric Hobsbawm's words: '[t]hrough Italy (according to Mazzini), through Poland (according to Mickiewicz), the suffering peoples of the world were to be led to freedom' (Hobsbawm 1962, 164).[6]

However, if Mazzini's political activism would seem to connect him to these Enlightenment figures, his sense of his own work was quite distinct from theirs. As early as 1836, Mazzini announced that France in the late eighteenth century had indeed established the universal principles of liberty and equality but that this was not enough, for the result has been fifty years of insurrection but not true revolution. A true revolution, Mazzini wrote, must offer a new social sphere but with a definite centre, 'a center to the individualities which jostle with each other inside it; a center to all the scattered rays which diffuse and waste their light and heat. Now, Mazzini continued, the theory which bases the social structure on individual *interests*'– that is, on those individual rights that the Enlightenment nationalist cosmopolitans exclusively emphasised – 'cannot supply this center':

> To find a center for all the many interests we must rise to a region
> above them, independent of them all. To close a provisional dispen-
> sation and organize a peaceful future, we must reconnect that center
> with something, eternal as Truth, progressive as its development in

the sphere of facts. To prevent the clash of individualities we must find an *aim* common to all, and direct ourselves towards it. (Mazzini 1966, 131)

Unlike the Enlightenment nationalist cosmopolitans, who (in Mazzini's portrait) fondly imagined a world of rights-bearing individuals in simple social contract with one another, Mazzini believed that rights-bearing individuals also needed a 'common aim'.[7] That aim, reiterated throughout Mazzini's writings, is what he often called 'Humanity', and the process of achieving it 'angelification'. As Ignazio Silone explains, 'Mazzini regarded life on earth as a continuous process of growth toward spiritual perfection, a process of "angelification". ... Humanity could not help advancing step by step along a pathway toward ultimate happiness and goodness which Providence had pre-surveyed' (Mazzini 1972, 13). Mazzini put it this way in his address 'To the Italian Working-Men' (the first in his well-known 1869 collection of essays entitled *The Duties of Man*):

> When I say that knowledge of their *rights* is not enough to enable men to effect any appreciable or lasting improvement, I do not ask you to renounce these rights; I only say that they cannot exist except as a consequence of duties fulfilled. (Mazzini 1966, 16)

In Mazzini's analogy, just as Christ sought to realise God's Kingdom on earth, so too should we perform these duties in order to achieve the perfection of humanity.

> Italian Working-men, my Brothers! When Christ came and changed the face of the world, ... he did not speak of utility or of self-interest to a people whom utility and self-interest had corrupted. He spoke of Duty, He spoke of Love, of Sacrifice, of Faith. ... [W]e live in an epoch like Christ's. We live in the midst of a society rotten as that of the Roman Empire, and feel in our souls the need of reviving and transforming it, of associating all its members and its workers in one single faith, under one single law, and for one purpose; the free and progressive development of all the faculties which God has planted in His Creatures. We seek the reign of God upon earth as in heaven, or better, that the earth shall be a preparation for heaven, and society an endeavor towards a progressive approach to the Divine Idea. (Mazzini 1966, 19)

Nations, for Mazzini, were indispensably part of this progressive approach to the Divine Idea. As he explained in the chapter 'Duties to Country' in *Duties*, '[y]our first Duties ... are, as I have told you, to Humanity,' but '[t]he *individual* is too weak, and Humanity too vast', at least as long as 'no means is found of multiplying your forces and your powers of action indefinitely' (Mazzini 1966, 51–2). 'But God gave you this means', he continued, 'when he gave you a Country, when, like a wise overseer of labour, who distributes the different parts of the work according to the capacity of the workmen, he divided Humanity into distinct groups upon the face of our globe, and thus planted the seeds of nations' (Mazzini 1966, 52). Governments have subsequently corrupted this Providential design, turning nations away from the Divine Idea and towards gross material gain. Italians, subsequently, '[w]ithout Country[,] ... have neither name, token, voice, nor rights, no admission as brothers into the fellowship of the Peoples' (53). Therefore, he announced to his fellow countrymen, '[y]ou cannot obtain your *rights* except by obeying the commands of *Duty*', the first of which is to build a nation.

> Our Country is our field of labor; the products of our activity must go forth from it for the benefit of the whole earth; but the instruments of labor which we can use best and most effectively exist in it, and we may not reject them without being unfaithful to God's purpose and diminishing our own strength. In laboring according to true principles for our Country we are laboring for Humanity; our Country is the fulcrum of the lever which we have to wield for the common good. If we give up this fulcrum we run the risk of becoming useless to our Country and to Humanity. (Mazzini 1966, 54–5).

Derek Heater accurately reports that for Mazzini 'the very purpose of the nation-state is to mobilise individuals for the effective discharge of their cosmopolitan duties to humanity' (1996, 92). However, Heater misrepresents the nature of those duties (and reveals his own constructivist bias, as well) when he writes that Mazzini (and his fellow 'visionary' Comte) 'allow[ed] their imaginations free rein to conjure images of a world society synthesized by the cohesive forces of historical evolution and religious faith' (92). As Mazzini emphasises, these duties are not to synthesise but to realise an essential humanity that is already present, if dormant. Nations and religions do not so much strive to cohere with one another as when they simultaneously undertake a common universal cause: the realisation of our God-given higher nature as human beings.

The essentialism underlying George Eliot's nationalist cosmopolitanism has also confused modern commentators. In Eliot's case, however, this is less because of her ramping up the metaphysics of that essentialism (which she sometimes did, though not nearly to the extent of Mazzini) than because her essentialism, to modern ears at least, often sounds close enough to modern ethnic essentialism to make her equally undeniable cosmopolitan leanings baffling. Consider the interpretive confusion surrounding her last novel *Daniel Deronda* (1876), in which the titular hero does not marry the heroine, Gwendolyn Harleth – even after she renounces the prejudices of her class – but instead heads off to the Levant to do what he can to re-establish a Jewish homeland. For much of the twentieth century Eliot's modern readers have mostly been perplexed by the curious internationalist plot: why should a novel of manners involve such a digression?[8] Terry Eagleton was among the first to take advantage of the emerging distinction between constructed and essentialist nationalisms to open a new line of criticism of Eliot as promoting a particularist essentialism when he argued in 1978 that in *Deronda* 'the voice of liberalism has become the voice of jingoist reaction' (Eagleton 1978, 125). This easy equation of Eliot's programme with ethnic essentialism has since become the norm. Some find in that essentialism an imperialist and racist nationalism. For example, Susan Meyer writes in her 1996 *Imperialism at Home: Race and Victorian Women's Fiction* that 'the proto-Zionist impulse of *Daniel Deronda*, like the British proto-Zionist enthusiasm as a whole, reveals a continuity with imperialist ideology, a belief in white racial superiority, and a subtle distaste for the Jews' (Meyer 1996, 187).[9] Others view Eliot's essentialism as also fundamentally particularising and homogeneous, but more in line with the organic communitarianism described by Ferdinand Tönnies in his 1887 *Gemeinschaft und Gesellschaft*. For instance, Bernard Semmel (1994) contends that by early in her career 'Eliot had become convinced that the *Gesellschaft* values of individualism and cosmopolitanism that prevailed in British liberal circles would impair both family affection and social cohesion'. 'Only a nation ... based on filial sentiment, perceived national kinship, and common historical traditions,' Semmel argued, 'could provide a realistic foundation for communal solidarity' (6). By the time of *Deronda*, according to Semmel, Eliot's specific target was the 'antinational' ideology of liberal intellectuals, against which she offered 'an almost Burkean 'politics of national inheritance''' (7). Eliot's Jews in *Deronda*, in fact, are meant as 'a model to counter the cosmopolitanism of liberal Englishmen' (11).[10]

However, to read Eliot strictly as an imperialist or as a communitarian is to continue to make the modern assumption that early (i.e. pre-constructivist) nationalism always entailed an exclusive, commitment to one particular essence. Without a doubt Eliot shared in some of the racist beliefs common in her day, but at the same time she, like Mazzini, ultimately envisioned a universal humanity absorbing all of our particular differences. She explained this belief to John Sibree in a February 1848 letter, for example.

> Extermination up to a certain point seems to be the law for the inferior races – for the rest, fusion both for physical and moral ends. ... The nations have been always kept apart until they have sufficiently developed their idiosyncrasies and then some great revolutionary force has been called into action by which the genius of a particular nation becomes a portion of the common mind of humanity. (Eliot 1954–78, 1.246)

Whatever particular qualities a race may have – qualities that lead to extermination or to fusion – the progressive realisation of the 'common mind of humanity' is deemed providential. Just a month later, Eliot wrote again to Sibree to celebrate the 1848 French Revolution: 'I thought we had fallen on such evil days that we were to see no really great movement,' she admits, 'but I begin to be glad of my date. I would consent, however, to have a year clipt off my life for the sake of witnessing such a scene as that of the men of the barricade bowing to the image of Christ "who first taught fraternity to men" ' (Eliot 1954–78, 1.253). Our particularities are temporary, but our universality – as the equally non-Christian Mazzini also used the figure of Christ to argue – will be final. In a February 1853 letter, immediately after expressing her interest in the Slavery question, 'and in America generally – that cradle of the future,' Eliot imagined a Mazzinian 'Humanity' to be the *telos* of the contemporary struggles.

> Is it not cheering to think of the youthfulness of this little planet, and the immensely greater youthfulness of our race upon it? – to think that the higher moral tendencies of human nature are yet only in their germ? I feel this more thoroughly when I think of that great Western Continent, with its infant cities, its huge uncleared forests, and its unamalgamated races. (Eliot 1954–78, 2.85)

A few decades later, in *Deronda*, Eliot remained committed to gradual race amalgamation and the realisation of a universal human essence. Her search for this final community, Patrick Brantlinger has written of

Deronda, 'leads to [a] nationalism ... that clashes with merely provincial, merely English narrowness' (1992, 270–1). Rather, she offers 'an *international* nationalism,' one, Brantlinger observes, 'that Eliot expresses in terms of *racial* unity or community, even though no race can be pure in the physical sense, so that the only possible unity is spiritual – that is, cultural' (272). Brantlinger's many qualifications are appropriate, for in *Deronda* Eliot's nationalist cosmopolitics is ambiguous (more so than Mazzini's certainly) about the final nature of the human universal: is it racial, spiritual, cultural? Consider some of the pronouncements made by Mordecai, the ailing Jewish mystic who helps Daniel Deronda (an orphan raised by English aristocrats) come to terms with his Jewish heritage. Familiar with the more radically cosmopolitan arguments that history has moved beyond nations, Daniel is nevertheless drawn to Mordecai's arguments for a Jewish nation. One of these is that a Jewish state will serve both to represent Jewish interests in the world as well as Western cosmopolitan interests in the East:

> Then our race shall have an organic centre, a heart and brain to watch and guide and execute; the outraged Jew shall have a defence in the court of nations, as the outraged Englishman or American. And the world will gain as Israel gains. For there will be a community in the van of the East which carries its culture and the sympathies of every great nation in its bosom. (Eliot 1987, 595)[11]

A second argument is that people need nations in order to develop fully as citizens, and that the world as a whole clearly benefits from these new nations and citizens:

> The degraded and scorned of our race will learn to think of their sacred land ... as a republic where the Jewish spirit manifests itself in a new order founded on the old, purified, enriched by the experience our greatest sons have gathered from the life of the ages. How long is it? –only two centuries since a vessel carried over the ocean the beginning of the great North American nation. The people grew like meeting waters – they were various in habit and sect – there came a time, a century ago, when they needed a polity, and there were heroes of peace among them. (Eliot 1987, 597)

Note that in both arguments Mordecai emphasises the kind of 'rights talk' that Mazzini associated with the Enlightenment, but that there is also always some suggestion that the world as a whole will gain as well.

Later in the book Mordecai emphasises this latter point, even soaring to Mazzinian heights when explaining to his sister Mirah the significance of the *Shemah* (the call in Deuteronomy to Israel that 'The Lord is Our God, the Lord is One'):

> Seest thou Mirah ... the *Shemah*, wherein we briefly confess the divine Unity, is the chief devotional exercise of the Hebrew; and this made our religion the fundamental religion for the whole world; the divine Unity embraced as its consequence the ultimate unity of mankind. See, then – the nation which has been scoffed at for its sep-arateness, has given a binding theory to the whole human race. Now, in complete unity a part possesses the whole as the whole possesses every part: and in this way human life is tending toward the image of the Supreme Unity. ... (Eliot 1987, 802)

In short, Mordecai's (and eventually Daniel's) language hovers between the older nationalist cosmopolitics of the Enlightenment (as depicted by Mazzini) and that of Mazzini: that is, between understanding nations as the means to achieving rights for individuals universally and under-standing nations as the means to achieving (in Mazzini's words) 'a centre', 'a common aim'.

It is in 'The Modern Hep! Hep! Hep!', the final essay of *Impressions of Theophrastus Such* (1879), that Eliot makes clear her commitment to the Mazzinian vision. Here again Eliot, through the speaker Theophrastus, makes the case for a Jewish state. She argues – much like Renan does a few years later – that the 'nobleness of a people' (Eliot 1994, 146) depends upon their allegiance to their memories of past greatness, her examples being the ancient Greek and Roman republics as well as the modern Greek and Italian republics (143–6). She adds also – like Mazzini – that 'an individual man, to be harmoniously great, must belong to a nation of this order'. And she is clear in her conviction that 'a common humanity is not yet enough to feed the rich blood of various activity which makes a complete man. The time has not come for cosmopoli-tanism to be highly virtuous,' she writes, 'any more than for communism to suffice for social energy' (147). Rather, '[w]hat is wanting is that we should recognise a corresponding attachment to nationality as legitimate in every other people, and understand that its absence is a privation of the greatest good' (147). The English should support the Jews in gaining what the English already have: 'the consciousness of having a native country ... the dignity of being included in a people which has a part in the comity of nations and the growing federation of the world; that sense of special belonging which is the root of human virtues, both public and private' (156). In her closing paragraphs, Eliot as Theophrastus recognises that 'the tendency of things is toward the quicker or slower fusion of races' and that '[i]t is impossible to arrest this tendency'. Rather, 'all we can do is to moderate its course,' thus giving nations time to cultivate the virtues and genius of each different people before their inevitable fusion together. '[I]t is in this sense that the modern insistence on the idea of Nationalities has value' (160), Eliot explains. This nationalism or 'spirit of separateness has not yet done its work in the education of mankind, which has created the varying genius of nations' (160).[12]

Not unlike Mazzini, Walt Whitman sought also to reconcile the individual rights associated with the Enlightenment, particularly in the Enlightenment's American instantiations as the Declaration of Independence and the Revolution, with the pursuit of some greater oneness. In the modern commentary on Whitman, however, that oneness is generally equated with the same kind of particularism that critics have also mistakenly read into Eliot's essentialism. For example, one of the most profound essays on Whitman, Allen Grossman's 1985 'The Poetics of Union in Whitman and Lincoln', presents both men as seeking (similar to much of the antebellum political and intellectual leadership of the United States) to 'reconcile the equality requirement of the Declaration of Independence with the continuity requirements of the Constitution' (183). With the southern states insisting that the Constitution justified not only preserving slavery within their own borders but also exporting it to the new western territories clamouring to join the Union, the reconciliation of American commitments to both the Declaration's individual liberties and the Constitution's federal union was no easy task. Grossman subsequently concludes that '[t]he contradiction between equality and perpetuation ... was more powerful' than what Lincoln and Whitman could offer' (202).

However, Grossman's readiness to equate Whitman's own vision of totality with Lincoln's desire to perpetuate a single nation is, again, to imagine the ambitions of nineteenth-century nationalist cosmopolitanism to be more relentlessly particularist than they actually were. Consider a few examples of how Whitman renders this challenge of reconciling liberties with unity. In the 1876 Preface to *Leaves of Grass*, Whitman does indeed seem committed to a strictly nationalist agenda.

> [T]he vital political mission of The United States is to practically solve and settle the problem of two sets of rights – the fusion, thorough compatibility and junction of individual State prerogatives, with the

> indispensable necessity of centrality and Oneness – the National Identity power – the sovereign Union, relentless, permanently comprising all, and over all, and in that never yielding an inch. ... (Whitman 2002, 655)

Whitman's programme of unity here could be read as strictly national-ist, particularly when one compares his language with the more abstract (and seemingly universal) language of Mazzini (as cited above): '[t]o find a center for all the many interests [by] ris[ing] to a region above them, independent of them all' (Mazzini 1966, 131).

A second example, however, reveals the nature of Whitman's unity to be more ambiguous. In his revisions of what began in the 1856 *Leaves of Grass* as 'Liberty Poem for Asia, Africa, Europe, America, Australia, Cuba, and The Archipelagoes of the Sea' and by 1881 became 'To a Foil'd European Revolutionaire', Whitman clearly grapples with the problem of an exclusive Enlightenment focus on liberties. But it remains dramat-ically unclear to him what is necessary to solve this problem. In the 1856 version, the poem insists dogmatically that 'Liberty is to be sub-served, whatever occurs' – that is until 'all life and all the souls of men and women are discharged from any part of the earth,' for '[t]hen shall the instinct of liberty be discharged from that part of the earth / Then shall the infidel and the tyrant come into possession' (Whitman Electronic Text Center). The 1881 edition, in contrast, begins with the same hearty line about liberty being 'subserv'd whatever occurs' but ends with not only a more robust assertion that liberty will somehow outlive both tyranny and death but also the indication that liberty alone does not clarify *what* 'you are for' or 'I am for myself, nor what any thing is for,' and that this *common aim* (to recall Mazzini's terminology) needs to be determined.

> Then courage European revolter, revoltress!
> For till all cease neither must you cease.
> I do not know what you are for, (I do not know what I am for
>   myself, nor what any thing is for,)
> But I will search carefully for it even in being foil'd,
> In defeat, poverty, misconception, imprisonment – for they too
>   are great.
> Did we think victory great?
> So it is – but now it seems to me, when it cannot be help'd, that
>   defeat is great,
> And that death and dismay are great.
>
> (Whitman 2002, 312)

A third example suggests, finally, that there are at least some occasions when Whitman is more confident that what we are all 'for' is indeed a common unity, and that this 'Oneness' that he pursues is not national but cosmopolitan, though achieved by way of nations. *Democratic Vistas*, an 1867 essay in response to Carlyle's (1867) 'Shooting Niagara; and After?' that evolved into an 1871 book, begins by recalling the principles to which the nineteenth-century nationalist cosmopolitan is committed:

> Sole among nationalities, these [United] States have assumed the task to put in forms of lasting power and practicality, on areas of amplitude rivaling the operations of the physical kosmos, the moral political speculations of ages, long, long deferr'd, the democratic republican principle, and the theory of development and perfection by voluntary standards, and self-reliance. (Whitman 1982, 929)

For Whitman, the challenge is to sustain the liberties of a democratic republic while also encouraging human development and perfection. That the social contract alone cannot meet this challenge is clear enough. But what does Whitman mean by this 'theory of development and perfection'?

> For after the rest is said ... – after the valuable and well-settled statement of our duties and relations in society is thoroughly conn'd over and exhausted – it remains to bring forward and modify everything else with the idea of that Something a man is, ... standing apart from all else, divine in his own right, and a woman in hers, sole and untouchable by any canons of authority, or any rule derived from precedent, state-safety, the acts of legislatures, or even from what is called religion, modesty, or art. (1982, 941)

There is a temptation, to which Richard Rorty has yielded among others, to interpret Whitman in such moments as offering the kind of constructivist civic nationalist that is so highly esteemed today: a civic religion that looks (in Rorty's version of Whitman) to 'the contingent future' (1998a, 19) rather than the past, and that 'redefines God as our future selves' (22). Mazzini's unifying essentialism may depend upon metaphysics or even theology for its significance, but Whitman's 'essence' seems to Rorty much more a creation of the human imagination than an appeal to otherworldly authority. Above, after all, Whitman explicitly rejects 'any canons of authority'.

However, while it is possible to read portions of Whitman that way, ultimately there are just too many Mazzinian indicators in Whitman's

writing about our 'Oneness' to support Rorty's constructivist interpretation. When, a few paragraphs after those cited by Rorty, Whitman heralds
a 'perfect individualism ... that deepest tinges and gives character to the
idea of the aggregate' (Whitman 1982, 942), the poet seems to associate
that individual perfection with metaphysical truth.

> I say the mission of government, henceforth, in civilized lands, is not
> repression alone, and not authority alone, not even of law, nor by
> that favorite standard of the eminent writer [Carlyle], the rule of the
> best men, the born heroes and captains of the race – but higher than
> the highest arbitrary rule, to train communities through all their
> grades, beginning with individuals and ending there again, to rule
> themselves. What Christ appear'd for in the moral–spiritual field for
> human-kind, namely, that in respect to the absolute soul, there is in
> the possession of such by each single individual, something so tran-
> scendent, so incapable of gradations, (like life,) that, to that extent, it
> places all beings on a common level ... – is tallied in like manner, in
> this other field, by democracy's rule that men, the nation, as a com-
> mon aggregate of living identities, affording in each a separate and
> complete subject for freedom, worldly thrift and happiness, and for a
> fair chance for growth. ... (1982, 947)

Once again, like Mazzini and Eliot before him, the non-Christian
Whitman appeals here to Christ specifically in order to clarify (for a pre-
sumably more orthodox readership) the universal redemptive role of the
nation-state in the tutelage of individuals in the pursuit of perfection, a
'merg[ing] into "the divine, vast, general law," ' a merging that is finally
a cosmopolitan programme. There is something 'topping democracy,'
Whitman writes, something that 'alone can bind' democracies 'and ever
seeks to bind, all nations, all men, of however various and distant lands,
into a brotherhood a family'. That something is love:

> It is the old, yet ever-modern dream of earth, out of her eldest and her
> youngest, her fond philosophers and poets. Not that half only, indi-
> vidualism, which isolates. There is another half, which is adhesive-
> ness or love, that fuses, ties and aggregates, making the races
> comrades, and fraternizing all. Both are to be vitalized by religion,
> (sole worthiest elevator of man or State,) breathing into the proud,
> material tissues, the breath of life. For I say at the core of democracy,
> finally, is the religious element. All the religions, old and new, are
> there. Nor may the scheme step forth, clothed in resplendent beauty

and command, till these, bearing the best, the latest fruit, the spiritual, shall fully appear. (1982, 948–9).

For Whitman, this religious pursuit of union between individual and aggregate (i.e the fraternising of the races) often involved a central role for an idealised United States. Lately many critics have tallied the nationalist and racist moments that inevitably crop up in Whitman's descriptions of the United States in this role.[13] One could indeed point to a few such moments in Whitman's most international poem, 'Salut Au Monde!' (composed in 1856, revised through 1881): the condescending attention to Africans in the Section 11 catalogue of peoples (Whitman 2002, 124–5), the special Section 12 dedicated entirely to reassuring the same that 'I do not prefer others so very much before you either, / I do not say one word against you away back there where you stand, / (You will come forward in due time to my side)' (125). These moments of condescension are isolated, however, and the poem moves relentlessly towards an assertion of human equality and unity. This is from the final section, Section 13:

My spirit has pass'd in compassion and determination around
   the whole earth,
I have look'd for equals and lovers and found them ready for me
   in all lands,
I think some divine rapport has equalized me with them
                                            (Whitman 2002, 125–6)

And, for Whitman, the United State's global role was ideally cosmopolitan, not imperial, as he explained in an 1846 about the Mexican War:

We pant to see our country and its rule far-reaching, only inasmuch as it will take of the shackles that prevent men the even chance of being happy and good – as most governments are now so constituted that the tendency is very much the other way. ... [B]ut the mere physical grandeur of this Republic ... is only desirable as an aid to reach the truer good, the good of the whole body of the people. (1920, 1.244)

Late in life, Whitman would report to his friend Horace Traubel that '[t]he chief reason for the being of the United States of America is to bring about the common goodwill of all mankind, the solidarity of the world' (Allen 1957, qtd 444). Nations, for Whitman as for Eliot and Mazzini, are only an aid to reach 'the truer good'.[14]

It is appropriate to conclude this appreciation of nineteenth-century nationalist cosmopolitics with Ernest Renan's lecture, 'What is a Nation?', delivered at the Sorbonne in 1882. For, by this time it was clear to some at least that nationalism was being preconceived in such a way that it would become the major obstacle, rather than the major avenue, to realisation of one world. '[R]ace is confused with nation' now, Renan announced at the beginning of his lecture, 'and a sovereignty analogous to that of really existing peoples is attributed to ethnographic, or, rather, linguistic groups' (Renan 1996, 42). Ironically, when he is remembered at all, Renan is usually remembered for his interest in ethnography, but Renan is quite clear in his remarks that, while 'I am very fond of ethnography, for it is a science of rare interest[,] ... in so far as I would wish it to be free, I wish it to be without political application' (49). Ethnography changes over time, Renan explains, so to describe states' frontiers by reference to ethnicity would be foolishly to make nations 'follow the fluctuations of [this] science [of ethnography]' (49). Renan goes on to show that language, religion, even geography 'cannot supply an adequate basis for the constitution of a modern nationality either' (50). Rather, '[m]an is everything in the formation of this sacred thing which is called a people,' primarily by cultivating collective memory and political consent. Renan then offers the kind of constructivist vision of the nation that we know so well today:

> A nation is therefore a large-scale solidarity, constituted by the feeling of the sacrifices that one has made in the past and of those that one is prepared to make in the future. It presupposes a past; it is summarized, however, in the present by a tangible fact, namely, consent, the clearly expressed desire to continue a common life. A nation's existence is ... a daily plebiscite, just as an individual's existence is a perpetual affirmation of life. That, I know full well, is less metaphysical than divine right and less brutal than so-called historical right. (53)

'We have driven metaphysical and teleological abstractions out of politics', Renan confidently asserts, and with that claim many contemporary commentators, partial to constructivist nationalism, might rest satisfied. Renan's plea to 'let the reign of the transcendants pass' and to consider settling questions of boundaries instead by consulting not ethnography or religion but the people living there (53–4) is where contemporary nationalist cosmopolitics also concludes.[15]

Yet, at the same time, Renan also seems to gesture backwards to the kind of progressive universalism upheld by the other nineteenth-century nationalist cosmopolitans. 'The nations are not something eternal,' Renan states, '[t]hey had their beginnings and they will end'. Like Eliot and Mazzini, Renan emphasises that '[a]t the present time, the existence of nations is a good thing, a necessity even. Their existence is the guarantee of liberty, which would be lost, if the world had only one law and only one master', But, again, like Eliot and Mazzini, Renan takes the next step:

> Through their various and often opposed powers, nations participate in the common work of civilization, each sounds a note in the great concert of humanity, which, after all, is the highest ideal reality that we are capable of attaining. (53)

That highest ideal reality was universal human perfection, the pursuit of which Renan, like the other nationalist cosmopolitans, held to be the very purpose of human existence (see Rose 1967).

Of course, not all nineteenth-century nationalists were also cosmopolitans. In an unfinished manuscript, Alexis de Tocqueville wrote that 'I am convinced that the interests of the human race are better served by giving every man a particular fatherland than by trying to inflame his passions for the whole of humanity.' Unlike Mazzini or Eliot or Whitman, Tocqueville did not believe those local affiliations might be tutored into global ones. Still, Tocqueville believed – like the nineteenth-century nationalist cosmopolitans – that this local work would nevertheless benefit all humanity.

> Man has been created by God (I do not know why) in such a way that the larger the object of his love the less directly attached he is to it. … There are but few who will burn with ardent love for the entire species. For the most part, the sole means by which Providence (man taken as he is) lets each of us work for the general good of humanity is to divide this great object into many smaller parts making each of these fragments a worthy object of love to those who compose it. (Clinton 2003, qtd 22–3)

Unlike so many contemporary commentators, who – when pressed – reveal themselves to believe that national and cosmopolitan allegiances differ fundamentally, Tocqueville, just as the other nineteenth-century universalists reviewed here, had little difficulty understanding nations as, at least potentially, 'smaller parts' of that 'general good of humanity'. That kind of humanist essentialism, although it may have its own problems, deserves to be reconsidered in its own right, as something quite different from the particularist essentialism that haunts the contemporary theoretical imagination. In this regard, the nineteenth-century nationalist cosmopolitans have something distinctive and important to offer us.

Notes

1. With the self at the centre, Nussbaum explains in her introduction, the series of concentric circles then surround family, neighbours, city, countrymen, world and '[o]ur task as citizens of the world will be to "draw the circles somehow toward the center" (Stoic philosopher Hierocles, 1st-2nd CE)' (Nussbaum 2002, 9). Beyond this, however, there is little agreement among the contributors. Sissela Bok suggests we are morally obligated to embrace all of the circles of humanity as quickly as possible, for, if the metaphor has sometimes been used 'to urge us to stretch our concern outward, ... more often it has been invoked to convey a contrasting view: that of "my station and its duties", according to which our allegiances depend on our situation and role in life and cannot be overridden by obligations to humanity at large' (Bok 2002, 39). The circles tell a cautionary tale for Michael Walzer, too, though the opposite one: the problem is not those who begin and possibly end with local duties or affiliations, but those who begin with supposed universal duties, and ignore real local ones. 'My allegiances ... start at the center', Walzer explains, 'by understanding what it means to have fellow citizens and neighbors; without that understanding we are morally lost' (Walzer 2002, 126).
2. Notably for Berlin, cosmopolitans, like nationalists, had their own fanatical myths, theirs was one of a rational utopia (1990, 213). More typically partisan was Karl Popper, who raged in *The Open Society and Its Enemies* (1971) that nationalism 'appeals to our tribal instincts, to passions and to prejudice, and to our nostalgic desire to be relieved from the strain of individual responsibility which it attempts to replace by a collective or group responsibility' (49).
3. Modern nationalist theory's struggle with (and triumph over) essentialism is an oft-told tale: see Eley and Suny (1996, 1–10), Ross Poole (1999, 1–8), Benjamin Barber (1995 158–68), and Michael Ignatieff (1993, 3–16). Incidentally, I have used Nussbaum as my representative contemporary cosmopolitan, but she is notably more generous to nationalists than most cosmopolitan theorists today: see Neilson (1999) and Karam (2001) on most cosmopolitan theorists' paranoia about nationalism.
4. Again, there were many kinds of nationalists in the nineteenth century, but I am contending that there was not the kind of ethnic nationalist that has served as the bogeyman for modern cosmopolitans and civic nationalists. More precisely, the very influential Volkisch nationalism developed by the German Romantics in the late eighteenth century has nothing to do with the ethnic nationalism one finds in the decades following the rise of social Darwinism and other race 'science', from about 1880 forward. On distinguishing between Herder and Hitler, see Ignatieff (1993, 85–6).

5. For a review of Mazzini's influence in nineteenth-century Britain in this regard, see Laura E. Nym Mayhall's summary of the relevant historiography (Mayhall 2001, 483–4).
6. Heater provides a number of similar examples of Enlightenment nationalist cosmopolitans (1996, 70–7). Like so many modern cosmopolitans, Hobsbawm in 1962 did not believe Mazzini and Mickiewicz were cosmopolitans at all; nationalism had hopelessly tainted their projects, and they were better understood in relation to 'Russian Slavophils … and the Germans who were subsequently to tell the world at some length that it would be healed by the German spirit'. The revolutionary French, in contrast, were right to regard Paris 'as the headquarters of all revolutions, and the necessary prime mover in the liberation of the world. To look to Paris was rational; to look to a vague 'Italy', 'Poland', or 'Germany' (represented in practice by a handful of conspirators and émigrés) made sense only for Italians, Poles, and Germans' (164). While never warming to Mazzini, thirty years later Hobsbawm did clarify that Mazzini's nationalism, unlike the kind that emerged in the period between 1880 and 1914, was not based upon race or ethnicity and was politically progressive (Hobsbawm 1992, 102).
7. Whether Mazzini was correct in characterising the Enlightenment nationalist cosmopolitans as indeed lacking an essentialist programme, I leave unanswered here. My suspicion is that many *did* have such an essentialist programme, and that there was more significant continuity between Enlightenment and nineteenth-century nationalist cosmopolitics than Mazzini allows. Because it helps to clarify my argument at several points, however, I will continue to work with Mazzini's version of Enlightenment nationalist cosmopolitics.
8. See Susan Meyer's summary of the major modern Eliot critics in her first chapter.
9. Other critics who fault Eliot for her commitment to British nationalism (and subsequent anti-semitism) include Heller (1983), Ragussis (1989) and Linehan (1992). Critics who fault Eliot for her commitment to Jewish nationalism include Said (1979). Meyer faults Eliot for both.
10. Graver (1984) and Wohlfarth (1998) offer similar readings of Eliot's nationalism. Wohlfarth, for example, reads Deronda's nationalism as intended as an admonishment to the British, who should be 'keeping alive the flame of national identity in the face of cosmopolitan dissemination' (1998, 205).
11. The reference to a 'court of nations' suggests that Eliot had in mind events such as the 'Don Pacifico Incident' of 1850, during which the Foreign Secretary, Lord Palmerston, sent the British navy to the aid of Pacifico, whose home in Athens had been ransacked and who claimed British citizenship by virtue of his birth in Gibraltar. Defending his actions to outraged French and Russian governments, Palmerston declared that 'a British subject, in whatever land he may be, shall feel confident that the watchful eye and the strong arm of England will protect him against injustice and wrong' (Thomson 1950, 155).
12. Interestingly, Eliot's speaker likens this argument to that made in *On Liberty* (1859) by John Stuart Mill, a nationalist cosmopolitan who, if space permitted, I would include among the four sketched here. 'A modern book on Liberty has maintained that from the freedom of individual men to persist in

idiosyncrasies the world may be enriched. Why should we not apply this argument to the idiosyncrasy of a nation, and pause in our haste to hoot it down?' (165).

13. Earlier in the twentieth century, modern critics tended to recognise both Whitman's cosmopolitan and national moments but could not resolve the paradox: see Arvin (1938, 283–9) and Asselineau (1983). More recently, modern critics have responded to Whitman's nationalism primarily, and much like Eliot's more recent critics, too. In 'The Body Politic in Democratic Vistas' (Harold Aspiz wrote in 1994) Whitman 'proposes a program of national eugenics to produce an inexhaustible supply of splendid individuals who would constitute the American body politic' (Aspiz 1994, 105), or (as Betsy Erkkila put it the same year) yokes his 'embarrassingly hawkish nationalism' to his 'prophetic poet[ry]' (Erkkila 1994, 60), or (as David Reynolds wrote in 1996) 'embrac[es] evolution, religion, capitalism, and occasional racism' in placing the future of the country in the hands of bards who 'sound almost like dictators' (Reynolds 1996, 483). Again, I am not contesting Whitman's occasional racism, only the critical tradition that has reduced Whitman's nationalism to racism.

14. Whitman's confidence in the United States specifically as an agent of cosmopolitanism wavered in his later years. The United States, he wrote in 1847, 'will regard human life, property, rights [and will] never be guilty of furnishing duplicates to the Chinese war, the operations of the British in India, or the extinguishment of Poland' (1920, 1.33). But in 1888, he shared his concern with Traubel that while '[i]t is true that there are a lot of us ... in whom there is developed a new cameraderie, fellowship, love; the farther truer idea of the race family, of international unity, of making one country of all countries: ... the trouble is that we do not hold the whip hand' (Traubel 1961–92, 3.43). 'While I love America, and wish to see America prosperous', he remarked to Traubel at another time, 'I do not seem able to bring myself to love America, to desire American prosperity, at the expense of some other nations or even of all other nations' (Traubel 1961–92, 1.6).

15. There are a few contemporary appreciations of Renan, and they emphasise his constructivist sympathies: for example, Weber (1992), Gossman (1982) and Pecora (2001).

References

Allen, G. W. (1957) *Walt Whitman Handbook*, New York: Hendricks House.

Arvin, N. (1938) *Whitman*, New York: MacMillan.

Aspiz, H. (1994) 'The Body Politic in Democratic Vistas', in E. Folsom (ed.), *Walt Whitman: The Centennial Essays*, Ames, IA: University Iowa Press.

Asselineau, R. (1983) 'Nationalism versus Internationalism in *Leaves of Grass*', in G. K. Hall (ed.), *Critical Essays on Walt Whitman*, Boston, MA: J. Woodress.

Bachem, R. (1967) 'Arnold's and Renan's Views on Perfection', *Revue de Litterature Comparee*, Vol. 41, 228–37.

Barber, B. (2002) 'Constitutional Faith', in M. Nussbaum (ed.), *For Love of Country?*, Boston, MA: Beacon Press, pp. 30–7.

Barber, B. (1995) *Jihan vs. McWorld: How Globalism and Tribalism Are Reshaping the World*, New York: Ballantine Books.

Berlin, I. (1990) *The Crooked Timber of Humanity: Chapters in the History of Ideas*, Princeton, NJ: Princeton University Press.

Bok, S. (2002) 'From Part to Whole', in M. Nussbaum (ed.), *For Love of Country?*, Boston, MA: Beacon Press, pp. 38–44.

Brantlinger, P. (1992) 'Nations and Novels: Disraeli, Eliot, and Orientalism', *Victorian Studies*, Vol. 35, No. 3 (Spring), 255–75.

Carlyle, T. (1867) 'Shooting Niagara: And After?', London: Chapman & Hall.

Cheah, P. (1988) 'Introduction Part II: The Cosmopolitical – Today', in P. Cheah and B. Robbins (eds), *Cosmopolitics: Thinking and Feeling Beyond the Nation*, Minneapolis, MN: University of Minnesota Press, pp. 20–43

Clinton, D. (2003) *Tocqueville, Lieber, and Bagehot: Liberalism Confronts the World*, New York: Palgrave Macmillan.

Eagleton, T. (1978) *Criticism and Ideology*, London: Verso.

Eley, G. and Suny, R. G. (1996), 'Introduction: From the Moment of Social History to the Work of Cultural Representation', in G. Eley and R. G. Suny (eds), *Becoming National: A Reader*, New York: Oxford University Press.

Eliot, G. (1994) *The Impressions of Theophrastus Such* ed. Nancy Henry, Iowa City: University of Iowa Press.

Eliot, G. (1987) *Daniel Deronda* ed. Barbara Hardy, New York: Penguin Books.

Eliot, G. (1954–78) *The George Eliot Letters*, 9 Vols ed. Gordon S. Haight, New Haven, CT: Yale University Press.

Erkkila, B. (1994) 'Whitman and American Empire', in G. M. Sill (ed.), *Walt Whitman of Mickle Street: A Centennial Collection*. Knoxville: University of Tennessee Press.

Gossman, L. (1982) 'Review of *Renan: Historien Philosophe* by H.W. Wardman', *History and Theory*, Vol. 21, No. 1, 106–24.

Graver, S. (1984) *George Eliot and Community: A Study in Social Theory and Fictional Form*, Berkeley, CA: University California Press.

Grossman, A. (1985) 'The Poetics of Union in Whitman and Lincoln: An Inquiry toward the Relationship of Art and Policy', in W. B. Michaels and D. E. Pease (eds), *The American Renaissance Reconsidered*, Baltimore, MD: Johns Hopkins University Press.

Heller, D. (1983) 'George Eliot's Jewish Feminist', *Atlantis*, Vol. 8, 37–43.

Heater, D. (1996) *World Citizenship and Government: Cosmopolitan Ideas in the History of Western Political Thought*, New York: St. Martin's Press.

Hobsbawm, E. J. (1992) *Nations and Nationalism since 1780: Program, Myth, Reality*, Cambridge: Cambridge University Press.

Hobsbawm, E. J. (1962) *The Age of Revolution: 1789–1848*, New York: Mentor Books.

Ignatieff, M. (1993) *Blood and Belonging: Journeys into the New Nationalism*, New York: Farrar, Straus, and Giroux,

Karam, J. T. (2001) 'Review Essay: Looking Within and Beyond the Nation', *Passages: An Interdisciplinary Journal of Global Studies*, Vol. 3, No. 2, 252–64.

Linehan, K. B. (1992) 'Mixed Politics: The Critique of Imperialism in Daniel Deronda', *Texas Studies in Language and Literature*, Vol. 34, 323–46.

Mayhall, L. E. N. (2001) 'The Rhetorics of Slavery and Citizenship: Suffragist Discourse and Canonical Texts in Britain, 1880–1914', *Gender and History*, Vol. 13, No.3 (November), 481–97.

Mazzini, G. (1972) *The Living Thoughts of Mazzini*, Westport, CT: Greenwood Press.

Mazzini, J. [sic] (1966) *The Duties of Man and Other Essays*, London: Everyman's Library.

McConnell, M. W. (2002) 'Don't Neglect the Little Platoons', in M. Nussbaum, (ed.), *For Love of Country?*, Boston, MA: Beacon Press, pp. 78–84.

Meinecke, F. (1970) *Cosmopolitanism and the National State* trans. R. Kimber, Princeton: Princeton University Press.

Meyer, S. (1996) *Imperialism at Home: Race and Victorian Women's Fiction*, Ithaca: Cornell University Press.

Neilson, B. (1999) 'Review Article: On the New Cosmopolitanism', *Communal/Plural: Journal of Transnational and Crosscultural Studies*, Vol. 7, No.1 (April), 111–25.

Nussbaum, M. (2002) 'Introduction: Cosmopolitan Emotions?'; 'Patriotism and Cosmopolitanism', in M. Nussbaum (ed.), *For Love of Country?*, Boston, MA: Beacon Press, pp. ix–xiv; 2–17.

Özkirimli, U. (2000) *Theories of Nationalism: A Critical Introduction*, New York: St. Martin's Press.

Pecora, V. P. (2001) 'Introduction', in V. P. Pecora (ed.), *Nations and Identities: Classic Readings*, Oxford: Blackwell Publishing, pp. 1–42.

Poole, R. (1999) *Nation and Identity*, New York: Routledge.

Popper, K. R. (1971) *The Open Society and Its Enemies. Vol. II The High Tide of Prophecy: Hegel, Marx, and the Aftermath*, Princeton, NJ: Princeton University Press.

Ragussis, M. (1989) 'Representation, Conversion, and Literary Form: Harrington and the Novel of Jewish Identity', *Critical Inquiry*, Vol. 16, 113–43.

Renan, E. (1996) 'What Is a Nation?', in G. Eley and R. G. Suny (eds), *Becoming National: A Reader*, Oxford: Oxford University Press.

Reynolds, D. S. (1996) *Walt Whitman's America*, New York: Vintage Books.

Rorty, R. (1998a) *Achieving Our Country: Leftist Thought in Twentieth-Century America*, Cambridge, MA: Harvard University Press.

Rorty, R. (1998b) 'Justice as a Larger Loyalty', in P. Cheah and B. Robbins (eds), *Cosmopolitics: Thinking and Feeling Beyond the Nation*, Minneapolis, MN: University of Minnesota Press, 45–58.

Saïd, E. (1979) 'Zionism from the Standpoint of Its Victims', *Social Text*, Vol. 1 (Winter), 7–58.

Semmel, B. (1994) *George Eliot and the Politics of National Inheritance*, New York: Oxford University Press.

Singer, P. (2002) *One World: The Ethics of Globalization*, New Haven, CT: Yale University Press.

Smith, D. M. (1994) *Mazzini*, New Haven, CT: Yale University Press.

Thomson, D. (1950) *England in the Nineteenth Century (1815–1914)*, Baltimore, MD: Penguin Books.

Tönnies, F. (1887) *Gemeinschaft und Gesellschaft: Abhandlung des Communismus und des Socialismus als empirische Culturformen*, Leipzig: Fues.

Traubel, H. (1961–92) *With Walt Whitman in Camden*, 7 Vols, New York and Carbondale, IL: Rowman & Littlefield and Southern Illinois University Press.

Walzer, M. (2002) 'Spheres of Affection', in M. Nussbaum (ed.), *For Love of Country?*, Boston, MA: Beacon Press, pp. 125–7.

Weber, E. (1992) 'Being Ernest: Reflections on the Timeliness of Some Outdated Ideas', *American Scholar*, Vol. 61, No. 4 (Fall), 575–83.

Whitman W. (2002) *Leaves of Grass and other Writings* ed. Michael Moon, New York: Norton Critical Editions.

Whitman, W. (1982) *Democratic Vistas in Poetry and Prose* ed. J. Kaplan, New York: Library of America.

Whitman, W. (1920) *The Gathering of Forces. For Love of Country?*, 2 Vols, ed. C. Rodgers and J. Black, New York: Putnam's Sons.

Whitman, W. (1856) 'Liberty Poem for Asia, Africa, Europe, America, Australia, Cuba, and The Archipelogoes of the Sea', *Leaves of Grass*, Electronic Text Center, University of Virginia Library. Available: http://etext.lib.virginia.edu/

Wohlfarth, M. E. (1998) 'Daniel Deronda and the Politics of Nationalism', *Nineteenth-Century Literature*, Vol. 53, No. 2 (September), 188–210.

8
Human Rights and Public Accountability in H. G. Wells' Functional World State

John S. Partington

> If democracy means economic justice and the attainment of that universal sufficiency that science assures us is possible today; if democracy means the intensest possible fullness of knowledge for everyone who desires to know and the greatest possible freedom of criticism and individual self-expression for anyone who desires to object; if democracy means a community saturated with the conception of a common social objective and with an educated will like the will of a team of football players to co-operate willingly and understandingly upon that objective; if democracy means a complete and unified police control throughout the world, to repress the financial scramble and gangster violence which constitute the closing phase of the sovereign state and private ownership system; then we have in democracy a conception of life for which every intelligent man and woman on earth may well be prepared to live, fight or die, as circumstances may require. (Wells 1939a, 70–1)

> The more socialisation proceeds and the more directive authority is concentrated, the more necessary is an efficient protection of individuals from the impatience of well-meaning or narrow-minded or ruthless officials and indeed from all the possible abuses of advantage that are inevitable under such circumstances to our still childishly wicked breed. (Wells 1940b, 137)

As has long been acknowledged, H. G. Wells was one of the twentieth century's most insistent advocates of a world state. From the publication of *Anticipations* in 1901 to his death in 1946, Wells evolved a political vision which rejected nationalism and free-market capitalism, and advanced global political institutions and (non-Communist) central planning as alternatives. In this chapter, I do not attempt to recapitulate Wells' world-state thinking in its entirety,[1] but I discuss an aspect of it that came late in Wells' thinking, and which has been relatively neglected by scholars of Wells' cosmopolitanism: the role of human-rights protection and government accountability.[2]

With the outbreak of the Second World War, Wells saw an opportunity to embark in a practical way upon his project for world unity. This possibility he called the 'Rights of Man' campaign and it was first raised during the discussion of Allied war aims in the first few months of the conflict. According to Wells, the immediate need for an Allied declaration of war aims arose out of memories of the Great War and the debacle of the post-war treaties. He made this clear as early as 30 September 1939 in a letter to *The Times* in which he identified 'the need for lucid world explanations that will save us from another repetition of the "settlement" of 1918–1920' (Wells 1939b, 238). He believed that the Great War had been prolonged by the fact that the enemy peoples were unsure of their fate in the event of an Allied victory. He felt this was again the case during the Second World War, only more so in view of the fact that many people could remember the punitive measures contained in the Versailles Treaty, especially the territorial readjustments, the 'war-guilt clause' against Germany and the heavy reparations imposed upon the defeated nations. Wells captured the mood of the enemy populations' quandary in *The Rights of Man* of 1940 when he wrote, regarding the German people, 'They are going to be liberated from the Nazi yoke, our leaflets tell them, and instead of being simply grateful about it and sabotaging Herr Hitler, they ask: "What then?" ' (Wells [1940c], 26). In order to answer this question, Wells sought 'to establish clearly defined unanimity of outlook, so that the common man everywhere and the decent enemy citizen may know where he stands' (Wells 1940a, 61).

I. Why human rights are necessary

Although the desire to avoid a repeat of the Versailles Treaty and the need to prepare a post-war settlement before the end of hostilities were the apparent reasons for Wells' advocacy of the 'Rights of Man', he had greater motives that made the campaign much more significant. By 1939, Wells had come to realise that his cosmopolitanism was open to abuse of the gravest kind. This was explicated in *The New World Order* when he wrote: 'The more highly things are collectivised the more necessary is a legal system embodying the Rights of Man' (Wells 1940b, 80).[3] In promoting human rights, Wells felt a part of that democratic tradition going back to the Magna Carta and Thomas Paine's *Rights of Man*. In *The Common Sense of War and Peace* he observed, 'It has been the practice of what are called the democratic or Parliamentary countries to meet every enhancement and centralisation of power in the past by a definite and vigorous reassertion of the individual rights of man' (Wells 1940a, 83). Some rightist critics, notably F. A. Hayek, have ridiculed Wells' 'Rights of Man' campaign as contradicting his general political philosophy:

> It is pathetic, but characteristic of the muddle into which many of our intellectuals have been led by the conflicting ideals in which they believe, that a leading advocate of the most comprehensive central planning like Mr H. G. Wells should at the same time write an ardent defence of the Rights of Man. The individual rights which Mr Wells hopes to preserve would inevitably obstruct the planning which he desires. (Hayek 1997, 63)[4]

What Hayek seems unable to realise, however, is that the 'Rights of Man' declaration was to be the yardstick by which the efficacy of Wells' world-state reforms were to be measured. There would be no possibility of a static society[5] being created because, through the charter of human rights, the actions of the world state would be constantly challenged and the 'Rights of Man' would, therefore, act as the motor to social change, not only defending human rights but being used as a legal mechanism to reinterpret those rights continually in a changing world.

In order to achieve the acceptance of the 'Rights of Man' charter worldwide, the humanistic tradition of Britain, France and the United States would have to be extended to the whole globe. During the 1930s, Wells had asserted that popular control of his proposed governing faculties could be achieved through consumer and employee groups,[6] and while this was not entirely rejected during the Second World War he did feel that it relied too much on the good faith of those in managerial positions within the government administration and he therefore noted that 'to guarantee that these [worldwide] commissions do not infringe the free spirit of mankind, it is necessary from the start to insist upon the primary importance of the Natural Universal Rights of Man, stated clearly and unambiguously' (Wells 1944, 55). In the Soviet Union, Wells saw an example of a centralised state suffering through over-reliance on good faith. There, owing to a lack of protective legislation (and the non-enforcement of the 1936 liberal constitution), such good faith had led to autocratic personal rule and the elimination of oppositional opinion, as 'Instead of loyalty to the objective, [the Soviet leaders] demand subservience to themselves' (Wells 1941, 44). Indeed, Wells' solution to the problem of Russian repression vies very closely with his general demand for the 'Rights of Man':

> The real and effective disapproval, distrust and disbelief in the soundness of the Soviet system lies [...] in the conviction that it can never achieve efficiency or even maintain its honest ideal of each for all and all for each, unless it has free speech and an insistence upon legally-defined freedoms for the individual within the collectivist framework. (Wells 1940b, 79)

With the outbreak of the Second World War, and particularly after 1941 when fascism and communism ranged their forces against each other, Wells realised the need for in-built guarantees which would protect the rights of individuals and minority groups throughout his world state and which would allow a definite popular voice to directly influence the bureaucracy. The alternative to such an accountable world state would inevitably 'be collectivism in the dark' (Wells 1939d, 148). Thus, in relation to his world-state project, the 'Rights of Man' campaign was aimed at establishing a check to absolute power strong enough to prevent the political repression and general authoritarian excesses of the totalitarian states. Wells hoped that the 'Rights of Man' would be a bulwark against the totalitarian usurpation of his world-state bureaucracy; a usurpation he saw increasing around the world:

> Throughout the whole world we see variations of this same subordination of the individual to the organisation of power. Phase by phase these ill-adapted governments are becoming uncontrolled absolutisms; they are killing that free play of the individual mind which is the preservative of human efficiency and happiness. The populations under their sway, after a phase of servile discipline, are plainly doomed to relapse into disorder and violence. Everywhere war and monstrous economic exploitation break out, so that those very same increments of power and opportunity which have brought mankind within sight of an age of limitless plenty, seem likely to be lost again, it may be lost for ever, in an ultimate social collapse. (Wells [1940c], 79–80)

Wells' opposition to tyranny at this time shows a lasting interest in the protection of fundamental human rights which he demonstrated during the Great War with his plea for a human-rights charter for colonial peoples,[7] and throughout the inter-war period when, for example, he condemned censorship by the BBC (Smith 1986, 316) and was occasionally seen 'mingling with hunger marchers during the Great Depression, to deter the police from baton-charging them' (Sherborne 1981, 190). His attitude during the Second World War was accurately captured in a letter to F. J. C. Happold on 4 October 1943 in which Wells writes, 'Power does not exist to enforce Law. Law exists to control Power, and the better the Law and the better the education, the less need is there for militancy and bossing' (Wells 1943a, 438). Wells' 'Rights of Man' campaign aimed not only at preventing the abuses of power that had been so rife throughout the inter-war period but also at setting in place a guarantee that his own world-state dogma could not be turned into a monolithic tyranny through bureaucratic unaccountability. Circumstances may have led Wells to tie his 'Rights of Man' campaign to the general movement for war aims, but when one sees the campaign as a part of Wells' general world-state proposals, it becomes simply 'an extension of his world order thinking' (Dilloway 1998, 4–5). Wells openly declared this fact in a letter to *Tribune* when he warned that 'this earth will be ruled entirely by pampered old lags, and that future World Commonwealth will remain a dream, [...] until one single Declaration of equal Human Rights has been made the fundamental law of a federated world' (Wells 1942c, 340).

II. The terms of the 'Universal Rights of Man'

Wells first advocated the 'Rights of Man' in a letter printed in *The Times* on 25 October 1939. Although he intended the letter to be a basic model for further debate, it resulted in his being flung into a great cosmopolitan brainstorm about the terms and phrasing of an ideal declaration of human rights. The *Daily Herald* took up the campaign and, as its then editor Ritchie-Calder explained, 'Wells agreed to introduce the arguments for each group of clauses with an article. We arranged in advance for the most eminent thinkers in Britain to intervene' (Ritchie-Calder 1967, 4), and the paper also published letters from the general public. The response to that publicity led to the establishment of a committee under Wells' chairmanship to hone the rights into a document acceptable to all the world's peoples. Soon, Lord Sankey took over the chairmanship and the Sankey Committee of the Rights of Man produced a revised draft of the document.[8] However, 'Wells kept working on the "Sankey Declaration" [...] for several years after the Sankey Committee had finished with it in 1940' (Wagar 1961, 46) and he 'had it distributed to three hundred editors in forty-eight different countries' and 'dropped [...] on microfilm into Occupied Europe' (Ritchie-Calder 1967, 4) as well as having it sent out to intellectual leaders and interested members of the general public throughout the world. Based on the global feedback, he refined his original ten points on successive occasions, making the wording acceptable for translation into all the major languages of the world[9] and attempting to create a human-rights document that respected cultural differences in every corner of the earth. He published a version of the rights in almost all of his books between 1940 and 1944 with slight amendments from draft to draft.

However, between his letter to *The Times* and the publication of the final 'Universal Rights of Man' in *'42 to '44* in 1944, six distinct versions of the declaration can be identified.[10] Although most amendments were concerned with the clarity of the language as a basis for the effective translation of the document, certain fundamental shifts also occurred in the nature of the rights themselves. Although these shifts were not necessarily Wells' own suggestions, he supported them absolutely. The amendments often affected his cosmopolitan policies and they ultimately made him reassess his notions of democracy and representation. By assessing the evolution of the charter, one is able to realise the process of Wells' thought between 1939 and 1944 and can thus understand his final utterances on governmental selection and accountability in a cosmopolitan world state. In order to assess the changes of emphasis in the Rights documents, it will be most convenient to print each clause of the original declaration and discuss alterations on a clause-by-clause basis. Following such a discussion, the final version of the 'Universal Rights of Man' will be printed.

> (1) That every man without distinction of race or colour is entitled to nourishment, housing, covering, medical care and attention sufficient to realise his full possibilities of physical and mental development and to keep him in a state of health from his birth to death. (Wells 1939c, 243)

In all versions of the declaration, the right of subsistence from birth to death for all people is guaranteed. Wells was a lifelong advocate of equal treatment for all the peoples of the earth and in a letter to Lord Esher in 1935 he confirmed that he 'demurs to any arbitrary distinctions between human beings on the score of race or colour' (Wells 1935, 46). By the final draft of the charter two important explications are made to this right: first, to dispel any confusion over the relative importance of men or women, it is declared that '[s]ince most languages have no pronoun that means both "man" and "woman", "he" will be written here to express both sexes' (Wells 1944, 45). Thus the rights apply equally to both genders. Second, to create an equal legal basis for all, regardless of mental and/or physical difference, it is declared that 'Human beings differ among themselves very widely, but in the eyes of the law they are all equal to one another' (Wells 1944, 46). This proviso guarantees the protection of minority or disadvantaged groups of all kinds, be they non-white, colonial or immigrant populations struggling to compete alongside wealthier or better-educated imperial peoples, or the mentally or physically disabled who might be unable to look after all their own needs. By inserting this umbrella statement, a more concise clause is possible with the original need to specify protection regardless of 'race or colour' becoming redundant. In a letter to Lance Corporal Hlope, a Zulu soldier fighting for the Allied cause in the Second World War, Wells demonstrates the depth of feeling he attaches to this plea for racial and cultural equality when he writes,

> I don't think you get a fair deal down there in South Africa. There are some fine coloured people there, not only the Zulus, but the Basuto and others, and there can be no peace in that part of the world until white men and coloured men learn to live and mingle on terms of equality. (Wells 1942a, 353)

As well as protecting the vulnerable in society, this clause aims to guarantee difference as, according to *The New World Order*, 'The more unequal and various their gifts, the greater is the necessity for a Magna Carta to protect them from one another' (Wells 1940b, 166).

This first right sets the tone of the whole document, asserting a 'biological' basis ('Everyone, male or female' [Wells 1944, 45]) as the one upon which deservedness of respect is determined. The declaration, except when specifically stated otherwise, applies to the most guilty criminal as well as the most innocent child, on the grounds that being human in the fundamental biological sense is the only criterion by which these rights are determined. This point is further reiterated in clause eleven of the final draft where it is asserted that 'The Rights of Man are in his nature and cannot be changed' (Wells 1944, 47).

(2) That he is entitled to sufficient education to make him a useful and interested citizen, that he should have easy access to information

upon all matters of common knowledge throughout his life and enjoy the utmost freedom of discussion. (Wells 1939c, 243)

This second clause, ultimately to be enshrined in clauses seven and eight of the final declaration, remained important throughout the charter's revisions, and indeed its principles were stressed at various times throughout Wells' writings. In *Men Like Gods*, for instance his 'Five Principles of Liberty' include the 'Principle of Unlimited Knowledge' and of 'Free Discussion and Criticism' (Wells 1923, 252–5), whereas *The Salvaging of Civilization* declares that 'the more co-operation we have in our common interests, the more necessary is it to guard very jealously the freedom of the mind, that is to say, the liberty of discussion and suggestion' (Wells 1921, 186). In his role as chair of the International P. E. N. Association, he was able to take a practical hand in defending such rights, making 'a real stand for liberty of expression and the solidarity and freedom of art and literature in Europe' (Wells 1933, 508)[11] and, when writing about the importance of scientific research to social progress, he extended such protection to include 'free questioning, free experiment, free publication and open discussion' (Wells 1935, 46).

Furthermore, education was also central to Wells' cosmopolitan philosophy. By insisting on the right to knowledge and information for all throughout life, the declaration was enshrining the principle of Wells' 'Permanent World Encyclopaedia' (Wells 1938, 58), a mechanism by which all the world's citizens would have access to all knowledge through the micro-photographing of texts and objects, and universal access to microfiche machines.[12] By making such a clause world law, the chances of Wells' educational reforms being initiated would be greatly advanced as demands for them would receive legal legitimacy.

In the final draft of the charter, a new clause was also introduced which appears to have sprung from this one. It refers to the protection of minors and declares, 'The natural protection of the young is the family into which it is born. If that protection is not given, the community must protect the child. A child ceases to be a minor when he is able to take a full share in the life of the community' (Wells 1944, 46). This additional clause takes into account cultural differences throughout the world that designate different ages as the time when a child reaches maturity. However, the principle of recognising the particular vulnerability of minors is an important one that the charter eventually came to acknowledge.

Although in *The Common Sense of War and Peace*, the declaration includes 'freedom of expression, discussion, association and worship'

(Wells 1940a, 85), in the final draft that right is reduced to free thought, discussion and worship. The question as to why the freedom of association was dropped from the final two drafts of the charter has been raised by several critics, notably Leon Stover. Wells gives no overt answer to this question in his writings on the 'Rights of Man' and one can only assume that the freedom of discussion included that of association. To be sure, Wells advocated the right of association elsewhere in his work, emphasising its value when discussing the formation of pressure groups to push for world government: '[w]herever there are two or three gathered together, there is the New World begun. [...] Large strong groups may attempt publications and the organization of their feebler, more scattered brethren' (Wells 1932, 39). However, the question remains ultimately unanswerable.

> (3) That he and his personal property lawfully acquired are entitled to police and legal protection from private violence, deprivation, compulsion and intimidation. (Wells 1939c, 243)

Throughout the various drafts of the declaration, the right to possess is enshrined (including a 'private dwelling, reasonably limited in size' [Wells 1944, 46]; see clause (6), below). In all cases, a citizen's property is guaranteed by police protection from violence or robbery, though by the final draft of the charter a private dwelling may be entered by the police upon the presentation of a legal warrant. The declaration is careful to exclude any protection of the right of inheritance, however, as Wells felt it was important to ensure 'that a man may not "found a family" on a property basis, since he shares the common inheritance of mankind and hands his own personal accumulations back to the community' (Wells 1944, 134). Thus, although Wells accepts the handing down of personal cultural or vocational possessions to one's heirs, wealth, including land, must be earned and not bequeathed. As well as abolishing unearned wealth, this addendum sought to restrain property 'whenever it infringes upon the liberty and free movement of others' (Wells 1935, 46) which inherited land, added to over generations, must threaten to do.

> (4) That although he is subject to the free criticisms of his fellows, he shall have adequate protection from any lying or misrepresentation that may distress or injure him. All registration and records about citizens shall be open to their personal and private inspection. There shall be no secret dossiers in any administrative department. All dossiers shall be accessible to the man concerned and subject to verification and correction at his challenge. A dossier is merely a memorandum;

> it cannot be used as evidence without proper confirmation. (Wells 1939c, 243)

This clause, although greatly truncated, remains unaltered in principle throughout the various charters and becomes merged with clause (8) in the final draft. These rights were recognised as fundamental by Wells as early as 1923 when in *Men Like Gods* he enshrined them in his 'Five Principles of Liberty' as the 'Principle of Privacy' and the principle that 'Lying is the Blackest Crime' (Wells 1923, 252–3). In the final charter, these principles are condensed thus: 'Secret evidence is not permissible [in court]. Statements in administrative records are not evidence unless they are proved. A man has the right to protection from any falsehood that may distress or injure him' (Wells 1944, 47).

It is worth noting that, although Wells thus advocated the protection of persons from blacklists and other secret dossiers, and allowed persons the right to see their personal files and have them corrected if fallacious, he does not outlaw the maintenance of 'registration and records about citizens' as such. From as early as 1905, in *A Modern Utopia*, Wells insisted that the state must keep account of all citizens' whereabouts and public activities, including their place of residence and employment, their criminal record, their marital status and even their location when travelling outside their place of normal domicile. In his utopia, universal fingerprinting and code-word identification are instituted for all citizens, both of which are demanded by public officials (in such places as employment exchanges) and the latter by hotels, employees and the like (see Wells 2005, 112–15). Although his utopia might be considered zealous in its range, Wells simply advocated the more efficient gathering and holding of information already generally held by public bodies, and given people's right to inspect and correct such information concerning themselves, Wells clearly saw a compromise in his proposals between the freedom of the citizen from 'lying or misrepresentation' and 'secret dossiers' and the right of the state to efficiently administer human affairs and keep tabs on transgressors.

> (5) That he may engage freely in any lawful occupation, earning such pay as the need for his work and the increment it makes to the common welfare may justify. That he is entitled to demand employment and to a free choice when there is any variety of employment open to him. He may suggest employment for himself and have his claim publicly considered. (Wells 1939c, 243)

Over the several drafts of the declaration, this clause received significant amendment. From having the right to look for work in this first statement, eventually it is acknowledged that 'the community must find him suitable work when he asks for it. It is his right'. Further, from having a choice of work among those occupations that contribute to the 'common welfare', by the final declaration this right is extended so that one may earn pay for the work 'that the desire of anyone for what he does may give him' (Wells 1944, 46) (with the exception of those occupations prohibited by clause (7), below). This extension of lawful occupations was clearly intended to benefit all types of artist, whose contribution to the common welfare is not quantifiable though it may be of major interest to individual purchasers. By insisting in the final declaration that 'No one shall be forced to work' (Wells 1944, 46), Wells counters Hayek's criticism that his advocacy of a central control of labour would limit the range of employment available and thus dictate occupations to some people (Hayek 1997, 63–4). In fact, given the guarantee of a healthy, interesting life, made in clause (1), above, the declaration permits those who can find no suitable occupation to remain idle at the state's expense until a satisfactory job becomes available.

(6) That he may move freely about the world at his own expense. That his private house or apartment or reasonably limited garden enclosure is his castle, which may be entered only with his consent, but that he shall have the right to roam over any kind of country, moorland, mountain, farm, great garden or what not, where his presence will not be destructive of its special use nor dangerous to himself nor seriously inconvenient to his fellow-citizens. (Wells 1939c, 243)

This freedom to go about was asserted in *Men Like Gods* as the 'Principle of Free Movement' (Wells 1923, 252). It remained intact throughout all the rights documents, though the individual's range became more widely defined and modes of transport were latterly included. Thus, in addition to those areas listed in the original clause are included 'river, lake, sea or ocean' and the means of travel is specified as 'by land, air or water' (Wells 1944, 47). (The specified right to a dwelling with legal protection is dealt with in clause (3), above.) Although not stated overtly, the implications of this right of free movement are quite far reaching. They are expressed in an undated letter that Wells wrote to the British Home Secretary in respect to Leon Trotsky's request for medical attention in Britain:

At present that tradition of free communication upon which we believe that all that is most worth while in civilisation rests, is being threatened and assailed as it has never been assailed before [...]. And Mr Trotsky seeks something very like asylum with us. (Wells *c*.1929–31, 353–4)

Combined with clause (1) of the charter, guaranteeing food, clothing, shelter and medical attention throughout life, this clause makes provision for the movement and care of people in times of political repression, and Trotsky's case, having been forced to flee from Russia and living as a political exile in Turkey, was a test of the British government's respect for such rights. The government's refusal to grant Trotsky refuge must surely have been an inspiration to Wells when drafting the 'Rights of Man', not to mention the large numbers of persecuted people being forced out of Germany during the Nazi era.

> (7) That he shall have the right to buy or sell without any discriminatory restrictions anything which may be lawfully bought or sold, in such quantities and with such reservations as are compatible with the common welfare. (Wells 1939c, 243)

In the ultimate declaration, this clause was incorporated with the right to earn money and formed clause (4). It was limited in the final declaration to supplying commodities which people could not acquire unassisted, though '*buying and holding and selling for profit without service is not lawful*. That is speculation'. Money may be earned where genuine service is provided to the community but 'forestalling, appropriation, hoarding and such strangling activities' (Wells 1944, 46; emphasis in the original) are considered exploitative, providing nothing new to society. The same exclusions to the right to buy were made by Wells in his letter to Lord Esher in 1935 when he condemned 'all forestalling, monopolization, sweating and other abuses of property' (Wells 1935, 46).

> (8) That a man unless he is duly certified as mentally deficient shall not be imprisoned for a longer period than three weeks without being charged with a definite offence against the law, nor for more than three months without a public trial. At the end of the latter period, if he has not been tried and sentenced by due process of law, he shall be released. (Wells 1939c, 243–4)

Throughout the six drafts of the charter, the right to personal liberty declared that the mentally insane were the only people who could be restrained indefinitely without having committed a crime, though several reservations were ultimately made to this. Thus, 'madness' had not only to be ascertained by a 'competent authority' and confirmed 'within seven days and considered again at least annually', but the individual in question had to be deemed 'a danger to himself or others' (Wells 1944, 47).

With regards the mentally able, the clause, again, was liberalised during its revision stages. Thus, whereas initially it proposed that a person could be held for no longer than three weeks without a charge, by the final draft this term had been reduced to twenty-four hours. Also, before a trial the accused was entitled to see the evidence against him or her and, if acquitted, could not be re-charged for the same offence. Although not mentioned in the original charter, drafts two to five assert that no one 'shall be conscripted for military or other service to which he has a conscientious objection' (Wells 1942d, 244), though drafts four and five added that 'to perform no social duty whatsoever is to remain unenfranchised and under guardianship' (Wells 1942d, 244–5). Interestingly, in the final version of this clause, conscientious objection has dropped out of the rights altogether and instead a new clause regarding duty and freedom asserts that 'Everyone must respect and protect the rights of everyone else according to his ability.' Whether the phrase 'according to his ability' was intended to encompass moral ability as well as physical and therefore protect conscientious objectors is left unstated, though it is declared in the same clause that 'No one shall be forced to work' (Wells 1944, 46) which may have been intended by Wells to allow for conscientious objection.

> (9) That no man shall be subjected to any sort of mutilation [*sic*] or sterilization except with his own deliberate consent, freely given, nor to bodily assault, except in restraint of his own violence, nor to torture, beating or any other bodily punishment; he shall not be subjected to imprisonment with such an excess of silence, noise, light or darkness as to cause mental suffering, or to imprisonment in infected, verminous or otherwise insanitary quarters, or be put in the company of verminous or infectious people. He shall not be forcibly fed nor prevented from starving himself if he so desire. He shall not be forced to take drugs, nor shall they be administered to him without his knowledge. That the extreme punishments to which he may be subjected are rigorous imprisonment for a term of not longer than 15 years or death. (Wells 1939c, 244)

This freedom from violence clause was simplified throughout the six drafts and in the final charter it is added that 'No one shall be punished vicariously by the arrest or ill-treatment of those for whom he cares' (Wells 1944, 47). Punishment by death is finally omitted from the declaration and becomes illegal under clause (1), guaranteeing the right to life. Wells' anger at the use of capital punishment and his realisation that cosmopolitan control was the only way of ending it is asserted in a letter to Marc Slonimsky in which he rails that 'The USA is a union of 48 national states with life & death powers over the citizens and the Sacco & Vanzetti case and the Scottsboro case and the Huey Long cases show how mischievously state freedom can deprive men of human rights' (Wells 1942b, 338). However, a curious deletion from later drafts of the charter is a maximum prison term. This is a curious omission that permits serious abuses of human rights. The fact that Wells included a limit in his original draft suggests that he was opposed to prison sentences for the duration of life and his objection, in later drafts of this clause, against mental torture can surely be assumed to protect individuals against literal life sentences.

> (10) That the provisions and principles embodied in this Declaration shall be more fully defined in a legal code which shall be made easily accessible to everyone. This Declaration shall not be qualified nor departed from upon any pretext whatever. It incorporates all previous Declarations of Human Right [*sic*]. Henceforth it is the fundamental law for mankind throughout the whole world. (Wells 1939c, 244)

This final clause, declaring the charter inalienable, was strongly reinforced by later drafts where the need for the charter to be 'more fully defined in a legal code' was rejected; the final charter was to be the overriding law to shape and mould all other legal codes. The rights 'are in his nature and cannot be changed' (Wells 1944, 47). Governments are defenders of the charter and not providers of rights and thus, as Wells wrote to A. D. Lindsay, 'The Universal Rights of Man is not a *declaration* of rights. It is an assertion of rights' (Wells 1943b, 427; emphasis in the original). In cases where the rights are not respected by governments, Wells is suggesting that those governments have no legitimacy, as 'it is the fundamental law for mankind throughout the whole world' (Wells [1940c], 84). This being the case, it became important to incorporate a democratic element into the clause to protect against 'all tyrannies and arbitrary governments' (Wells 1935, 46). Thus,

> [T]he appointment from time to time of these protectors of these rights shall be made according to the ways of the people, whether by elder men, by election of representatives, or in a common meeting, or by lot, or otherwise, according to the custom of the country. (Wells 1944, 48)

The final draft of the charter allowed for government selection by any number of methods for two reasons: first, Wells sought the charter's respect by all cultures of the world, and this would include those peoples who had not adopted Western-style democratic institutions; and second, Wells himself was not satisfied with the mass-electoral method of choosing governing representatives. In a functional world state, Wells felt electoral democracy to be unsuitable and sought other methods of popular representation. By phrasing the democratic clause in the terms that he did, Wells was allowing the possibility of its application to a functional world state and permitting himself to experiment with alternative ideas of government selection.

Following the changes of position over the course of the lengthy debate and several amendments that were made to the original 'Rights of Man' document, a cosmopolitan version was arrived at and published in '42 to '44 as listed in the following section.

III. The universal rights of man

1. Right to live

Everyone, male or female, has the rights asserted in this declaration. (Since most languages have no pronoun that means both 'man' and 'woman', 'he' will be written here to express both sexes.) Everyone is a joint inheritor of the world in its entirety, of earth and sea and of all that mankind has accumulated before his birth – knowledge, inventions, powers and possibilities. He is the child of mankind, and he has an equal right to food, covering and medical care and to do all that he can do for the world from birth to death. Human beings differ among themselves very widely, but in the eyes of the law they are all equal to one another.

2. Protection of minors

The natural protection of the young is the family into which it is born. If that protection is not given, the community must protect the child. A child ceases to be a minor when he is able to take a full share in the life of the community.

3. Duty and freedom

Everyone must respect and protect the rights of everyone else according to his ability. No one shall be forced to work. But the community must find him suitable work when he asks for it. It is his right.

4. Right to earn money

He has a right to earn money. He may earn the pay that his work for the community is worth, or that the desire of anyone for what he does may give him. He may have pay for calling attention to a product or conveying it to those who might not get it unless he did so. *But buying and holding and selling for profit without service is not lawful.* That is speculation. It gains only by creating want. It has been the curse of the old order that is passing away. Such gains can be got only by forestalling, appropriation, hoarding and such strangling activities. It is equally unlawful for private individuals and public administrative bodies.

5. Right to possess

A man may enjoy his lawful gains, and the community must give them full protection from violence or robbery. He or his family may possess a private dwelling, reasonably limited in size, which may be entered only with his or their consent except by someone with a warrant as the law may direct.

6. Freedom to go about

A man may go anywhere in the world at his own cost. So long as his movement does not trespass upon the private domain of any other citizen, harm, disfigure or encumber what is not his, interfere with its proper use, or seriously impair the happiness of others, he has the right to come and go wherever he chooses, by land, air or water, over any kind of country, mountain, moorland, river, lake, sea or ocean, in this, his world.

7. Right to know

He has a right to the teaching and information and news necessary for him to make the fullest use of his powers.

8. He has the right to free thought, discussion and worship

9. Personal liberty

This is what the English and American law calls the right of *Habeas Corpus*. It requires careful study by those unused to legal action.

Unless a man is found by a competent authority to be a danger to himself or others, through madness, a finding which must be repeated within seven days and considered again at least annually, he cannot be held prisoner for more than twenty-four hours unless he is charged with a definite offence. He shall not be held prisoner for more than three months without a trial. At a reasonable time before his trial, he shall be given a copy of the evidence against him. At the end of these three months, if he has not been tried and found guilty, he shall be acquitted and released. No man shall be charged again for the same offence. Secret evidence is not permissible. Statements in administrative records are not evidence unless they are proved. A man has the right to protection from any falsehood that may distress or injure him.

10. Freedom from violence

No one shall be subject to any sort of mutilation except with his own deliberate consent, freely given, nor to forcible handling, except in restraint of his own violence, nor to torture, beating or any bodily ill treatment. No one shall be punished vicariously by the arrest or ill treatment of those for whom he cares. No one shall be imprisoned with verminous or infectious people. But if a man himself is a danger to the health of others, he may be cleansed, disinfected, put in quarantine or otherwise restrained.

(11) The Rights of Man are in his nature and cannot be changed. Rulers, rajahs, governments, directors, are no more than servants of those rights. In some things it is good for them to restrain us. The rule of the road, for example, or the protection of money from forgery, in laying out streets and ways, or guarding public health. But all such convenient small things can be talked over and altered if those who are appointed to protect our rights decide to change them. What cannot be changed are the rights written down in the ten Articles before this one. And the appointment from time to time of these pro-tectors of these rights shall be made according to the ways of the peo-ple, whether by elder men, by election of representatives, or in a common meeting, or by lot, or otherwise, according to the custom of the country.

These are the universal rights of all human beings. They are yours whoever you are. Your elders, rajahs, governments and rulers are bound by this Law. We are all bound by this Law. It is the fundamen-tal law of a new free world that dawns on mankind. (Wells 1944, 45–8)

This evolution of the declaration of the 'Rights of Man', taking into consideration the opinions of many intellectual leaders and members of the general public from all parts of the world, is amazingly slight consid-ering that the initial charter was the work of Wells alone. Nonetheless,

the changes that occurred were important in creating a universal document acceptable to all the world's cultures and thus moving away from a
narrowly parliamentary-democratic, Eurocentric charter.

Few human-rights campaigners have remembered Wells' activities
when writing about post-war developments. However, Lord Ritchie-
Calder believed that the 1948 Universal Declaration of Human Rights
'contains the substance and meaning of the Wells debate' (Ritchie-Calder
1967, 6) and James Dilloway has gone further, asserting that Wells'

> World Declaration was the true forerunner of today's Universal
> Declaration of Human Rights and of the two binding International
> Covenants that now underpin it – those on Economic, Social and
> Cultural Rights and on Civil and Political Rights, respectively – as
> well as of a long series of Conventions and other instruments, many
> of them legally binding on accession and subject to periodic checking
> on performance. (Dilloway 1998, 2)

Teru Hamano has suggested that Wells' greatest achievement was
getting copies of the various drafts of the 'Rights of Man' into the hands
of President Franklin Roosevelt who reflected their influence in his 'Four
Freedoms' of 6 January 1941 and the Atlantic Charter of 10 August 1941
(Hamano 1998, 12),[13] both of which asserted the Allies' responsibility
for guarding human rights and protecting them in international law
after the war. With Wells' final draft of the 'Rights of Man' being
produced in 1944, Dilloway has recorded the process by which it may
have achieved international law:

> Six months before the death of H. G. Wells in 1946, the first part of
> the first UN General Assembly, held at Westminster, had before it a
> draft Declaration of Rights and Freedoms. In the same year the UN
> Commission on Human Rights was set up and on 10 December 1948
> the present Universal Declaration was adopted by 50 countries.
> (Dilloway 1998, 8)

In recent years, Wells has finally received some public credit for his
human-rights activities. In 1999, the esteemed human-rights lawyer,
Geoffrey Robertson, reflecting on the evolution of international law over
the past century, said of Wells' *The Rights of Man* that it 'must be
accounted one of the twentieth century's most influential books'
(Robertson 1999, 22) and, in 2000, Francesca Klug, a director of the Human
Rights Act Research Unit and 'one of the driving forces behind the 1998
[British] Human Rights Act',[14] acknowledged Wells' place in human-rights

history, stating that 'with the exception of H. G. Wells' wartime initiative there was no significant lobby for a bill of rights during the last two centuries in the UK until the late 1960s' (Klug 2000b, 152).[15]

Despite the ultimate success of his 'Rights of Man' charter, Wells had desired much more. As was stressed at the start of this chapter, human rights was simply one aspect of his world-state campaign. In addition to world legal protection, he sought global accountability for the cosmopolitan structures he advocated. This was particularly reflected in the ambiguous final clause of the declaration, which allowed for a diversity of governmental selection methods. In the final section of this chapter, Wells' own preferred method of global accountability for a functional world state will be discussed.

IV. Popular representation in a functional world state

In clause (11) of the final 'Rights of Man' document, Wells universalises the processes of government appointment so as to appeal to all cultures, both democratic and non-democratic. His watchword for government appointment can be said to have been 'representational' rather than 'parliamentary' or narrowly 'democratic'. By adopting the 'representational' principle, Wells was allowing for experimentation in the selection of governors. Although such an experimental position aimed to appeal to the diverse cultures of the world, Wells also sought to allow himself the opportunity to devise a selection method that would continue within the broadly democratic tradition while putting an end to the situation where, '[a] citizen had to vote for one Party or the other, and, except for the excitement of faction or the shabby little personal rewards of the spoils system, he got nothing for it' ([Wells] 1943c, 11). During the course of the war, and his campaign for the 'Rights of Man', Wells evolved a position that met his demand satisfactorily.

With the existence of the National Government in Britain and the approach to coalition government in 1940, Wells began to consider governmental accountability. Aware of the role that patriotism played in protecting governments from general criticism in times of war, Wells suggested taking advantage of the public mood to alter the way in which politicians were scrutinised. He believed it was possible to criticise individual ministers without destabilising the government:

> It is a logical but often disregarded corollary of the virtual creation of All-Party National Governments and the suspension of electoral contests, that since there is no Opposition, party criticism should give place to individual criticism of ministers, and that instead of

throwing out governments we should set ourselves to throw out individual administrative failures. (Wells 1940b, 129–30)

However, the mechanism for such a criticism of individual ministers did not exist in Britain during the war and so Wells suggested extra-parliamentary mobilisation of opinion to deal with deadwood politicians:

> We can insist upon men who have done things and can do things, and whenever an election occurs we can organise a block of non-party voters who will vote if possible for an outsider of proved ability, and will at any rate insist on a clear statement from every Parliamentary candidate of the concrete service, if any, he has done the country, of his past and present financial entanglements and his family relationships and of any title he possesses. (Wells 1940b, 130)

Such pressure on individual politicians could be organised by 'an active Vigilance Society,' whose job it would be to 'begin the elimination of inferior elements from our public life' (Wells 1940b, 131). This type of activity is far from representing an alternative to the general election method of selecting politicians. However, the notion of thorough accountability and penetrating criticism from the general public was at the core of Wells' reforms of the electoral system and from these criticisms it is possible to see the direction in which his thought process was going *vis-à-vis* governmental selection. In *The Outlook for Homo Sapiens* Wells began considering the notion of permanently sitting electors passing judgement on politicians after every act they perform. There he wrote, 'the consent of the governed in a democracy can never be a finally silenced and irrevocable consent. It must be *a continuing consent*. It must be subject to sustained revision and renewal' (Wells 1942d, 39; emphasis in the original). Wells was clearly feeling around for a mechanism by which to put an end to the 'elected dictatorship' of parliamentary democracy. By the time he produced his last major revision of the rights document, he had found that mechanism.

When thinking through his ideas on government selection, Wells considered the nature of his proposed world state – a series of functional enterprises serving the needs of consumers – and saw parallels with the organisation of large-scale business corporations. Hence, Wells believed it would be possible to create a governing system based upon contemporary ideas about serving consumers' needs. Thus, in *'42 to '44*, he wrote:

> As big business systems grow, even under the incubus of private ownership, their working approximates more and more closely to the

necessary forms, ministries and administrations of a world-wide socialist order. The ordinary big department store chain, for instance, has to solve problems almost identical with those the distributive ministry of a socialist state will have to face. It finds its book department failing to attract a crowd; it is unsure about a particular line of goods upon which it thinks of embarking; it wants to know why people do not seem eager to consume the refreshments it provides and whether there is anything needed about the establishment that would make the customers happier.

A politician would lock all the doors and ask the customers to elect a general manager, either the old one or a new one. And much good that would do!

No competent businessman would do anything of the sort. He would get answers to his questions from Samples of his Consumers. He would call in the art of various experts who would make a number of unobtrusive enquiries and return with what Mr Tom Harrisson calls a 'Mass Observation' report, or he would make a 'Gallup Poll' of the people who came into his shop and of the people who might do so and didn't, upon these important questions. The Sample Method is a very necessary one for the unified human future. (Wells 1944, 42–3)

By demanding, on the one hand, a permanently sitting group of citizens responsible for criticising politicians and, on the other hand, a sample method of enquiring about the needs and wants of the consumer society, it did not take a great leap of the imagination for Wells to reconsider an idea he briefly advocated in 1903 in *Mankind in the Making*: government by jury. His proposals in *Phœnix* are surprisingly similar to those of forty years earlier and were inspired by the same considerations.

Wells envisaged the jury system of government to 'be as much of a world sovereign as a unified world will need'. Through creating a pyramidal society, with business and administrative bodies existing on a global, national and regional level, the world jury 'will be the apex of the system and below it there will be a great variety of sectional Juries representing national, local and professional consumer needs', or, more specifically, '[t]he Grand Jury may do its work as a whole, or in sections, or in special groups associated with representatives of the Ministries and corporations' (Wells 1942e, 91). As in the judicial system, however, Wells was unwilling to allow such a jury government to make laws willy-nilly. As he wrote to Lindsay, 'it is not proposed to give a jury *power*. "Power" like "powers" has to pass out of the human imagination' (Wells 1943b, 427; emphasis in the original). Rather, such a government would

184 John S. Partington

play a regulatory role, intervening in society only when cases were put before it to consider, and with no personal or class axe to grind. He cited the kind of jury he had in mind in *God the Invisible King* in 1917:

> The idea of the law court will have changed entirely from a place of dispute, exaction and vengeance, to a place of adjustment. The individual or some state organisation will plead *on behalf of the common good* either against some state official or state regulation, or against the actions or inaction of another individual. (Wells 1917, 144; emphasis in the original)

As he explained to Lindsay, the jurors 'are assessors drawn from all sorts of places who have not developed any special class consciousness. Before they can do that they will disperse automatically and give place to another jury' (Wells 1943b, 427).

The significant difference between Wells' jury proposals of 1903 and those of 1942 is that in the former year, Wells advocated juries of electors selecting politicians to govern on a national level whereas in the latter year the jury itself might be the governing body, regionally, nationally and/or globally. However, this change in scale and role does not discredit Wells' earlier thoughts on jury government, as during the Second World War he still foresaw, below the government level, a wide range of administrative roles being played by juries, some regulating affairs and making decisions directly, others interviewing candidates and selecting specialists and managers to make decisions on behalf of the consumers they represented. Furthermore, regardless of the role of the jury in question, the process of selection often applied equally to both purposes.

When discussing the selection method for a world jury, Wells stated, 'I will not pretend to any special knowledge' of the best way of appointing a jury from the millions of individuals eligible to be called upon. However, he believed that '[t]here must be a great body of human experience on record for selecting men for the military draft, and in the conduct of lotteries, which could be easily and rapidly co-ordinated.' While offering a sketch of the method by which a world jury could be drawn, he admitted his ignorance of the task and asserted that it could be 'done effectively by any actuarial expert' (Wells 1942e, 90). Wells' suggestion for selection ran as follows:

> [I]f you map your world into two and a half million areas of approximately equal population and select twenty thousand of these areas by lot, and if you then select a man by lot from each of these areas, or

better, have a prompt election in that area of a few select men and then take one of those by lot, and if this is done quickly without any unnecessary publicity you will be able to assemble a body of Consumers far more authoritative than any electoral body now in existence. (Wells 1942e, 90)

As cumbersome as such a sizeable jury may seem, Wells maintained that '[t]here is now no mechanical impossibility, with loud speakers and so forth, in as many as twenty thousand people or more coming to a conference together.' Even with regards the 'language difficulty', he declared that that problem 'was not insurmountable at Geneva [i.e. in the League of Nations Assembly]' (Wells 1942e, 91).

Wells' reference to the holding of 'a prompt election' may appear at first sight to be a contradiction to his desire to end the power of party machines and the manipulation of traditional electoral politics. However, by referring to *Mankind in the Making* and its proposals for selecting governors, we can see how Wells, by ensuring that 'this is done quickly without any unnecessary publicity', intended avoiding such a return to accepted democratic ways. Wells' proposals were expressed thus:

> [The jury] could hear, in public, under a time limit, the addresses of such candidates as had presented themselves, and they could receive, under a limit of length and with proper precautions for publicity, such documents as the candidates chose to submit. They could also, in public, put any questions they chose to the candidates to elucidate their intentions or their antecedents, and they might at any stage decide unanimously to hear no more of and to dismiss this or that candidate who encumbered their deliberations. [...] The Jury between and after their interrogations and audiences would withdraw from the public room to deliberate in privacy. (Wells 1903, 271–2)

As well as hearing evidence from the candidates themselves, Wells proposed that objections could be heard from any member of the public with clear evidence against a candidate. Thus,

> [P]rovision might be made for pleas against particular candidates; private individuals or the advocates of vigilance societies might appear against any particular candidate and submit the facts about any doubtful affair, financial or otherwise, in which that candidate had been involved. (Wells 1903, 272)

Once a world jury had been assembled, either drawn by lot or selected by a regional sub-jury, its work would be straightforward:

> The various producing, distributing and other corporations will present their cases for any readjustment [of the law], the Jury will question, discuss and decide. It will also consider any rational complaints and grievances that may be submitted to it by petition, grievances for which the ordinary law does not provide, and it will, if necessary, amend the law. (Wells 1942e, 91)

By creating a governing system in which individual governors are far removed from the enfranchised population (and by enfranchised is meant those eligible to sit on a jury), new structures for the lobbying of the jury would have to come into being. Large corporations would, by their nature, quickly adapt lobbying practices and, as with the aforementioned vigilance societies, Wells foresaw the proliferation of consumer associations designed to watch and criticise the bureaucratic bodies producing for and administrating the world, as 'any association can proceed by petition' (Wells 1942e, 91). A world jury would sit permanently, though 'at the expiration of a reasonable period, a year perhaps, or three years or seven years, another Jury might be summoned' (Wells 1903, 272), and during the interim period between juries, the outgoing jury 'may appoint committees to control particular matters that will function until the next Grand Jury takes them over' (Wells 1942e, 91).

By promoting the idea of a world government-by-jury, Wells was hoping to end electoral politics altogether. He despised the power of party machines and the manipulation of the electorate by party propagandists and politically motivated newspapers. Further, he thought that the selection of a government on a world scale would be reduced to irrelevance if the system of general election was used, as once 20,000 elected delegates were assembled, the individual constituencies that they represented would become irrelevant. As no individual politician would be able to defend the needs of his or her constituency, the principle of electoral politics becomes absurd. With a jury system, however, being replaced after a short time ('a year perhaps, or three years or seven years'), Wells hoped to overcome narrow interests and believed that the plucking of individuals at random from diverse areas of the globe would guarantee disinterested cooperation based on commonsense and the moral will to do the right thing. The unpredictable nature of the jury would protect it from manipulation by lobby groups, especially those organised by the functional world bureaucracies that Wells hoped would manage the goods and services of the world, though without holding absolute power over global affairs. In such a way the 'jury would be the sovereign in the new world' (Smith 1986, 433).

With his advocacy of guaranteed human-rights protection and global government by jury, Wells put the finishing touches to his world-state proposals. In light of the abuses of human rights by the totalitarian regimes of Europe and Asia and the criticisms that Wells' world-state ideas received from the likes of George Orwell (Orwell [1941])[16] and Hayek, these political additions to his cosmopolitanism were absolutely fundamental in making Wells' ideas suitable for a post-war world of reconstruction.

Notes

1. For detailed analyses of Wells' cosmopolitanism, see Wagar 1961 and Partington 2003. A recent volume, Feir 2005, is deserving of no consideration at all, being poorly researched, partisan in the extreme and riddled with factual errors.
2. Over the years there have been few articles published on Wells' interest in human rights, though these have not contextualised the issue within his general world-state thinking (see Ritchie-Calder 1967; Smith and Stone 1989; Dilloway 1998; Hamano 1998; Robertson 1999; Klug 2000 a,b).
3. As early as 1904, Wells was warning the Fabian Society leadership of the potential threat to individual liberties posed by centralised bureaucratic institutions: 'I am inclined to say that where any class of people have relations of authorities [*sic*] over any other class, then any abuse of the first fair propositions of that relation that can be imagined, will presently be found in being' (Wells 1904, 25).
4. Hayek's criticisms are made against Wells' 1939 Rights document. It is difficult to account for this, as he must surely have been aware that the charter was revised several times throughout the war with its final version being published the very year he made his criticisms, in 1944.
5. Wells analysed the dichotomy of the 'static' and the 'kinetic' society in his early works, writing his first full-blown 'kinetic' utopia in 1905, with *A Modern Utopia* (see Partington 2002). By the standards of Wells' later thinking on human rights, that utopia was flawed owing to its lack of legal mechanisms holding the rulers, or 'samurai', to account. In emphasising the likelihood of the emergence of a temperamentally committed ruling class, working selflessly for the good of society, he ignored the human frailty that comes with the assumption of power (and especially absolute power), and which requires regulation by an independent legal system. The 'Rights of Man' initiative, coming towards the end of Wells' life, was thus a crucial ingredient in his general world-state thinking, and one heavily neglected by scholars of Wells' political ideas. For Wells' discussion of 'a classification of temperaments' early and late in his career (using much the same terminology in both instances), see Wells 2005, 178–82 and Wells 1942e, 39–51.
6. See Partington 2003, 101–25 for a detailed discussion of Wells' earlier thoughts on education and employees' rights as means of empowering citizens in his world state.

7. In 1918, Wells had called for 'a common law for Africa, a general Declaration of Rights, of certain elementary rights, and we want a common authority to which the black man and the native tribe may appeal for justice' (Wells 1918, 46).
8. Wells resigned the chairmanship of the committee as it 'inhibited his right to participate. [...] In truth, it remained his committee' (Smith and Stone 1989, 24). The members of the Sankey Committee were Wells, Lord Sankey, Ritchie-Calder, Sir John Orr, Lord Horder, Barbara Wootton, Norman Angel and Francis Williams (Smith 1986, 431).
9. According to David C. Smith, the declaration was translated into Czech, Welsh, French, Danish, Spanish, German, Icelandic, Russian, Italian, Polish, Gujerati, Hausa, Swahili, Arabic, Urdu, Hindi, Bengali, Ganda, Yoruba, Basic English, Zulu and Greek by 1944 (Smith 1986, 444).
10. Draft 1: Wells 1939c, 243–4; Draft 2: Wells 1940b, 139–45; Draft 3: Wells [1940c], 78–84; Draft 4: Wells 1940a, 81–9; Draft 5: Wells 1942d, 242–8; and Draft 6: Wells 1944, 45–8.
11. For a discussion of Wells' international activities as chair of P. E. N., see Schenkel 2005, 100–4.
12. For a full discussion of Wells' proposed revolution in world education, see Partington 2003, 87–100. For a discussion of Wells' 'Permanent World Encyclopaedia' as a precursor to modern technological educational devices, see Mayne 1994, and more narrowly as a precursor to the world wide web, see Gardner 1999.
13. It should not be forgotten that the Universal Declaration of Human Rights was proposed by the late president's wife, Eleanor Roosevelt, as an American delegate to the United Nations in 1948.
14. From the biographical blurb in Klug 2000b, I.
15. See also Klug 2000a, 8 and my reply Partington 2000, 37–8.
16. For a detailed discussion of Orwell's criticisms of Wells, see Partington 2004, 45–56, or for a summary, see Partington 2003, 14–15.

References

Dilloway, J. (1998) *Human Rights and World Order: Two Discourses to the H. G. Wells Society with some Additional Material*, rev. edn, Nottingham: H. G. Wells Society.

Feir, G. D. (2005) *H. G. Wells at the End of His Tether: His Social and Political Adventures*, New York: iUniverse.

Gardner, M. (1999) 'The Internet: A World Brain?', *Skeptical Inquirer* (January–February), 12–14.

Hamano, T. (1998) 'H. G. Wells, President Roosevelt, and the Universal Declaration of Human Rights', *Life & Human Rights*, Vol. 9 (Autumn), 6–16.

Hayek, F. A. (1997) *The Road to Serfdom*, London: Routledge.

Klug, F. (2000a) 'in the Footsteps of H. G. Wells: The Great Author Called for a Human Rights Act; 60 Years Later, We Have It', *New Statesman*, 9 October, p. 8.

Klug, F. (2000b) *Values for a Godless Age: The Story of the UK's New Bill of Rights*, Harmondsworth: Penguin.

Mayne, A. (1994) 'Critical Introduction', in H. G. Wells (ed.), *World Brain: H. G. Wells on the Future of World Education*, London: Adamantine, pp. 1–70.

Orwell, G. [1941] 'Wells, Hitler and the World State' [August], in (1981) *Down and Out in Paris and London, The Road to Wigan Pier, Homage to Catalonia, Essays and*

Journalism: 1931–1940, Essays and Journalism: 1940–1943, Essays and Journalism: 1944–1945 and Essays and Journalism: 1945–1949, London: Book Club Associates, pp. 567–71.

Partington, J. S. (2000) 'The Debt to H. G. Wells', *New Statesman*, 30 October, pp. 37–8.

Partington, J. S. (2002) '*The Time Machine* and *A Modern Utopia*: The Static and Kinetic Utopias of the Early H. G. Wells', *Utopian Studies*, Vol.13, No.1, 57–68.

Partington, J. S. (2003) *Building Cosmopolis: The Political Thought of H. G. Wells.* Aldershot: Ashgate.

Partington, J. S. (2004) 'The Pen as Sword: George Orwell, H. G. Wells and Journalistic Parricide', *Journal of Contemporary History*, Vol. 39, No. 1 (January), 45–56.

Ritchie-Calder, Lord (1967) *On Human Rights*, London: H. G. Wells Society.

Robertson, G. (1999) *Crimes Against Humanity: The Struggle for Global Justice.* London: Lane / Penguin.

Schenkel, E. (2005) 'White Elephants and Black Machines: H. G. Wells and German Culture', in Patrick Parrinder and John S. Partington (ed.), *The Reception of H. G. Wells in Europe*, London: Thoemmes Continuum, pp. 91–104.

Sherborne, M. (1981) 'Wells, Plato, and the Ideal State', in John S. Partington, (ed.) (2003), *The Wellsian: Selected Essays on H. G. Wells*, [Oss]: Equilibris, pp. 189–98.

Smith, D. C. (1986) *H. G. Wells: Desperately Mortal*, New Haven, CT: Yale University Press.

Smith, D. C. and Stone, W. F. (1989) 'Peace and Human Rights: H. G. Wells and the Universal Declaration', *Canadian Journal of Peace Research*, Vol. 21, No.1 (January), 21–6 and 75–8.

Wagar, W. W. (1961) *H. G. Wells and the World State*, New Haven, CT: Yale University Press.

Wells, H. G. (2005) *A Modern Utopia* ed. Gregory Claeys and Patrick Parrinder. London: Penguin.

Wells, H. G. (1944) *'42 to '44: A Contemporary Memoir upon Human Behaviour during the Crisis of the World Revolution*, London: Secker & Warburg.

Wells, H. G. (1943a) Letter to F. J. C. Happold, 4 October, in David C. Smith (ed.), (1998), *The Correspondence of H. G. Wells: Volume 4, 1935–1946*, London: Pickering & Chatto, pp. 438–9.

Wells, H. G. (1943b) Letter to A. D. Lindsay, 4 August, in David C. Smith (ed.) (1998), *The Correspondence of H. G. Wells: Volume 4, 1935–1946*, London: Pickering & Chatto, pp. 426–7.

[Wells, H. G.] (1943c) *The Rights of Man: An Essay in Collective Definition*, Brighton: Poynings.

Wells, H. G. (1942a) Letter to Lance Corporal Hlope, 24 November, in David C. Smith (ed.) (1998), *The Correspondence of H. G. Wells: Volume 4, 1935–1946*, London: Pickering & Chatto, pp. 352–3.

Wells H. G. (1942b) Letter to Marc Slonimsky, 20 August, in David C. Smith (ed.) (1998), *The Correspondence of H. G. Wells: Volume 4, 1935–1946*, London: Pickering & Chatto, pp. 337–8.

Wells, H. G. (1942c) Letter to the Editor, *Tribune*, 18 September 1942, in David C. Smith (ed.) (1998), *The Correspondence of H. G. Wells: Volume 4, 1935–1946*, London: Pickering & Chatto, pp. 339–40.

Wells, H. G. (1942d) *The Outlook for Homo Sapiens: An Unemotional Statement of the Things That Are Happening to Him Now, and of the Immediate Possibilities Confronting Him*, London: Readers Union/ Secker & Warburg.

Wells, H. G. (1942e) *Phœnix: A Summary of the Inescapable Conditions of World Reorganisation*, London: Secker & Warburg.

Wells, H. G. (1941) *Guide to the New World: A Handbook of Constructive World Revolution*, London: Gollancz.

Wells, H. G. (1940a) *The Common Sense of War and Peace: World Revolution or War Unending*, Harmondsworth: Penguin.

Wells, H. G. (1940b) *The New World Order: Whether It Is Attainable, How It Can Be Attained, and What Sort of World a World at Peace Will Have to Be*, London: Secker and Warburg.

Wells, H. G. [1940c] *The Rights of Man, or What Are We Fighting For?*, Harmondsworth: Penguin.

Wells, H. G. (1939a) *The Fate of Homo Sapiens: An Unemotional Statement of the Things That Are Happening to Him Now, and of the Immediate Possibilities Confronting Him*, London: Secker and Warburg.

Wells, H. G. (1939b) Letter to the Editor, *The Times*, 30 September, in David C. Smith (ed.) (1998), *The Correspondence of H. G. Wells: Volume 4, 1935–1946*, London: Pickering & Chatto, p. 238.

Wells, H. G. (1939c) Letter to the Editor, *The Times*, 23 October, in David C. Smith (ed.) (1998), *The Correspondence of H. G. Wells: Volume 4, 1935–1946*, London: Pickering & Chatto, pp. 242–4.

Wells, H. G. (1939d) *Travels of a Republican Radical in Search of Hot Water*, Harmondsworth: Penguin.

Wells, H. G. (1938) *World Brain*, London: Methuen.

Wells, H. G. (1935) 'Letter to Lord Esher', 2 November, in David C. Smith (ed.) (1998), *The Correspondence of H. G. Wells: Volume 4, 1935–1946*, London: Pickering & Chatto, pp. 46–9.

Wells, H. G. (1933) 'Letter to Prospective Members of P. E. N.', 27 November, in David C. Smith (ed.) (1998), *The Correspondence of H. G. Wells: Volume 3, 1919–1934*, London: Pickering & Chatto, pp. 508–9.

Wells, H. G. (1932) *After Democracy: Addresses and Papers on the Present World Situation*, London: Watts.

Wells, H. G. (*c.*1929–31) 'Letter to J. R. Clynes M. P.', in David C. Smith (ed.) (1998), *The Correspondence of H. G. Wells: Volume 3, 1919–1934*, London: Pickering & Chatto, pp. 353–4.

Wells, H. G. (1923) *Men Like Gods*, London: Cassell.

Wells, H. G. (1921) *The Salvaging of Civilization*, London: Cassell.

Wells, H. G. (1918) *In the Fourth Year: Anticipations of a World Peace*, London: Chatto & Windus.

Wells, H. G. (1917) *God the Invisible King*, London: Cassell.

Wells, H. G. (1904) 'Letter to Beatrice Webb', 29 April, in David C. Smith (ed.) (1998), *The Correspondence of H. G. Wells: Volume 2, 1904–1918*, London: Pickering & Chatto, pp. 24–7.

Wells, H. G. (1903) *Mankind in the Making*, London: Chapman & Hall.

9
Towards a Cosmopolitics of Heterogeneity: Borders, Communities and Refugees in Angelopoulos' Balkan Trilogy

Lasse Thomassen

I. Angelopoulos, heterogeneity and borders

What do three films by the Greek art film director Theo Angelopoulos have to do with questions of cosmopolitanism? And why is a political theorist like myself interested in Angelopoulos' films? The short answer is that Angelopoulos' three films from the 1990s, also referred to as the 'Balkan Trilogy' – *The Suspended Step of the Stork* (1991), *Ulysses' Gaze* (1995) and *Eternity and a Day* (1998) – are interventions in the debate on immigration, asylum and borders in today's Europe (Horton 1997a, 71).[1]

The aim of this chapter is both theoretical and political. In terms of the former, I argue that the notion of heterogeneity helps us in understanding the nature of borders and communities. This notion, which I take from the works of Jacques Derrida and Ernesto Laclau, refers to what escapes the logic of inside/outside, thus putting into questions the borders of communities whose identities rest on this logic (Derrida 2002; Laclau 2005, chapter 5).[2] Heterogeneity refers to a leftover from the constitution of identities and distinctions, a leftover that simultaneously helps constitute them. For Derrida and Laclau, identity is constituted through relations of difference. If the identities are to be stabilised, the totality of differences must be fixed so that the play of differences is stopped. Yet, this is only possible through the exclusion of a radical difference, one that is heterogeneous to the system of differences and, as such, cannot be represented within the system of differences (because it would have merely continued the play of differences). The heterogeneous is not simply the outside of an inside; it cannot be represented according to the inside/outside dichotomy. It is this radical difference that Derrida and Laclau refer to as heterogeneity. It makes possible the representation of what it simultaneously escapes and undermines, namely clear and distinct identities. It makes possible the spatial representation of identities and the borders between identities, yet also refers to the limit of this spatialisation. Being at one and the same time the condition of possibility and the condition of impossibility of the identities and limits of communities, heterogeneity highlights the fact that the latter are the result of contingent, historical struggles and will remain so.

The notion of heterogeneity raises important political questions in relation to immigration, asylum and nationalist discourses in contemporary Europe and beyond. As I argue, in his Balkan Trilogy, Angelopoulos provides us with a strong critique of Fortress Europe and of nationalist discourses. In the films, refugees are represented as heterogeneous: unable to find their place in a world divided into national communities by political borders they are neither simply excluded nor simply included. This is the political aim of the chapter. However, as I also argue, Angelopoulos' humanist openness to the other – to the illegal immigrants living at the bottom of our societies, for instance – must be paired with a scepticism about the possibility of eliminating exclusion altogether. This negotiation of inclusion and exclusion is what I refer to – with a term from Derrida – as cosmo*politics* (Derrida 2006, 220). I do not use this term in the same way as Derrida, who uses it to criticise a cosmopolitan politics which is still linked to the (nation)state. My point in keeping the term 'cosmopolitics' is to stress the impossibility of an inclusive mechanism – whether a state or not – that does not also involve some exclusion.

Here it is not a question of either being true to or betraying Angelopoulos. I take his work as a privileged site of thinking about the transformation of borders and communities because they attempt to make visible in a new way that which is invisible in the present, that which cannot be represented according to existing conceptual categories. Yet, I also argue that, pushed to its limits, problems emerge in Angelopoulos' discourse, problems that cannot simply be glossed over as mistakes or oversights – although they may also be that – but are, rather, irresolvable problems that one must nonetheless try to negotiate.

Theo Angelopoulos is at once a Greek, a European and a Balkan film director. Although his characters and landscapes are often indistinct and without clear national features, he has been preoccupied with Greek history, tradition and mythology, and his films often ask the question of what it means to belong to the Greek community. This is not a specifi-cally Greek question, however. Rather, his films pose the question of what it means to be at home anywhere in the world. They do so, among other things, by making the protagonists travel across borders in space and time until their (ethnic and national) identities become indistinct. Angelopoulos is also a European film director. The films in his Balkan Trilogy are voyages in and across Europe or, rather, at the limits of what we usually understand as Europe, namely the Balkans. They are also voy-ages back and forth in time, thus putting into question the dominant narratives of the history of the borders and identities of European nation-states. Finally, by focusing on the Balkans as the margins of Europe, Angelopoulos decentres the centre and makes us see it in a new light. Indeed, in his films, the Balkans is not something outside of Europe but instead shown to be an essential – geographical, cultural and political – part of Europe.[3]

In the following section, I primarily deal with the Balkan Trilogy, and especially *Eternity and a Day*. In the film immediately preceding the Balkan Trilogy, *Landscape in the Mist* (1988), one of the protagonists asks: 'What is the meaning of borders?' The Balkan (or Border) Trilogy seeks to answer this question in relation to, among other things, geographical and political borders (Schulz 2001, 117). Angelopoulos' first films from the late 1960s and early 1970s were overtly political and concerned with collective problems of what is to be done. Between this early political period and the latest period of existential films about borders and com-munities, there was a middle period of more personal films. Although his latest films are not overtly political in a traditional sense – for instance, they do not attempt to provide any answers – they take place against a political backdrop framing the lives of the characters of the films. As such, Angelopoulos is still of political interest. Indeed, the Balkan Trilogy asks important political questions about the identity and boundaries of communities in the wake of the rise of nationalist and xenophobic discourses in Europe since the fall of the Berlin Wall. It shows how borders have eroded and been rebuilt in Europe during the past fifteen years. Moreover, I argue that the real political value of Angelopoulos' films lies not so much in whether they provide solutions to problems or not, but in their attempt to make visible what is invisible in the present.

In the next three sections, I look at Angelopoulos' treatment of borders, refugees and communities, respectively. In the last two sections of the chapter, I then address some of the political implications of my argument.

II. Borders

The theme of borders – including national and political borders – is central to Angelopoulos' Balkan Trilogy. It is worth noting, however, that Angelopoulos himself emphasises that the borders in his films are not geographical, but 'personal' borders. For instance, according to Angelopoulos, *Eternity and a Day* is not about a physical border – that between Greece and Albania, between the official Europe and its backyard – but, rather, about a border between life and death: 'Borders are simply divisions, between here and there, between then and now. In this film it is a question of a division between life and death. It's a demarcation line' (Bachmann 2001, 106). Like his other films, *Eternity and a Day* is about the passing of spatial and temporal borders, in this case the literal passing away of the poet Alexander, the film's protagonist who is terminally ill, and who is only waiting to go into a hospice the following day. *Eternity and a Day* is not only about Alexander's passing away from life to death, though. In the film, the border between life and death is interweaved with political and national borders and the lives of refugees. For the Albanian refugees in the film, passing the physical and political border between Albania and Greece is a matter of life and death in two ways. First, in the sense that it is only by crossing the border into Greece that the refugees have a chance of making a living.[4] And, second, in the sense that the physical crossing through the land-mined no-man's land around the border proves fatal to some of them. As such, *Eternity and a Day* shows how physical and political borders influence the personal lives of people, that is, how their lives are literally and figuratively framed and enclosed by these borders.

This is also the case in the two other films in the Balkan Trilogy. *The Suspended Step of the Stork* takes place among refugees stranded in a small town on the border between Greece and Albania. The film and the refugees are, as the title suggests, suspended in this border area. The physical border is a river separating the two countries and even separating a man and a woman as they are getting married standing on each side of the river. The physical presence of the border in the river makes visible the significance of the border and what it does to people's minds and lives. As one of the main characters says about the refugees when he observes how they fight among themselves: 'It's the border that drives them mad. The Boundaries.' The border is not only a physical but also a mental presence. *The Suspended Step of the Stork* is an invitation to cross borders, however. The protagonist, a journalist who has come to find a story in the region, is transformed at the end of the film and starts crossing borders and reaching out to the refugees. This is made evident, for instance, in the use of the camera in the final scene where the journalist is seen approaching the river from the Greek side while the camera moves across the river in reverse, as it were, thus inviting the viewer to cross the border. This is the first time that we see the river from the other (Albanian) side, thus gesturing towards the transformation in the protagonist.[5]

Ulysses' Gaze, too, is a film about borders and border crossing, and here too a personal journey and border crossing is intertwined with the crossing of physical and political borders in the Balkans. As in *The Suspended Step of the Stork*, many of the borders in *Ulysses' Gaze* are rivers. The protagonist is told by a friend in Belgrade that 'Yugoslavia is full of rivers', suggesting that what was once Yugoslavia is now divided by political and national borders. However, in the film, the rivers are not only used to separate people but also to travel along to new places and to meet people – in short, to communicate. Thus, at the point where people and communities are separated, there is also the possibility of crossing borders and of travelling to the other side.

III. Refugees

The refugee theme is central to Angelopoulos' Balkan Trilogy. As he argues: 'Emigration and diaspora, refugees chased away from their home-land, crossing borders and seeking shelter, these are among the most burning social issues of our time' (in Fainaru 2001b, 76). The refugees in his films are a heterogeneous excess created by the organisation of polit-ical space into distinct nation-states. In all three films, we witness how refugees gather around and across the border between Greece and Albania, caught in a no-man's land. In *Eternity and a Day*, the protago-nist, Alexander, saves an Albanian boy from being caught by the police in Thessalonica, Greece. The boy thereby eludes the policing of political borders. Later in the film, Alexander also saves the boy from the mafia who catch Albanian street children in order to sell them off to rich, Western couples. In the first case, Alexander tries to save the boy from the symbolic structure of political sovereignty (the law); in the second case, he tries to save him from the flows of capital (money).

The boy refers to himself as *xenitis*, a Greek poetic expression meaning an outsider, someone living in exile, or, more precisely and importantly, some-one who is a stranger everywhere (Bachmann 2001, 108). The boy is, thus, not just a foreigner – someone who can be determined as one of 'them' as opposed to one of 'us' – but a stranger everywhere, that is, a stranger to the division between 'us' and 'them' or between 'home' and 'foreign'.

Alexander is trying to create a space for that which is foreign and heterogeneous. However, doing so, he is forced to rely on the very same
structures he is trying to escape. For instance, he uses money to buy back
the Albanian boy from the mafia, and when, at the end of the film, the
boy is sent off in the back of a truck on a ship (going to America), the
boy will still be caught up within the symbolic system of global capitalism. Moreover, Alexander and the boy do not speak the same language.
One could say that their relationship is outside language; yet, there are
attempts to use language to communicate, as for example with the term
xenitis. In none of these cases, resistance to existing oppressive structures
is possible from beyond or outside of those structures. We are dealing
with a subversion of them, rather than simply going beyond them.

Notice also that one cannot simply oppose borders and closure to
openness. For instance, the border exposes the refugees to danger and
death; yet, once crossed, the border also protects them against the death
they have escaped. The protection they receive on the Greek side of the
border is of course a mixed blessing: they must escape the sovereignty
(the state, the police, the law) that, at the same time, upholds the border
that protects them. The inclusion of the refugees is only possible insofar
as they are subsumed to the system of identities and divisions (borders,
states and so on) that, *at the same time*, excludes them. Their relationship
to inclusion and exclusion is undecidable, being simultaneously
included and excluded. Moreover, getting rid of borders can be a way of
asserting power; indeed, the inequalities and injustices that follow in
the wake of, especially economic, globalisation depend on the undermining of the borders of the nation-state, which allow strong states and
businesses to benefit from the free movement of capital and labour.
Therefore, we are not dealing with a simple opposition between, on the
one side, a logic of borders and divisions and, on the other side, a world
without borders.

The life and death of the refugees are linked to capitalism and
national identity in one additional and important way in the film. In a
scene in which Alexander and the Albanian boy find the boy's friend,
Selim, dead in the harbour, we see a small aircraft carrying a streamer for
a credit card from a Greek bank. The name of the card and the bank –
Ethnokarta, Ethniki Trapeza tis Ellados: National Card of the National
Bank of Greece – reappears in a scene later in the film. In the latter scene,
Selim's friends gather together in a building under construction in order
to burn Selim's clothes and bid him a last farewell. Alexander is there
too, and when he steps out into the street, we see a poster for the same
credit card and bank. Thus, in these two scenes, the life and death of

refugees are intertwined with capitalism and with the ethnos and the national community. The solution to the refugees' problems, it would seem, is the transformation of capitalism and of national communities and borders.

How this can be done may become evident if we consider the scene where the Albanian children burn the dead boy's clothes. In this scene, the distinction between inside and outside is subverted. The children, who are outsiders and excluded from the Greek community, create their own provisional community around the fire – their own 'inside', as it were. The community of Albanian children is at once excluded from the Greek community and exists within it. This is also made visible in the structure of the building in which they have the fire. As the building is only halfway finished, it is not clear whether the children are actually outside or inside; that is, the building does not have the structure that can establish a clear inside or outside. Like the building site, the community of refugees is a community under construction, a floating community that does not get settled down within determined borders, rather than an already constituted community. It is my contention that this precisely highlights the heterogeneous character of the refugees: they cannot be subsumed to a logic of inside/outside, that is, a logic of clear and stable borders between the respective identities of different communities.

The community of refugee children in *Eternity and a Day* is a community of those who are strangers everywhere, *xenitis*. They are neither simply Greek nor simply Albanian (or of some other determinable national identity). They cannot be recognised according to national distinctions. They are the neither/nor of the either/or – the neither Greek nor Albanian, neither European nor non-European. It is the discourse of national and political borders that forces a false choice on the refugees: are you foreigners or part of us? Are you Europeans or non-Europeans? And so on; thus representing the refugees in terms of 'us' and 'them', 'inside' and 'outside'. Although these discourses also speak of the outside, for them, the outside affirms and reaffirms the inside. Talk of an outside, of what is foreign and strange can be a way of policing the borders of the inside, so that while this outside is very much present within the discourse, it in no way threatens the inside. As Derrida writes, '[t]he "dialectics" of the same and the other, of outside and inside, of the homogeneous and the heterogeneous, are ... among the most *contorted* ones. The outside can always become again an "object" in the polarity subject/object, or the reassuring reality of what is outside the text; and there is sometimes an "inside" that is as troubling as the outside may be reassuring' (Derrida 2002, 67). The representation of something or someone as an outside(r) may be a way to respond to the heterogeneous that cannot be determined according to the logic of inside/outside. The heterogeneous – those who are strangers everywhere, *xenitis* – put into question the inside/outside distinction insofar as they continuously escape it. This is linked to how we understand what it means to be home and what it means to be a stranger, to which I now turn.

IV. Communities

The theme of belonging is central to Angelopoulos' films. He asks questions such as: What is a stranger? What does it mean to be home? Commenting on this, Angelopoulos has said that 'the stranger is not he who comes from the outside. To me, exile was always internal' (in Levieux 1998, my translation).[6] If the stranger cannot come from the outside, it is because there is no fully constituted home, or inside, in relation to which there can be an outside and in relation to which he can be a stranger. The distinction between home and stranger, us and them, inside and outside, is blurred because neither of the two poles is fully constituted as an entity with clear limits. The stranger is not a stranger as opposed to home or as opposed to us, nor is the stranger someone who is estranged from his home, but a stranger everywhere – *xenitis*. The stranger is in all of us as part of what it means to be home – a home out of joint.[7]

Yet, Angelopoulos also argues that ' "Home" for me is the place where we feel a balance in ourselves and between ourselves and the world – the feeling we've at last found a place where we're at ease' (quoted in Romney 1999). And, 'For me, the voyage is the only way of discovering myself [*moi-même*]' (quoted in Estève 1995, 171, my translation). Here we arrive at a hiatus in the interpretation of Angelopoulos' Balkan Trilogy and its view of communities and borders and of journeys and homes. There are two different conceptions of community and home at work in Angelopoulos' films, I argue. The protagonists in his films all undertake a journey or voyage in search of something. They may be in search of a home, and they may be crossing borders in order to arrive at a place of balance where they can feel at ease. This is one way of reading Angelopoulos' films and his own comments about them. Maria Rovisco (2004), for instance, interprets *The Suspended Step of the Stork* in this way: as a homecoming, as the discovery of one's identity after a period of destabilisation. Thus, while she acknowledges the transitional character of the refugee community in *The Suspended Step of the Stork*, she nonetheless believes that the refugees are able to feel at home here. Although I do not want to dispute that one may be able to come to terms with the transitional and unstable character of home, what is problematic is to think of the journey as a homecoming or a discovery as this assumes an already constituted and a given home or a self.

Another way of reading Angelopoulos' films is to stress the never-ending character of the journey and the search. If there is no home, if we are strangers everywhere (*xenitis*), then the search is not a search for an authentic home, but rather a displacement of the category of 'home'. We cross borders, but not in order to eventually arrive home. You may undertake the journey in order to create a dialogue with those on the other side: with the ones beyond the border or with the strangeness in yourself. In either case, what is true of the journey is also true of Angelopoulos' films: 'my films never really end. To me they are all "works in progress." Like building sites' (in Bachmann 2001, 102). And here we might add: like the community of refugees, like communities that are not self-identical, but out of joint (Horton 1997b, 109). 'For me', Angelopoulos says, 'every film is a voyage, everything is voyage, search. Knowledge comes to me during the voyage' (in Bachmann 2001, 109; see also Schulz 2001, 122). The protagonists in the three films in the Balkan Trilogy are all transformed in one way or the other by the journeys they undertake. The search, the journey is then what creates knowledge of and dialogue with the other. Not as an end-goal, but as a process, and therefore as something that must be continued. So, when asked what he is looking for, the protagonist in *Ulysses' Gaze* answers, 'Something that may not even exist', that is, not something lost to be recuperated. The same pattern of individuals searching for something that they do not know what reoccurs in Angelopoulos' other films. If the home is out of joint from the very beginning, then there is no home to arrive at or return to.[8]

Conceptions of community and borders are linked to conceptions of homes and journeys. In *Ulysses' Gaze*, the protagonist's friend says, 'God's first creation was the voyage. Then came doubt and nostalgia.' If the journey comes first, that is, if journey is prior to home, then the journey cannot start from home, and any nostalgic search for a lost home would be a mistake. And yet, the journey also seems to presuppose a home, as a starting point or a telos, in order to be a journey in the first place. It is a journey that puts the home into question at the very moment it presupposes it, making it impossible to imagine a journey that is neither to nor from a home. The journey, then, is both prior to and dependent on the home, and *vice versa*. What we are witnessing in Europe today is too much nostalgia and too little doubt, to use Angelopoulos' terms. The changes in the world and the breaking down of old borders have not been met with doubt about the nature and necessity of discourses of national communities and their borders; on the contrary, these have been reasserted and sometimes reinvented. What we seem to need is doubt about the necessity and essentiality of identities and borders. The answer to the mutual imbrication and subversion of journey and home is not nostalgia, but doubt about the need for a home that can be distinguished from the stranger, the journey. ... Instead, what we have witnessed in the Balkans and what we find across Europe today – nationalism, xenophobia, racism – is the nostalgia for a lost home, an authentic anchor in a sea of doubt as an answer to the question of where the journey is from and to.

V. Inclusion, exclusion and cosmo*politics*

Angelopoulos' Balkan Trilogy represents refugees as a heterogeneous excess from the division of political space into distinct communities by clear and stable borders. At the same time, there is an aporia at work: openness requires some closure, and yet the two sides are also opposed. It means that, strategically as well as conceptually, we cannot simply oppose closure to openness, home to journey. The task for the social critic is to focus on the heterogeneous elements and on what they make possible, and this is precisely what Angelopoulos is doing: making visible the heterogeneous excess from capitalism and nationalism. Focusing on these elements makes us able to imagine things otherwise, that is, to see possibilities for social and political transformation. The heterogeneous is the other side of the contingency that must be suppressed in order for existing frameworks – conceptual schemes, legal institutions, political borders and so on – appear natural and necessary. To highlight the heterogeneous, then, is to show the contingency of these frameworks and, thereby, the possibility of their transformation. This negotiation is what I refer to as a cosmo*politics*, because it brings to the fore the continuous political negotiation of the tension between inclusion and exclusion without ever being able to fully overcome that tension. Cosmo*politics*, understood in this sense, would be an alternative to the alternative between either the nation-state, and the exclusions associated with it, or a universally inclusive cosmopolitanism. As opposed to most accounts of cosmopolitanism, it would acknowledge the significance of belonging; and as opposed to communitarian and nationalist discourses, it puts into question the possibility and desirability of stable and fixed identities and borders.

In Angelopoulos' Balkan Trilogy, the refugees signal us towards the contingency of political borders. Although the image of the refugee in his films is bleak, the figure of the refugee is nonetheless also the starting point for thinking of the transformation of the space of the nation-state. The refugees occupy a position in-between, neither inside nor outside the community, that is, they are heterogeneous to political and national distinctions. The refugees make visible the violence, symbolic as well as physical, which institutes the borders of political and national communities. Angelopoulos' films represent what the borders of communities do to people's lives. The films attempt to make visible – through the realistic image – that which bears witness to the contingency of the identity and the limits of the community. However, the effect of the images is not a realistic representation of the heterogeneous, which would be impossible, but rather the creation of poetic images forcing the viewer to reflect on the images. Angelopoulos' films combine realistic, almost documentary, images (for instance, the sequence shot) with the suggestive power of poetic images. The suggestive power is based on the realistic images, but exceeds them (Horton 1997a, 5–6). Thus, the images of Angelopoulos' films, and indeed the films themselves, are not closed totalities. This forces the viewer to become active in the interpretation of the images and of the films – to fill the gap, as it were, between the realistic image and its poetic and political interpretation (Horton 1997a, 8). Hence, as argued above, the cinematic representation of heterogeneity forces the viewer to reflect on the historical conditions of this state of affairs and on how it could be transformed. In short, making visible the refugees as a heterogeneous excess forces the viewer to reflect on the contingency of the borders of our communities and on the violence that instituted them (see Fainaru 2001a, viii).

Heterogeneity, then, can be the point of entry for the reading of a text or, as in this case, a film, because it opens up the representational framework of the text or film. As such it is a point of entry for a writerly rather than a readerly reading of a text or a film, in Roland Barthes' sense of the terms (Barthes 1972, 249–60). Moreover, the endings of Angelopoulos' films are open to further interpretation and search by the viewer. For instance, the conclusion of *Eternity and a Day* is left open-ended: at the end of the film, we do not know what the poet Alexander will do next, and whether the film's depiction of his life is complete. In this sense, Angelopoulos' films are writerly films. They force the viewer to participate in the creation of the meaning of them, rather than passively consuming them. Although his films are largely devoid of suspense, Angelopoulos uses the suspension of images and action – for instance, the extensive use of long sequence shots – in order to force the viewer to reflect, not on what will happen next, but on the situation depicted in the film and to take a stand for or against what is happening. Obviously this also creates a challenge for anyone claiming to have understood Angelopoulos' films. Like communities, they remain suspended, in-between, and we do not arrive at a definite interpretation of the films because such an interpretation is impossible. And, like the interpretations of Angelopoulos' films, the negotiation of the tension between inclusion and exclusion remains incomplete.

Eternity and a day offers an alternative, however, namely the community of refugee children. This is a community without stable or clear limits, a community that is not like an inside to an outside. It is a community without a fixed centre; for instance, it is scattered across the city, only gathering momentarily. This image of a community, I will argue, is a way to start thinking about community, borders, inclusion and justice in terms of heterogeneity.

However, given that one cannot simply oppose closure to openness, the journey to the home and so on, this new community cannot be a cosmopolitan community if by that we mean the breaking down of borders or the breaking up of homes. This is not to say that post- and supra-national institutions should *prima facie* be rejected. On the contrary, in many cases such institutions will be preferable to the nation-state. Moreover, there may be good reasons for supra-national institutions to curb capitalism and rogue states. Thus, Angelopoulos himself suggests that the positive aspect of the European Union is that it leads to the abolition of national borders; the problem, he argues, is that, so far, this has only happened at an economic and not at a political level (Fainaru 2001d, 147).

Cosmopolitanism may be a step away from the exclusions that follow from national borders, but we should not therefore think that cosmopolitanism could do away with exclusions as such. There is no inclusion – of refugees, for example – without exclusion. And the possibility of undertaking a journey, especially if this is to be an equal possibility for all, must itself be supported by certain structures. There are certain journeys that are less desirable than others, for instance the refugees' journeys leaving them exposed to death. Inclusion and openness do not come out of nowhere; they must first be instituted, and this will involve some exclusion. Therefore the task is not simply to oppose exclusion but also to question *which* exclusions are made, and the *way* in which they are made. The question is how we react to the fact that exclusion is constitutive, that is, to the conceptually and strategically aporetic relationship between inclusion and exclusion.

My contention is that this requires that we think *otherwise* about inclusion and exclusion, borders and communities. With regard to this, Robert Goodin has put forward a critique of contemporary models of inclusion. According to Goodin, one of the problems with current uses of the terms inclusion and exclusion is that they work with a flawed notion of unity and inclusion. 'The true source of our anxieties ...', Goodin (1996, 344) writes, 'lies not in the practice of exclusion but in that of inclusion', because 'the problem of exclusion is that there *is* an inclusive community'. Hence, 'the solution is not to make our communities more inclusive but rather to change their nature' (Goodin 1996, 344). Since we tend to think of inclusion as emanating from a (nation-state) centre, the inclusion of the otherwise excluded merely confers a marginalised status upon the latter (348). As a consequence, Goodin proposes a new concept of the state. He envisages 'a system of multiple, overlapping "sovereignties," with lots of different levels and places one might lodge an application or an appeal' (364). For the people who nonetheless fall outside the sovereignty and protection of any state, 'we will need some agency ... to take residual responsibility for those who find no one else to take care of them' (366). 'This would not be an over-arching authority. It stands beneath, not above, the other elements of this larger network', in order 'to pick up the pieces that inevitably get left behind' (366). For Goodin, inclusion becomes a matter of adding new institutions – 'with lots of different levels and places' – as well as institutions to pick up the pieces and leftover. Although Goodin acknowledges the constitutivity of exclusion for inclusion, the problem with his proposal is that those who are residually included remain marginalised, which was what Goodin wanted to avoid in the first place. The task cannot simply be to add yet another inclusive institution. Rather, the task must be to rethink the relationship between inclusion and exclusion, and, on this basis, to rethink the way we build our institutions – precisely the task Goodin set himself. Rather than relegating the residuals to marginal positions within the system of inclusion or denoting them as foreign and thereby excluding them, thinking *differently* about inclusion/exclusion involves rethinking our notions of community, limits and inclusion in light of the heterogeneous remainders from our traditional ways of thinking about these things. This involves a renegotiation of community and home, including their decentring. It is for this reason that I have suggested that we take the status of refugees as the starting point for rethinking the way in which the boundaries of our communities are constituted.[9] Two, not incompatible, strategies are possible here. First of all, one has to ask why, today, social and political problems are often couched in terms of 'us' versus 'them'. It is necessary to criticise those discourses and instead use a language of humanity or, better, hybridity. Moreover, taking up Goodin's idea of a pluralisation of sovereignties, one could seek to create a plurality of sites and forms of inclusion and of contestation of exclusions. Inclusion and exclusion would then not be a matter of either/or, of either inclusion or exclusion, thus facilitating the continuous negotiation of the unstable relation between inclusion and exclusion.

VI. Heterogeneity and cosmo*politics*

As mentioned in the previous section, there has been a certain shift in the politics of Angelopoulos' films. As he says: 'I used to believe in politics. I now consider myself a non-believer' (in Romney 1999, 10). More specifically, there has been a shift from traditional Marxism to a certain humanism, where individuals represent a humanity shared by all. This is reflected in the protagonists of his films. Where they used to be collectives, they are now individuals. Nonetheless, as I have argued, the stories of individuals are set against a political context framing the lives of the individuals. Yet, there is an important ambiguity in Angelopoulos' films. His earlier films depicted collectives as, on the one hand, ultimately unrepresentable entities without clear limits and identities and, on the other hand, as mere representatives of History, thus in effect reducing the collectives to representatives of an underlying teleology of History. In his later works, including the Balkan Trilogy, this ambiguity disappears, but a new one emerges. In the later films, the protagonists are no longer collectives but individuals, often played by well-known actors, such as Marcello Mastroianni, Harvey Keitel and Bruno Ganz, thus stressing the individuality of the characters. Although this shift from collectives to individuals can be seen as a shift to a more bourgeois individualistic ideology, the individuals also become the faces – the vehicles and representatives – of a universal humanism. Yet, in Angelopoulos' Balkan Trilogy, there is also a displacement of space (of nation, community and so on) reflecting the idea of a home that is not fully constituted and cannot be represented. Both the earlier and the later films are, thus, political, even if in different ways (Jameson 1997, 86–94). What is important here are the different ways of being political: it can refer to the representation of History or a universal humanity, or it can refer to the making visible of the heterogeneous, that which cannot be represented in the present. In the latter case, politics refers to the negotiation of the aporetic relationship between inclusion and exclusion identified earlier, which is the starting point for a cosmo*politics* rather than a cosmopolitanism understood as a universal community, whether based on a Communist ideal or on a concept of humanity shared by all. I take the importance of Angelopoulos' Balkan Trilogy as an intervention in the debates about migration and national identity in this sense.

The humanism in Angelopoulos' films is connected to certain notions of home, language and communication. For instance, *Ulysses' Gaze* is the story of a search for 'a lost glance, a lost innocence', namely the less complicated world of the past (in Fainaru 2001c, 94–5, 97). Similarly, although Angelopoulos does not want us to go back to life in the village, he has a romantic view of life in the village: 'What do I want to happen [in Greece]? I simply want our life here to become more human. As you know we have lost so much in Athens. Crime, pollution, traffic, the impersonality of the city, so much. We need to return to those places to find much of what is still important, authentic to our lives' (in Horton 1997a, 206; cf. also ibid., 11). Angelopoulos opposes Athens to life outside the city, where the former is a deformed and distorted version of the true Greece represented by the latter (Horton 2001, 88). Although this romantic view in no way entails an image of an ethnically clean Greece, it seems to me to suggest a wrong approach to community. It suggests a harmonious image of social life, an image which historically has often functioned to hide underlying conflicts.

This romantic view is related to Angelopoulos' view of language and communication. He sees language and communication as a means to cross borders, to reach out and touch, and be touched by, the other. He states:

> I want a new politics in the world with vision. And this will not be a simple matter of balancing an economy and the military. It must be a new form of communication between people. (Horton 2001, 83; see also ibid., 88 and Horton 1997a, 208)

In all three films in the Balkan Trilogy, the hope of communication with the other is central: crossing the river at the end of *The Suspended Step of the Stork*, travelling across and along rivers in *Ulysses' Gaze* and exchanging words across language barriers in *Eternity and a Day*. Moreover, language and communication is a means to open ourselves to the other and decentre our selves. What I would like to insist on here is that this opening up to and inclusion of the other cannot be absolute; it is always conditional on its institutionalisation, involving the simultaneous exclusion of others. Communication, then, is not transparent or universal, but always proceeds in a particular idiom, even if we may never be completely 'at home' within that idiom.

There can be no going back or forward to a situation of non-exclusion and non-violence. What we need in this regard is a bit of doubt about the possibility of getting rid of exclusion. This argument for the constitutive necessity of borders and exclusions is not an argument for the necessity of any *particular* borders or exclusions or any particular *kinds* of borders or exclusions. From the unavoidability of borders and exclusions nothing follows about the justifiability of any particular borders or exclusions. Concrete borders and exclusions are precisely the contingent results of historical political and social struggles. Likewise, we may be able to create more inclusive societies than the societies in which we live today, but this depends on concrete political interventions in concrete circumstances. What political theory can attempt to do is to provide us with a different way of approaching these questions, a different way of seeing, by showing us what cannot be seen in the present.

The notion of heterogeneity is an attempt to do just this. It forces us to reflect on the borders that we have created, and on the exclusions that we have made. And it forces us to try to imagine things otherwise, for instance a Europe that is no Fortress Europe *and* a Europe that is strong, sovereign and protective against global capitalism and rogue states. In this regard, it is not enough to break down existing borders and divisions; one needs to break with a certain way of thinking identity, community and home, as argued above. To use the argument from Derrida's *The Other Heading*, identity is marked by *différance*: identities cannot be spatialised completely through their difference with other differences; there is something escaping their constitution, making them to come (*à-venir*). This decentring is depicted as journeys across space and time in Angelopoulos' films, thus making identities untimely and out of joint. Of course, here one should not oppose space and time; there is also a representation of time that is spatial, for instance a certain representation of the history of the nation as evolving teleologically from a determinate starting point.

This argument does not imply that we can do justice to the heterogeneous, however, because exclusion and violence cannot be eliminated. In other words, since the heterogeneous is heterogeneous to institutions of justice (law), doing justice to the heterogeneous is always deferred, to-come (Derrida 1990, 969f). We cannot represent the heterogeneous in a manner that does justice to it, representing it as it 'really' is in its 'essence', because it has no essential identity. Likewise, we cannot do justice by creating a new home for the heterogeneous, because the heterogeneous is what escapes and resists the creation of a home. Rather than a cosmopolitan inclusion of the other, we need a cosmo*political* negotiation of the relationship between inclusion and exclusion. To justice there is always a tomorrow escaping any attempt to make justice determinate and present. This futural excess over the present is also expressed in the paradoxical formulation of the title *Eternity* and *a Day*. 'How long does tomorrow last?' the poet Alexander asks. The answer he gets is, 'An eternity and a day.' The most we can do is to represent the heterogeneous in a (necessarily) distorted way, whether artistically or politically. And this means that our representations as well as our institutions are marked by this impossibility of doing justice to singularity. As such, the possibility of their contestation, of their subversion, must be, as far as is possible, built into them. For instance, the identities of our communities must be contestable through the contestation of the immigration and asylum policies supporting, and supported by, them.

We might be tempted to think that some refugees are more heterogeneous than others, for instance stateless refugees. There is nothing inherently heterogeneous about refugees, however, and refugees 'are' not heterogeneity. The term heterogeneity is merely a non-synonymous substitute I use to refer to things that occupy a certain position in relation to conceptual and representational distinctions within a given discourse. The figure of the refugee, as represented in Angelopoulos' Balkan Trilogy, does not enjoy an essential privilege in relation to the category of heterogeneity, even if I have used it as an example of the latter here. In this regard, one must avoid, as far as possible, any ontologisation of the refugee as heterogeneity or of the category of heterogeneity itself. There is an inescapable tension between the impossibility of representing the heterogeneous and the figure of the refugee as represented by Angelopoulos, for instance. This is a productive tension, however, because it calls attention to the essential danger of any attempt to represent what cannot be represented, whether as a political strategy or merely as the attempt to grasp the unrepresentable with categories such as 'unrepresentable' and 'heterogeneity'. Heterogeneity, for instance, does not take us beyond representation; it is, rather, an internal limit to representation. This tension or paradox should not lead to passivity or defeatism, but to the celebration of the open-ended character of cosmo*politics*. What is more, although I have privileged the figure of the refugee in the preceding, the refugee is only one among several possible sites of political transformation, none of which can be privileged *a priori*.

The refugee is not an essential part of a cosmo*politics*. Nor are Angelopoulos' films essentially privileged starting points for thinking differently about borders and communities, even if he does provide us with one possible representation of these.

Acknowledgements

Thanks to Lars Tønder, Beatriz Martínez, Marina Prentoulis, Davide Panagia and Peo Hansen for their comments on earlier versions of the chapter.

Notes

An earlier and different version of this chapter appeared in 2005 as 'Heterogeneity and Justice: Borders and Communities in Angelopoulos' *Eternity and a Day*', *Contemporary Justice Review* (2005) Vol. 8, No. 4, 381–95.

1. Angelopoulos' most recent film, *Trilogy: The Weeping Meadow* (2004) also takes up the issue of migration, which was also present in some of his earlier films, including *Landscape in the Mist* (1988).
2. Laclau explicitly links heterogeneity to the constitution of the limits and identities of communities. For an exploration of this – including in relation to Derrida's work – see (Thomassen 2005, chapter 6).
3. On Angelopoulos in relation to 'Balkan Cinema', see (Iordanova 1996, 888).
4. Hence, this is also why it is ultimately impossible to distinguish between (political) refugees and (economic) immigrants, as if the former were a matter of life or death and the latter merely a matter of economic comfort. As a consequence, I use the term 'refugees' to refer to both groups in the following section.
5. For a similar reading of *The Suspended Step of the Stork*, see Ishaghpour 1992, although he distinguishes between (1) the guards guarding and upholding the border, (2) the refugees who are looking for a home, and (3) the disappeared politician, whom the journalist has come to find, and who has rejected the ideology of borders, home and the 'proper' ('idéologies du "propre"', Ishaghpour 1992, 168). Compare Maria Rovisco's (2004) different interpretation of this film.
6. Angelopoulos (2004, my translation) says the same about himself: 'I have always felt as if I were in exile in my own [proper] country, a kind of interior exile. I have never found my home [domicile], a place where I feel in harmony with myself and with the world. Like my characters, I feel lost'.
7. For a related analysis of the use of 'home' in political discourse, see Honig, 1996. See Derrida 1992, 9–10, on the idea of identity as always different from itself.
8. The difference between the two interpretations of Angelopoulos' films could be expressed as the difference between Heidegger's phenomenological and Derrida's deconstructive view of language. See Angelopoulos' comments on Heidegger and language in (Schulz 2001, 121). On this, see also (Ravetto 1998).
9. For a similar attempt to do this, see (Critchley 2005).

References

Angelopoulos, T. (2004) 'Entretien avec Theo Angelopoulos', *Le Monde* 13 July.

Bachmann, G. (2001) 'The Time that Flows by: *Eternity and a Day*', in D. Fainaru (ed.), *Theo Angelopoulos: Interviews*, Jackson, MS: University Press of Mississippi, pp. 101–12.

Barthes, R. (1972) *Critical Essays* trans. R. Howard, Evanston, IL: Northwestern University Press.

Critchley, S. (2005) 'True Democracy – Marx, Political Subjectivity and Anarchic Meta-politics', in L. Tønder and L. Thomassen (eds), *Radical Democracy: Politics between Abundance and Lack*, Manchester: Manchester University Press, chapter 13.

Derrida, J. (2006) 'Hostipitality', in L. Thomassen (ed.), *The Derrida–Habermas Reader*, Edinburgh: Edinburgh University Press, pp. 208–30.

Derrida, J. (2002) *Positions*, 2nd edn, trans. A. Bass, London: Continuum.

Derrida, J. (1992) *The Other Heading: Reflections on Today's Europe* trans. P.-A. Brault and M. B. Naas, Bloomington, IN: Indiana University Press.

Derrida, J. (1990) 'Force of Law: The "Mystical Foundation of Authority" ' trans. M. Quaintance, *Cardozo Law Review*, Vol.11, No.5.

Estève, M. (1995) 'Le regard d'Ulysse de Théo Angelopoulos', *Esprit*, Vol. 18, No. 10, 172–5.

Fainaru, D. (2001a) 'Introduction', in D. Fainaru (ed.), *Theo Angelopoulos: Interviews*, Jackson, MS: University Press of Mississippi, pp. vii–xvii

Fainaru, E. (2001b) 'Silence Is as Meaningful as Any Dialogue: *The Suspended Step of the Stork*', in D. Fainaru (ed.), *Theo Angelopoulos: Interviews*, Jackson, MS: University Press of Mississippi, pp. 75–82.

Fainaru, D. (2001c) 'The Human Experience in One Gaze: *Ulysses' Gaze*', in D. Fainaru (ed.), *Theo Angelopoulos: Interviews*, Jackson, MS: University Press of Mississippi, pp. 93–100

Fainaru, D. (2001d) '… And about All the Rest', in D. Fainaru (ed.), *Theo Angelopoulos: Interviews*, Jackson, MS: University Press of Mississippi, pp. 123–49.

Goodin, R. (1996) 'Inclusion and Exclusion', *Archives Européennes de Sociologie*, Vol. 37, 2.

Honig, B. (1996) 'Difference, Dilemmas, and the Politics of Home', in S. Benhabib (ed.), *Democracy and Difference: Contesting the Boundaries of the Political*, Princeton: Princeton University Press, pp. 257–77.

Horton, A. (2001) 'National Culture and Individual Vision', in D. Fainaru (ed.), *Theo Angelopoulos: Interviews*, Jackson, MS: University Press of Mississippi, pp. 83–8.

Horton, A. (1997a) *The Films of Theo Angelopoulos: A Cinema of Contemplation*, Princeton, NJ: Princeton University Press.

Horton, A. (1997b) ' "What Do Our Souls Seek?": An Interview with Theo Angelopoulos', in A. Horton (ed.), *The Last Modernist: The Films of Theo Angelopoulos*, Westport, CT: Praeger, pp. 96–110

Iordanova, D. (1996) 'Conceptualizing the Balkans in Film', *Slavic Review*, Vol. 55, No. 4, 882–90.

Ishaghpour, Y. (1992) 'Le pas suspendu de la cicogne: la musique du paysage', *Les Temps Modernes*, Vol. 47, No. 548, 162–74.

Jameson, F. (1997) 'Theo Angelopoulos: The Past as History, the Future as Form', in A. Horton (ed.), *The Last Modernist: The Films of Theo Angelopoulos*, Westport, CT: Praeger, pp. 78–95.

Laclau, E. (2005) *On Populist Reason*, London: Verso.

Levieux, M. (1998) 'Pour Théo Angelopoulos, l'exil a toujours été intérieur', *Journal l'Humanité*, 25 May.

Ravetto, K. (1998) 'Mytho-poetic Cinema: Cinemas of Disappearance', *Third Text*, Vol. 3, 55.

Romney, J. (1999) 'Make it Yellow', *Sight and Sound*, Vol. 9, No. 5, 8–11.

Rovisco, M. (2004) *European Films of Voyage: Nation, Boundaries and Identity*, Oxford and New York: Berghahn Books.

Schulz, G. (2001) 'I Shoot the Way I Breathe: *Eternity and a Day*', in D. Fainaru (ed.), *Theo Angelopoulos: Interviews*, Jackson, MS: University Press of Mississippi, pp. 117–22.

Thomassen, L. (2005) 'In/Exclusions: Towards a Radical Democratic Approach to Exclusion', in L. Tønder and L. Thomassen (eds), *Radical Democracy: Politics between Abundance and Lack*, Manchester: Manchester University Press, chapter 6.

Part IV
Revisiting Kant

Part IV

Revisiting Kant

10
Soul and Cosmos in Kant: A Commentary on 'Two Things Fill the Mind ...'

Howard Caygill

Zwei Dinge erfüllen das Gemüt mit immer neuer und zunehmender Bewunderung und Ehrfurcht, je öfter und anhaltender sich das Nachdenken damit beschäftigt: der bestirnte Himmel über mir und das moralische Gesetz in mir. Beide darf ich nicht als in Dunkelheiten verhüllt oder im Überschwenglichen, außer meiner Gesichtskreise suchen und bloß vermuten; ich sehe sie vor mir und verknüpfe sie unmittelbar mit dem Bewußtsein meiner Existenz. Das erste fängt von dem Platze an, dem ich in der äußeren Sinnenwelt einnehme, und erweitert die Verknüpfung, darin ich stehe, ins unabsehlich Große mit Welten über Welten und Systemen von Systemen, überdem noch in grenzenlose Zeiten ihrer periodischen Bewegung, deren Anfang und Fortdauer. Das Zweite fängt von meinem unsichtbaren Selbst, meiner Persönlichkeit an und stellt mich in einer Welt dar, die wahre Unendlichkeit hat, aber nur dem Verstand spürbar ist, und mit welcher (dadurch aber auch zugleich mit allen jenen sichtbaren Welten) ich mich nicht wie dort in bloß zufälliger, sondern allgemeiner und notwendiger Verknüpfung erkenne. Der erstere Anblick einer zahllosen Weltmenge vernichtet gleichsam meine Wichtigkeit als einer tierischen Geschöpfs, das die Materie daraus es ward, dem Planeten (einem bloßen Punkt im Weltall) wieder zurückgeben muß, nachdem es eine kurze Zeit (man weiß nicht wie) mit Lebenskraft versehen gewesen. Der zweite erhebt dagegen meinen Wert als einer Intelligenz unendlich durch meine Persönlichkeit, in welcher das moralische Gesetz mir ein von der Tierheit und selbst von der ganzen Sinnenwelt unabhängiges Leben offenbart, wenigstens soviel sich aus der zweckmäßigen Bestimmung meines Daseins durch dieses Gesetz, welche nicht auf Bedingungen und Grenzen dieses Leben eingeschränkt ist, sondern ins Unendliche geht, abnehmen lasst. (Kant 1959, 186)

Two things fill the mind with ever new and increasing wonder and awe, the more often and constantly reflection concerns itself with them: the starry heavens above me and the moral law within me. I need not seek or intimate them beyond my horizon, shrouded in darkness or clothed in exaltation; I see them both before me and tie them immediately with the consciousness of my existence. The first begins from the place I occupy in the external world of sense, and extends the ties in which I stand into the unfathomable immensity of worlds beyond worlds and systems within systems and then into the limitless times of their periodic motion, their beginning and continuation. The second begins with my invisible self, my personality, and shows me in a world that has true infinity, but is discernible only through the understanding and with which (through which but at that the same time with all those visible worlds) I know myself to be tied in a universal and necessary and not just, as there, in a contingent way. The first view of a countless multitude of worlds annihilates my significance as an animal creature, which must give back to the planet (a mere point in the universe) the matter from which it came, the matter which is for a little time provided with vital force, we know not how. The latter, on the contrary, infinitely raises my worth as that of an intelligence by my personality, in which the moral law reveals a life independent of all animality and even of the whole world of sense – at least so far as it may be inferred from the final destination assigned to my existence by this law, a destination which is not restricted to the conditions and boundaries of this life but reaches into the infinite. (Kant 1993a,169)

The most cited sentence from the works of Kant is found in the conclusion of *The Critique of Practical Reason*. Apparently relaxing after the rigours of sustained reflection on the moral law, Kant mused on the 'Two things that fill the Mind ...' Yet, this seemingly perspicuous and innocent meditation contains within it many layers of significance and points of perplexity that have been overlooked. The meditation upon the perplexities of the text offers a point of entry into a Kantian physiology that links soul and cosmos in ways far stranger than would be expected from the author of the paralogisms of psychology and the cosmological antinomies in the 'Transcendental Dialectic' of the *Critique of Pure Reason*. It also provides a point of departure for an examination of Kant's medical philosophy whose influence on early nineteenth-century romantic medicine and even upon the allegedly anti-romantic pathology of Rudolf Virchow is enormous but still little understood.

I. The infinite analogy

In order to motivate the close work of commenting upon the paragraph and analysing how it works and what its tropes and terms mean, it might be useful to stress the completely overlooked perversity of Kant's parallel between the 'starry heavens' and the 'moral law'. It is necessary to ask what exactly it was that Kant saw when he looked up at night. From his subsequent description of the heavens in the same paragraph it would appear that Kant saw something that was seen by very few others in his century. From his place in the 'external world of sense' Kant moves from his vision of the stars – 'I see them before me' – to an *'Unabsehlich-Große'* an unsurveyable magnitude' of 'worlds beyond worlds and systems within systems and then into the limitless times of their periodical motion, their beginning and their continuation' (Kant 1993a, 166). Apart from the evocation of what in the *Critique of Judgement* will be called the experience of the – 'mathematical sublime' and beyond the contrasting tropes of worlds *beyond* worlds and systems *within* systems that intimate their periodic motion, the description of the infinite universe is clear and definite. Yet, this was very much a deviant view, one for holding which, 150 years before Kant, Giordano Bruno was put to death. Kant is thus comparing the moral law with a deviant and heretical view of universe, one not widely accepted among scientists and philosophers at the time, let alone the general public (and would not be for at least another century), and one that would have been met with sensations of distaste and even horror. The question then arises of why Kant should want to compare the majesty of the moral law that he has just reverently described in the *Critique* with what many contemporary readers would have regarded as an abhorrent, and even despised view of the heavens?

One possible approach to an answer lies in the analysis the aesthetic structure of the sentence and the paragraph that follows it. Following the analysis developed by Kant in the *Critique of Judgement*, it is possible to ask whether the sentence and paragraph obeys the rules of the beautiful or the sublime. In the case of the beautiful, one whose logic seems to have been automatically assumed in most readings of the sentence, the relationship between the two terms – starry heavens and moral law – is understood in terms of an analogy. According to section 59 of the *Critique of Judgement* the hypotyposis of symbol and analogy was identified as one of the structures underlying the experience of the beautiful. In section 59, Kant distinguishes between two species of hypotyposis: schema and symbol – both share the generic characteristic of 'presentation', but differ according to mode. The schema presents intuitions to concepts, whereas the symbol presents them 'according to analogy'. In analogy, judgement has a double function, 'first in applying the concept to an object of a sensible intuition, and then, second, in applying the mere rule of its reflection upon that intuition upon quite another object' (Kant 1988, 222, section 59).

As an analogy, the moral law stands in the same relation – applies the same rule of reflection – to the finite subject, as do the starry heavens. In this case, it is infinity which serves as the rule of reflection applied analogically to both the starry heavens and the moral law.

The analogical experience has for Kant a number of specific character-istics. It is usually associated with the beautiful, the analogy being iden-tified etymologically as 'proportion' and in the tradition issuing specifically from Baumgarten, with harmony. For Kant, the beautiful consists in the experience of harmony, whether this is located in the object or, more commonly for Kant, in the harmony of the *Gemütskräfte*. However, when the rule of reflection in question is infinite, then strange things happen to the analogy. Proportion is established on the basis of disproportion – neither infinity being commensurable with the other – and indeed adopts almost an antagonist relation between the rules of relationship. The analogy of infinity loses its proportioned, harmonic quality, and begins to approximate more fully to the sublime. The sub-lime is characterised by a pulsar movement, variously described in the *Critique of Judgement* in terms of inhibition and discharge, and repulsion and attraction. At infinity, the beautiful become sublime, and the move-ment of the sublime stabilises in the harmony of the beautiful. Returning to the specific analogy of the conclusion to the *Critique of Practical Reason*, the terms of the analogy are the 'starry heavens' and the 'moral law' and the predominant rule of relation is 'infinity'. Both the starry heavens and the moral law relate to the finite subject as 'things' which 'fill the mind with ever new and increasing wonder and awe'. The analogy is clear, but every term in it is far from being so. We shall return below to what Kant means by 'mind' (*Gemüt*) and to the extent to which it is empty and can be filled, as we shall with the by no means self-evident notions of the 'ever new,' 'increase' and of course 'wonder and awe'. The analogy also consists in both the moral law and the starry heavens possessing the property of being immediately visible to a finite subject – *'ich sehe sie vor mir'* 'I see them before me'. By virtue of this visibility the finite subject can *'verknüpfe sie* unmittelbar mit dem *Bewußtsein* meiner Existenz' 'tie them immediately with the consciousness of my existence'. Yet, at this point the analogy begins to complicate itself, especially with the reference to *'Bewußtsein meiner Existenz'* a formula which brings the *Gemüt* back into the equation, 'consciousness of my existence' being one of its defining properties. A complication emerges in so far as the prevailing rule of reflection is infinity, but is supplemented by a second analogy according to which 'immediate visibility' and 'consciousness of my existence' – the *Gemüt* – is the rule of reflection that sustains the analogy. It is also the *Gemüt* that would be filled by the infinities of the starry heavens and the moral law.

Before examining the meaning of *Gemüt*, it is necessary to look more closely at the work of infinity as a rule of reflection. This requires the putting into question of the very nature of the analogy at work in the passage under discussion. The notion that the moral law and the starry heavens are the equivalent terms of an analogy is shaken by the horrific character of the infinite starry heavens that Kant saw before him. In place of the harmonious experience of the beautiful, the analogy between the starry heavens and the moral law emerges as rather more perverse, being driven by a polar opposition between its terms. This experience brings the analogy into the orbit of the sublime, with its pulsatory movement described in the *Critique of Judgement* in terms of a *Hemmung* (inhibition following repulsion) of the vital forces and their *Ergießung* (discharge following attraction) (section 23), a movement which gives increase, since the overcoming of an inhibition provokes a greater discharge. Read in these terms, the passage in question may be situated within the corporeal experience of polar pulsation of the sublime rather than the harmonising experience of the beautiful. The terms of the analogy possess a reversed polarity,[1] with the experience moving between disgust at the infinity of the universe and reverence for the moral law: the *Hemmung* provoked by the disgusting spectacle of unlimited 'worlds beyond worlds and systems within systems' enhances the *Ergießung* achieved when the gaze turns to the moral law. In this view, consciousness of existence, or *Gemüt*, is 'filled' by 'new and increasing wonder and awe' with each, enhanced experience of inhibition and discharge.

Suspending the prejudices of decades of reading of this paragraph as a beautiful analogy, and turning to it afresh, it does indeed seem as if it is structured in terms of a sublime pulsation. Indeed, the overall organisation of the paragraph is pulsar. Kant provokes a series of pulses between the starry heavens and the moral law that are staged in terms of 'the first' (the starry heavens) and 'the second' (the moral law), and which produce an effect of emptying and filling that, we shall see not coincidentally, echoes that of the *Anfang* and *Fortdauer* of the infinite and repeatedly new universe. This same pulsar movement of 'the two things' 'fills' the *Gemüt* with 'ever new and increasing wonder and awe' precisely in so far as it provokes its *Hemmung* and *Ergießung*. The pulsar experience also takes the form of repulsion, an emptying or shying away of the *Gemüt* before the object, and attraction, the filling of the *Gemüt*, even to the point of overflowing in *Ergießung*.

The first pulsar movement is evident in the successive sentences beginning 'Der erste *fängt* von ... an' 'The heavens begin ...' and 'Der zweite *fängt* von ... an' 'The latter [moral law] begins ...'. The first sentence effects a movement of reduction and limitation – literally *Hemmung*. The place where I stand gazing up at the heavens and whose ties I extend to the universe is rendered insignificant before what Leopardi would call the 'sterminatory' scale of the cosmos. Kant describes this experience of disorientation more vividly in his discussion of the breakdown of measurement in the sublime of section 26 of the *Critique of Judgement*. There he moves from the measurement of a tree by the scale of the human body, to that of a mountain by the tree, to that of the earth by the mountain, to that of the solar system by the earth, to the milky where the measurement breaks down before *'die unermeßliche Menge solcher Milchstraßensysteme unter dem Namen der Nebelsterne* [the immeasurable set of such milky ways that are called nebulae]'. The breakdown of human measure before the starry heavens would itself be a demoralising and disorienting experience, one compounded by Kant by adding to the intimations of spatial infinity, the limitless temporal repetitions of the universe. Arriving at this extreme *Hemmung*, where the limitless of the starry heavens disrupts the tranquility of stargazer, Kant provokes a polar switch.

At the point of repulsion and self-loss before the immensity of the starry heavens, Kant summons up the moral law. The latter begins from the invisible self, the 'person' – the stage of development that in the *Religion Within the Limits of Reason Alone* is held to succeed animality and humanity (Kant 1960, 21). The point of view of personality reveals a 'true infinity' one implicitly opposed to the 'false infinity' of the starry heavens. The true infinity is discernible by the understanding through the presence of 'universality and necessity' – the fundamental quantitative and modal properties of any legitimate judgement of the understanding according to Kant. In this movement, the repulsion provoked by false infinity of the starry heavens is countered by the true infinity of personality (here playing the role adopted by imagination in the third *Critique*). Before the starry heavens, consciousness of existence is disrupted by the infinite vastness of the universe and its contingent links with it; from the standpoint of the moral law, however, consciousness of existence is experienced as universal and necessary. In the sublime movement between the two, consciousness of existence is emptied and filled, each time anew and with an increase. It is a movement to which Kant, in the *Critique of Judgement*, gives the name 'life'.

In the subsequent two sentences of 'Two things fill the mind ...' Kant augments the pulsar movement of the analogy by repeating it at an enhanced level, at the same time making explicit the links between the analogy and the stages of animate life. The first glimpse of countless world-sets 'annihilates my significance as an animal creature'. The extreme case of *Hemmung*, annihilates the significance of my animal life in a peculiar way, namely by reminding me that the matter of my animated body must be restituted to the planet: 'the matter out of which it came must be returned to the planet (a mere point in the universe)'. The sight of the starry heavens reminds the stargazer of their mortality and reduction of matter. The prospect of the reduction to matter, the annihilation of animal life provokes a small turn in the sentence towards the question of life. The matter of the animate body must be returned to the planet (without increase it would seem) ' which is for a little time provided with vital force (*Lebenskraft*), we know not how ...'. The sight of the starry heavens intimates the annihilation of this life and the reduction of stargazer to matter, but at same time raises the question of the meaning of that life, and the mystery of animate matter or 'life'. With this second reflection, nested within the annihilation, the *Hemmung* begins to turn towards *Ergießung*.[2]

From the repulsive intimations of annihilation, loss of animal life, reduction to matter and death provoked by the spectacle of the starry heavens, Kant turns to their opposite. Annihilation of my significance is succeeded by the contrary 'raising of my worth'. The sterminatory sense of the fragility of my matter-bound animal life is succeeded by 'personality' or my worth as an 'immortal intelligence,' a sense that reveals a 'consciousness of existence' or life that is 'independent of animality and from the sensuous world'. Yet instead of remaining with this exhalted

Ergießung, Kant begins the turn back towards limitation by qualifying the 'purposive determination of my existence through this law' that is not 'limited to the conditions and limits of life' but reaches into the infinite, with the phrase 'as least in so far as'. The cycle of *Hemmung* and *Ergießung*, repulsion and attraction, is thus set to recommence, as the exaltation of personality begins to be shrouded by the shadows of the limits of animal life.

The recommencement of the movement between the starry heavens and the moral law is part of the ineluctable movement of human life between the repulsion of *Hemmung* and the attraction of *Ergießung*. For the polar opposites of the starry heavens and the moral law oscillate between animality and personality – there is not a direct location of the human in this paragraph. The human is not mentioned since it provides the setting upon which the movement between animality and personality is played out – indeed, the human is this playing out. The *Gemüt* that is filled and emptied by the movement between animality and personality is the human soul, that can never be entirely emptied or filled, but is itself the movement of emptying and filling, the mysterious 'vital force'. Cosmos and the soul are closely linked in this movement, with the starry heavens prompting the gaze 'above me' and the moral law 'within me'. This perplexed gaze, turning in and out of the body, sees itself as at once animal and immortal, is confused in turn by the shadows and the exalted light. Repulsive strophe prompts attractive counter-strophe whose unstable excess provokes repulsive counter-strophe, an unstable polar oscillation oriented towards infinity but ever failing that point where the sublime oscillation settles into the harmony of the beautiful.

It is precisely such perplexities of the soul that the critical philosophy was supposed to relieve us of. The section of the *Critique of Pure Reason* on the 'Systems of Cosmological Ideas' – 'The Antinomy of Pure Reason' – showed that the cosmos could not be an object of experience. Why be terrified by the infinite universe in 1786 if it had been shown in 1781 that it could not be an object of experience? The therapeutic contribution of the *Critique* was intended to liberate the soul from concerns about the temporal and spatial beginnings and ends of the universe, its atomic or non-atomic composition, and its implications for freedom. An enlightenment thinker such as Christian Wolff could comfortably link the soul and the cosmos with a phrase such as 'Before we can understand what the soul is ... we must first learn what the constitution of the world is', thereby taking for granted that both soul and cosmos were possible objects of experience and thus knowledge, (Wolff 1719, section 540).

In contrast, Kant's position is far less secure. Disqualifying the cosmos and the soul as objects of experience in the 'Transcendental Dialectic' he acknowledged their peculiar character arising from their links with the infinite. Wolff's understanding of the cosmos as finite permitted it to be an object of knowledge from which could be deduced the knowledge of the soul; Kant's understanding of the cosmos disrupted both its own status as an object as well as that of the soul. What emerges in the *Critique of Practical Reason* is that the universe is a peculiar 'thing' – not a possible object of experience but nevertheless present through the affects of wonder and awe. The universe, like the moral law, is an impossible object of experience that Kant can nevertheless 'see before me'. Perhaps it is this spectral quality of the cosmos that contributes to the uncanny affects that it provokes in the soul, abnegation before and exaltation above it. In order to understand this better it is necessary to move the focus of the commentary from the infinite and its sublime analogies to an inquiry into the notion of seeing that which is not a possible object of experience.

II. Light and the cosmos

The starry heavens are infinite, but within my horizon; neither shrouded in darkness nor exalted they are object of vision – I see them before me and tie them immediately with 'the consciousness of my existence'. We may return to the question posed earlier of what it was Kant saw when he looked up at the night sky, but now inflecting it from *what* he saw to *how* he saw it. But what was it that enabled Kant to see the stars before him and not their light? It is light that enabled Kant to link his perception of the stars and the infinity of the cosmos, light is both of the object – it is that which is shown – and of the subject, being that which is seen. It is light, also, that allows for the 'immediate consciousness of my existence' that is *Gemüt*, suggesting further that the relationship between light and *Lebenskraft*, the cosmos and the soul, between cosmology and physiology, is more intimate than has been suspected. Kantian 'enlightenment' is not simply a question of knowledge, but involves an understanding of the nature of the cosmos and, closely related to, the mystery of the soul, or how matter may come to be infused with life.

The inquiry into the link between seeing the light of the stars and the 'consciousness of my existence' that it provokes raises the question of the relationship between soul and cosmos. This is a complex and a little-explored area of Kantian research that reveals a physiological dimension to his thought that, although inconspicuous, continues to inform the critical philosophy. A preliminary outline of the mutual implication of cosmology and physiology that is hinted at in the 'Two things fill the mind ...' passage may be sketched by a reading of the early and much neglected text: *Universal Natural History and the Theory of the Heavens* (1755), whose conclusion anticipates that of the second *Critique* and the late, and also much neglected *Opus Postumum* (Kant 1993b). The comparison reveals a startling continuity in Kant's thought regarding the soul and the cosmos that tacitly informs the analogy between the starry heavens and the moral law.

The *Universal Natural History and the Theory of the Heavens* finds Kant looking to the night sky, with Thomas Wright's *An Original Theory and New Hypothesis of the Universe* (1750) in hand. This time he is concerned by the discrepancy between the regularity established in the motions of the planets and the apparent spatial disorder of the stars. The apparent disorder of the stellar skyscape is a function of the Copernican revolution that has bestowed order upon the movement of the erstwhile wandering planets only to set the stars adrift from the 'hollow spheres of the heavens'. For the starry heavens are no longer, as claimed in our passage, 'above us' but all around us. What is more, for Kant, departing from observations on the Milky Way, not only we, but also the stars and even the galaxies are in motion. The scale of the universe is also disorienting, since Kant entertains the conjecture that the Milky Way is just one of a vast number of galaxies, and that the visible nebulae might themselves be distant galaxies (or 'world orders') all of which are in motion. Kant anticipates his observation in the *Critique of Practical Reason* with the thought of the infinity of the cosmos:

> If the greatness of a planetary world edifice, in which the earth as a grain of sand is hardly noticed, moves the intellect into admiration, with what astonishment will one be enchanted if one considers the infinite amounts of worlds and systems which fill the totality of the Milky Way; but how this astonishment *increases* [my emphasis] when one realises that all these immeasurable star orders again form the unit of a number whose end we do not know and which perhaps just as the former is inconceivably great and yet again is only the unit of a new minute system. (Kant 1981, 108)

From this experience, Kant tries to derive this infinite object from an infinite cause operating through a single 'divine presence' expressed in the three cosmological principles of matter and the forces of attraction and repulsion.

Kant resumes the theme of what it is we see when we look at the night sky in the fascinating section VII of part II 'From the Creation in the Entire Extent of its Infinity according to Space as well as Time'. Here Kant argues that light – the what and how of seeing – is made up of fine matter impelled by the movement of the forces of attraction and repulsion. The forces of attraction and repulsion working upon matter not only constitute 'the systematic constitution among the fixed stars of the Milky Way' but also the mode by which this constitution is made visible. Force and matter are not only the ontological constituents of the cosmos, but also the condition of the possibility of their being visible. However, this visibility also has within it invisibility. For the play of forces is not only constitutive but also potentially destructive – an imbalance of the forces of attraction and repulsion can either scatter the universe through space, or bring it into a concentrated collision: they can 'remove [world orders] from their positions and bury the world in an inevitably impending chaos' (Kant 1981, 150). The periodicity of the universe mentioned in the conclusion of the second *Critique* is none other than the destructive and constructive work of the forces of attraction and repulsion, correcting and disrupting the amassing of matter in the cosmos. For force in general is a quality of matter, and attractive force 'precisely that universal relation which unites the parts of nature in one space; it also stretches out over the entire extension of that space into all the reaches of its infinity' (Kant 1981, 150). Kant then makes the physical claim that underlies his later metaphysical proposition in the *Lectures on Metaphysics* 'Light is reality, darkness is negation, shadow is limitation, for it is a darkness that is bounded by light' (Kant 1997, 232). For given that light is fine matter, its motion towards us is subject to the forces of attraction and repulsion. If the attractive force of its object exceeds the attractive force of the rest of the cosmos, then the light will not escape the object and will not be visible to us. Kant relates light to the constant dispersal of matter that constitutes the universe. We cannot see chaos since it emits no light, we can only see creation through the emission of matter of which we are ourselves a part. Kant appears in the *Universal Natural History* to endorse two incompatible positions. The first concerns the acceleration of light on its journey through the universe, arriving at a limit of absolute speed or divine presence. According to this version, the cosmos is the 'infinite space of divine presence – buried in a silent night'. This version of the cosmos offers a physical correlate to intelligible 'personality' whereas that of material dispersal corresponds to what Kant in 1755 called 'this Phoenix of nature'. In this view, light is the fine part of the matter thrown off from the burning stars that is scattered by the force of repulsion and then re-gathered by the force of attraction, to be scattered again ... For ' the unification of so infinite an amount of fire store-houses as are these burning suns ... will scatter the stuff of their masses, dissolved by the unspeakable glow ... and the materials become available through these mechanical laws for new formations ...' (Kant 1981, 160). According to this view, the universe explodes and collapses; all we can see is the explosion – as the fine matter of light rushes through us. As one system begins collapsing, its phosphorescent fine matter is not impelled sufficiently to reach us, although another, in creative explosion impels its light through us – we can only by definition see 'reality' or creation, we cannot see destruction because the emission of light is a condition of creative explosion.

In the first account of the cosmos light is impelled by divine grace, in the second it is fine matter impelled into motion by emission of matter by a burning sun. Kant does not make a decision for either one of these positions, but leaves them both in place, offering the cosmological equivalent for the distinction between personality and animality that structures the conclusion of the *Critique of Practical Reason*. Indeed, and here we anticipate somewhat the discussion of the next section, Kant also situates the soul within these cosmic history. There is the immortal soul of the cosmos viewed as the space of divine presence, and the other soul that is a part of the movement of the cosmos. Kant asks at one point, 'With what kind of awe must not the soul look at her own being when she considers that she still has to live through all these changes.' In this view the soul too is part of the movement of matter driven by the forces of attraction and repulsion. The movement between attraction and repulsion located in the soul as the movement of *Hemmung* and *Ergießung* is also the movement of the cosmos, with the *Ergießung* of matter through combustion that generates sufficient repulsive force for matter – fine and otherwise – to escape the attractive force of the star and be drawn by that of the cosmos always restricted by the *Hemmung* of attractive force that would contain the emission of matter. The former (i.e. the Ergie βung) is the death of the star, is a departure from the order of reality, the latter (i.e. Hemmung) its life, the reconstitution of its matter.

Kant's claim in the conclusion to the *Critique of Pure Reason* that we must return our matter to the planet needs to be situated in this context. The destruction of death is but one part of the periodic movement through which the soul too must live. The possibility thus emerges of reading the affects of the soul in terms of the movement of repulsive and attractive force that constitutes the dynamic of the universe. Thus, the gaze oriented without into the starry heavens and the gaze oriented within, into the soul, are but two views of the same cosmic dynamic. Whereas the version of the unity of soul and cosmos is relatively crudely expressed in the early *Universal Natural History*, it is nevertheless clear that Kant is willing to see animate life and the soul as part of the wider, cosmic history of the expansion and contraction of matter through the play of attractive and repulsive forces. This is perhaps even clearer in the late *Opus postumum*.

Before moving to consider the cosmological dynamic in terms of the soul and the sophisticated medical physiology to which it gives rise in the *Opus postumum* it is necessary to consider again the account of light, which although consistent with the earlier version has undergone a further development. Once again, whenever Kant looked to skies, whether in the 1750s, 1780s or 1790s, he saw fiery store-houses burning themselves out and casting their light across the universe for reconstitution into new worlds – the starry heavens above present the monstrous glow of self-destructive, fire-creating matter. However, Kant's account of light has changed somewhat, since it is no longer consistently identified with fine matter (and consistency should not be expected too much from the jottings that make up the *Opus postumum*) but with the oscillation of fine matter. Kant indeed sways between a particle and wave account of light, inclining on the whole more to the latter. Light is carried on waves through the fluid matter of ether, but is also the cause of the patterns adopted by ether. In the case of the starry heavens 'since the generation of all cosmic bodies requires a preceding fluid state, and, since this latter is now preserved (at least) by the light of the sun, one may regard the fire-element as a type of matter which moves and is contained by all bodies; by means of heat and light it is the cause of all fluidity' (Kant 1993b, 20–1).[3] Light is characterised by 'free progressive and oscillatory motion' transmitted as a wave through the ether. It is a wave, however, that moves by means of a pulsar movement of attraction and repulsion yet one which is incremental, constantly augmenting itself. Here Kant points to a combination of the two views of the cosmos opposed to each other in the *Universal Natural History*. For now the motion of light is continuous, its attractive and repulsive forces proportioned: 'That light be no discharging motion (*ejaculatio*) of a matter but an undulatory motion (*undulatio*)' (Kant 1993b, 174). Light no longer obeys the sublime restriction and discharge – *Hemmung* and *Ergießung* – but is a continuous and augmentative oscillation. The universe thus obeys both physical laws and the laws of divine presence, as a self-augmenting proportion, this unified cosmology has its equivalent in the soul with the experience of the beautiful. The latter, as Kant will later show in the third *Critique*, is manifest in the augmentation of the feeling of life.

III. The life of the soul

The subject of the conclusion to the *Critique of Practical Reason* is the *Gemüt*, a term often translated as 'mind' – especially in its ubiquitous use in the *Critique of Pure Reason* – but whose meaning was by no means so restricted or even fixed. Since the term is drawn from medieval mysticism, one of the earliest recorded uses being by Master Eckhart, and given Kant's own use of the Latin equivalents *anima* and *animus*, the translation 'soul' is to be preferred.[4] However, it too does not do full justice to the properties of the term, and Kant is careful to distinguish *Gemüt* from *Seele* or the hypostatisation of the soul as substance (*anima*) by describing it as *animus* or the 'capacity to effect the unity of empirical apperception' and spirit (*Geist*).[5] This capacity is exercised by the *Gemütskräfte* or *Gemütspowers* variously classified but always involving sensibility, imagination understanding and reason. Yet more than this, *Gemüt* is a physio-philosophical concept that does not obey the distinction of sensibility and intelligibility, mind and body, but is itself identified as life. In the *Critique of Judgement Gemüt* is described as 'all life (the life principle itself), and its hindrance or furtherance has to be sought outside it, and yet in the man himself, consequently in connection with his body'(Kant 1988, 131, section 29).[6] The *Gemüt* as 'life principle' is also described as the *Inbegriff of* knowing, desiring and affect (Kant 1977b, 429) and has two origins the 'receptivity of impressions' and the 'spontaneity of concepts'; the latter provoke the two affects of the *Gemüt*, sensation and reflection (Kant 1993, A50/B74). An example of its operation is the affect of pleasure in the beautiful in which the experience of a beautiful object, illustrated by Kant in terms of 'a regular and appropriate building', 'quickens' the subject's 'feeling of life' or awareness of its own existence.

The filling of the *Gemüt* with wonder and awe at the sight of the starry heavens and the moral law is to be understood in terms of quickening the 'consciousness of existence' of the 'life principle'. Its operation in the key of the beautiful is signalled by the combination of the properties of constant repetition of the (receptive) perception and (spontaneous) reflection (*je öfter und anhaltende sich das Nachdenken damit beschäftigt ...*), and the fact that this is experienced in terms of 'constantly new' and augmentative affect (*mit immer neuer und zunehmender Bewunderung und Ehrfurcht*). The association of the *Gemüt* with the 'life principle' is evident not only from the rehearsal of its properties in the first two sentences – from augmentative repetition of affect to 'consciousness of existence' but also in the fact the two objects that it contemplates resolve by the end of the paragraph into two understandings of life. The paragraph unfolds the spectacle of the life principle moving from the vision of impossible objects to reflections on life itself. Through the reflection of the *Gemüt* the 'starry heavens' resolve into a reflection on animality and the restitution of the body's matter to the planet and the departure of its inexplicable *Lebenskraft;* the reflection upon the 'moral law' in its turn is expressed in terms of personality and a life 'independent of the world of the senses' one that, determined by the moral law, is infinite, unlimited by the 'conditions and limits of this life'. But the life of the *Gemüt* that has these reflections is neither of these, neither animality nor personality, yet somehow the scene of the play of both conceptions of life.

The conclusion to the *Critique of Practical Reason* ties sensible and intelligible life in the human *Gemüt* or 'principle of life'. Yet this tie involves a relationship to the cosmos, since the *Gemüt* itself is a part of the cosmos. Kant remains an heir to the close alignment of physiology and cosmology established by Paracelsus. His interest in animal economy – the connection between the outer and the inner relations of soul (evinced in the 'starry heavens' and 'moral law') is evident in both the *Universal Natural History* and the *Opus postumum*. It gives rise, in both texts, to a sustained discussion of 'animal economy' or physiology in the narrow sense, a discussion that provides the conditions of the possibility for medical therapy. In the former it appears in the guise of the fantastical reflection on life that makes up the third and final part of the text, one organised in terms of a reflection upon the life of the inhabitants of the various planets/stars.

Kant uses the theme of terrestrial and extra-terrestrial life as a conceit through which to explore the relationship between physiology and cosmology. He claims that

> the distances of the celestial bodies from the sun embody certain relationships which in turn entail a decisive influence on the various characteristics of thinking natures that are found there; whose manner of operating and feeling is bound to the condition of the material with which they are connected ... . (Kant 1981, 183)[7]

The reference to the restitution of the matter of the body to the planet in the passage from *Critique of Practical Reason* is thus founded in the general claim that the characteristics of the matter of the body are inseparable from the material conditions of the planet, and these in turn are inseparable from the material conditions of the cosmos. Kant correlates these characteristics with the 'measure [intensity] of the impressions which the [external] world evokes' in the body and these in turn with 'the properties of the relation of their habitat to [the sun], the centre of attraction and heat' (Kant 1981, 184). The sun's gravity – its force of attraction – and the 'repulsive force' of its heat together provide the conditions for the propagation of fine matter (light) (Kant is writing before the crucial invention of the concept of energy), which determines the life of the body. Kant is 'certain that this heat produces specific relationships in the materials of those celestial bodies in proportion to their distance from the soul' and thus experiences of body and soul on the different planets.

Kant takes as his 'general reference point' the example with which he is most familiar: human life on earth. Abstracting from the 'physical construction' of human beings or their 'moral traits', he restricts his investigation to 'what limitations his ability to think and the mobility of his body, which obeys that [former] would suffer through the properties of the matter to which he is linked and which are proportioned to the distance from the sun' (Kant 1981, 186). He then restates this physio-cosmological proposition even more emphatically:

> Whatever the infinite distance between the ability to think and the motion of matter, between the rational mind and the body, it is still certain that man – who obtains all his notions and representations through the impressions which the universe through the mediation of bodies evokes in his soul, both in respect of their meaning and of the readiness to connect and compare them, which man calls the ability to think – is wholly dependent on the properties of that matter to which the Creator joined him. (Kant 1981, 186)

Both the reception of the universe into the *Gemüt* and thinking is 'wholly determined' by the properties of matter – the particular balance of attractive and repulsive force (gravity and heat) that obtains in our part of the universe. This balance is, of course, not uniform throughout the cosmos, thus raising the possibilities of other forms of life, other forms of thinking and movement.

Kant discusses human physiology in terms of states and relations: the former comprises an amalgam of traditional and innovative medical concepts, the latter the notion of their interrelation or 'animal economy'. The units of human physiology are the Hippocratic fluids and fibres (sometimes 'nerves'). These are subject to the prevailing physical forces of attraction and repulsion, although the balance between them is different in the case of each individual. Human nature is characterised in terms of the 'unbending of the fibres, and in the sluggishness and immobility of fluids which should obey its stirrings' (Kant 1981, 187). The resistance of matter expressed in fibral inflexibility and the sluggishness of the humoral fluids stiffens the 'forces of the spirit into a similar dullness'. But the intensity of life – the degree of vivacity as opposed to dullness, depends upon 'excitation' expressed as 'animal economy' or the relationship between the 'forces of the human soul' and the matter to which 'they are most intimately bound'. He continues, 'this specific condition of the stuff has a fundamental relation to the degree of influence by which the sun in the measure of its distance enlivens them and renders them adapted to the maintenance of the animal economy'(188). This consists in the 'necessary relation to the fire, which spreads out from the centre of the world system to keep matter in the necessary excitation' (188). Life thus consists in the excitation of the matter that makes up the body, present in the forces of the soul and in the relations between the bodily humours and the suppleness and flexibility of its fibres.

In the *Universal Natural History* the concept of life and of animal economy is relatively underdeveloped, but its leading characteristics are clear. The character of life is intimately tied with the attractive and repulsive properties of matter that prevail on the planet Earth. The excitation of matter expressed as heat and light determines both the motion of the body and of thought. Thus, when Kant at one point in his discussion compares reason and the ability to judge with 'flashes of sunshine when thick clouds continually obstruct and darken its cheerful brightness' he is not mobilising a standard Enlightenment metaphor, but is being literal.

In the *Universal Natural History* Kant's understanding of animal economy is framed in terms of humours and fibres. The concept of life is relatively imprecise, even though he is prepared to mitigate the rigour of his physio-cosmology by appeals to the hope of a 'future life'. In the *Opus postumum* the concepts of soul and life are far more fully developed, and expressed now in terms drawn almost exclusively from modern medical physiology with explicit reference to the 'life principle' of Paracelsus.[8] The references to humoral fluids have disappeared, and the discussion of life, soul and cosmos is conducted almost entirely in modern terms.

One of the leitmotifs of the *Opus postumum* is the transition from metaphysics and transcendental philosophy to the discipline of physics. By the latter, however, Kant intends what previously had been known as 'physiology'. Thus Kant's 'physics' comprises both the 'moving forces of matter' in general – physics in the narrow sense – and the influence of these forces 'on the subject' 'In which, the body is thought of as animated and matter as animating' (Kant 1993b, 145). In this physics, questions relating to life and the soul thus form a major consideration. These considerations are framed in terms of the new understanding of the cosmos outlined above. The plenum of the ether oscillates through waves of attraction and repulsion, and the vital force is understood in terms of the 'concussive motion of an all penetrating matter' (Kant 1993b, 66).[9] Kant does not wish fully to embrace the mechanistic understanding of life in terms of physical forces that he identifies with the physiologist Hildebrandt (author of the *Lehrbuch der Physiologie*, 1799) but neither does he wish to adopt the Stahlist view of a totally immaterial vital principle. Living bodies contain a 'vital principle' but one which is connected in some way with ether. Kant reflects upon this principle in terms of Paracelsus' and Van Helmont's notion of the vital principle as the '*archeus*' – a term that was later re-adopted by Virchow. Kant noted that '[l]ife, however, stems from a distinct substance, from an *archeus*, (animated matter is contradictory), and organic bodies stand, through the ether, in the relation of a higher organ toward each other' (Kant 1993b, 184). The orientation of the *archeus* or 'life principle' according to the ether accords it an polar, oscillatory character of attraction/repulsion. This is described at one point – in the context of the 'transition to physics' in terms of an oscillation between the life/death, sickness/health polarities: 'the [characteristic] phenomenon of a species which preserves itself in space and time is the continuation of the genus and the alternating death and life of its individuals. Sickness forms the constant transition between the two' (Kant 1993b, 118).

In a subsequent note Kant reflects upon the polar character of the life principle at greater length. He wrote that '[o]ne can think of *health* and *sickness* with regard to organic bodies (not organic matter) since they possess a vital force, be it vegetative or animal, and for this reason also death or decay' (Kant 1993b, 197). The vital force moves between attraction and repulsion that is transmitted through the ether.[10] The vital principle is thus related to the cosmos, physiology to cosmology, although Kant is no longer convinced about the way in which this is achieved. Life is linked to an 'inner final cause' but its relationship to the cosmos is left open: 'It remains undetermined whether this encompasses the entire universe and hence underlies [everything] in cosmic space – as a world soul, as a unifying principle of all life (which thus must not be called *spirit*) or whether several be arranged hierarchically' (Kant 1993b, 197).

The old relationship of soul and cosmos is no longer valid – life is now both animated and animating – life generates life. In Kant's terms 'by the word "soul" is understood not merely a living or animated substance, but something which animates another substance (matter)' (182). Whether this property is a cosmic world soul, or whether it is product of individual life in interaction, the new view of life is consistent with the new view of the cosmos explored in the *Opus postumum*. Life is interactive and augmentative – just as the oscillations that make up the flow of ether do not consume but enhance each other. Vital force, consistent with the state of human physiology at time, is no longer, as in *Universal Natural History*, a product of excitability, but its cause.[11]

The implications of these changes in the understanding of the life principle and its relationship to the cosmos are apparent in the changed understanding of 'animal economy' or *zoonomy* evident in the *Opus postumum*. In the context of another of the many discussions of the transition to physics, this time from the 'metaphysical foundations' Kant is unambiguous concerning the physiological dimension to his new physics. He defines, 'Physics [as] the empirical science of the complex of the moving forces of matter. These forces also affect the subject – man – and his organs, since man is also a corporeal being. The inner alterations thereby produced in him, with consciousness, are perceptions; his reaction on, and outer alteration of, matter is motion' (Kant 1993, 103). The new physics has four divisions that relate closely to the schema of physiology proposed by Campanella and adopted to some extent by Descartes. The first concerns 'matter and bodies, according to their moving forces'; the second, the formal elements of the forces (mechanical or dynamic); the third 'organised and organising matter' and the fourth 'will power'.

Zoonomy comprises the third part of the new physics and is classified twice, according to the four *animalische Potenzen* or three *Lebenspotenzen*. The first three elements are common to both classifications – the animal powers add a fourth 'on the organisation of a whole of organic beings of different species'. The three main parts of zoonomy comprise '(1) on nervous power as a principle of excitability (*incitabilitas Brownii*); on muscular power (*irritabilitas Halleri*); on a force which preserves all the organic forces of nature as a constant alteration of the former two of which *one* phenomenon is heat'(103). Here, excitation and irritation – identified with the medical doctors and physiologists Brown and Haller – provide the polar opposition whose play constitutes life – one expressive the other reactive. Both in their turn are situated cosmologically according to what is identified in the second classification as the ether: the third vital power 'which brings both forces into active and reactive, constantly alternating, play; one all-penetrating, all moving etc., material, of which heat is one phenomenon' (103). Thus the physiological and cosmological are linked in Kant's new physiological physics into a polarised vital principle whose oscillation is informed by the cosmic ether, and whose play, like that of the ether, does not consume but augments itself.

Yet even in the *Opus postumum* Kant places above the order of life a divine order in which we participate in a higher form of life, the life of *spirit* rather than the life of *soul*. At this point he self-consciously distinguishes his position from that of Spinoza, for whom the order of God and World – spirit and soul – are inseparable. Kant however, although sometimes touching upon the notion of God as the plenum of the world, ultimately separates them, insisting upon 'the necessity of the division of the complex of all beings (of everything that exists): *God and the world*' (Kant 1993, 214). This separation becomes of that between soul and spirit, for '[i]n man there dwells an active principle, arousable by no sensible representation, accompanying him not as soul (for this presupposes body) but as spirit, which, like a particular substance, commands him irresistibly according to the law of moral–practical reason'(214). The assertion of the distinction between God and the world clearly shows Kant's extreme reluctance to move towards a rigorous physiology, a step that would be taken by his radical successors – Virchow in medicine and Nietzsche in philosophy. But his awareness of the problems arising from such a division was acute. It is in the context of this awareness that the apparent analogy or contrast between the starry heavens above and the moral law within, soul and spirit, world and God should begin to be read anew.

Notes

1. Kant's fascination with the properties of polarity and the nature of the experience of its reversal has been little noted. It is however central, and thematised as such, in *What is Called Orientation in Thinking*, and implicitly at work in a number of other places.
2. The contrast with Leopardi is again constructive, since for the poet of *la ginestra* there is no second reflection but only the annihilation. For more extended readings of Leopardi, see Caygill 2000.
3. In the *Opus postumum*, Kant returns to the Cartesian view of the important of heat is stimulating the motion of matter. At one point he even supplements the ether with 'caloric' – 'matter without gravity and not displaceable, but which moves all matter internally, renders matter elastic but also cohesive ... it is extended in the whole of cosmic space', (Kant 1993b, 37).

4. Etienne Gilson described *Gemüt* in terms of disposition and stablity, the 'stable disposition of the soul which conditions the exercise of its faculties' (Gilson 1955, 444).

5. This is most clearly carried through in Kant's 1796 letter to the medical doctor Sömmering on his '*The Organs of the Soul*, an early attempt to localise cerebral functions (Kant 1977a, 255–9).

6. The explicit Paracelsian and thus medical–physiological provenance of 'the life principle itself' will be shown below.

7. Here Kant anticipates some of the themes of recent anthropic cosmology, see Barrow and Tipler 1986.

8. Kant was extremely well informed about contemporary debates in medicine and human physiology. This is apparent above all in the discussions of Georg Ernst Stahl (1660–1754) and Friedrich Hoffmann (1660–1742) and their respective vitalist and mechanical views of human physiology as well the controversial medical doctrine of John Brown (1733–88), all discussed in his address 'On Philosopher's Medicine of the Body' in Kant 1986, especially 231–2.

9. In this view Kant is even prepared to view heat less as the cause of the repulsive force that 'expands and disperses matter' but as 'the mere effect of the repulsion of a matter set in motion' (Kant 1993b, 215).

10. See Kant (1993b, 197) for his mapping of the polar characteristics of life onto sexual reproduction (ibid., 182).

11. See Kant (1993b, 142) for his qualification of the generally augmentative nature of the interactions of vital force in the case of sexual intercourse which uniquely 'erodes' *aufreibt* vital feeling.

References

Barrow, J. D. and Tipler, F. J. (1986) *The Anthropic Cosmopological Principle* Oxford: Oxford University Press.

Caygill, H. (2000) 'Surviving the Inhuman', in S. Brewster et al. (eds), *Inhuman Reflections: Thinking the Limits of the Human*, Manchester and New York: Manchester University Press.

Gilsen, E. (1955) *History of Christian Philosophy in the Middle Ages*, New York: Random House.

Kant, I. (1997) *Lectures on Metaphysics* ed. K. Ameriks and S. Naragon, Cambridge: Cambridge University Press.

Kant, I. (1993a) *Critique of Practical Reason* tr. Lewis White Beck, New York: Library of Liberal Arts, Macmillan Publishing.

Kant, I. (1993b) *Opus Postumum* ed. E. Förster and M. Rosen, Cambridge: Cambridge University Press.

Kant, I. (1988) *Critique of Judgement* trans. J. C. Meredith, Oxford: Oxford University Press.

Kant, I (1986) *Kant's Latin Writings* trans. Mary J. Gregor, ed. Lewis White Beck, New York: Peter Lang Publishing.

Kant, I. (1983) *Critique of Pure Reason* trans. N. K. Smith, London and Basingstoke: Methuen.

Kant, I. (1977a) *Schriften zur Anthropologie, Geschichtsphilosophie, Politik und Pädagogie* 1st edn, W. Weischedel, Werkausgabe VI. XI, Frankfurt am Main: Suhrkamp.

Kant, I. (1977b) *Schriften zur Anthropologie, Geschichtsphilosophie, Politik und Pädagogie,* 2nd edn, W. Weischedel Werkausgabe VI. XII, Frankfurt am Main: Suhrkamp.

Kant, I. (1960) *Religion within the Limits of Reason Alone* trans. T Greene and H. H. Hudson, New York: Harper Torchbooks.

Mann, G. et al. (ed.) (1985) *Samuel Thomas Sömmering und die Gelehrten der Goethezeit* Stuttgart: G Fischer.

Wolff, C. (1999) *Vernünftige Gedanken von Gott, der Welt, und der Seele des Menschen, auch allen Dingen überhaupt* (1719) in *Christian Wolff: Metaphysica Tedesca* ed. R. Ciarfordone, Milan: Rusconi.

Wright, T. (1750) *An Original Theory and New Hypothesis of the Universe.* London: Printed for the Author and sold by H. Chapelle 1750. Reproduced in fascimile edition with introduction by M.A. Hoskin, London: Macdonald 1971.

11

Goethe's 'Enhanced Praxis' and the Emergence of a Cosmopolitical Future

Diane Morgan

The recent interest generated by the topic of cosmopolitics is no doubt owing to it being pertinent to major contemporary issues such as globalisation, global citizenship, human rights and international (or transnational) democracy (see for instance Archibugi 2003; Breckenridge et al. 2002; Cheah and Robbins 1998; Held 2002; Stengers 1997). Critical attention has tended to focus on the works of Immanuel Kant, particularly on his *Political Writings*, as he seems most clearly to presage the advent of a 'new world order' which breaks away from the confines of the nation-state. Indeed, in his 'Perpetual Peace' essay of 1795/6, Kant famously wrote the following inspiring, and, one might add, optimistic, words:

> The peoples of the earth have thus entered in varying degrees into a universal community, and it has developed to the point where a violation of rights in one part of the world is felt everywhere. The idea of a cosmopolitan right is therefore not fantastic and overstrained; it is a necessary complement to the unwritten code of political and international right, transforming it into a right of humanity [*zum öffentlichen Menschenrechte*]. (Kant 1994, 107–8)

Such sentiments, and such a political project, might seem far removed from Goethe's interests and concerns. Indeed, it is, maybe, surprising to see Goethe's methodological approach to nature associated at all with 'Kantian' cosmopolitics. Enthusiastic readers of Goethe, such as Nietzsche, would no doubt profess to find abhorrent the coupling of the

cheerful, overflowing 'Dionysian' who says 'Yes!' to life with that supposedly arid 'automaton of duty', and whose inflexible and formalistic
categoricals destroy all vital self-affirmation (Nietzsche 1990, 134).[1]
Indeed, Nietzsche went so far as to claim that Kant was the very
'antipodes of Goethe' (Nietzsche 1990, 114). This view of the diametrical opposition between Goethe's and Kant's standpoints is wholeheartedly agreed with by Oswald Spengler. In *The Decline of the West* Spengler
in effect concurs with Nietzsche's opinions on the vast difference
between Goethe and Kant when he writes:

> Plato and Goethe represent the philosophy of becoming [*die Philosophie
> des Werdens*]; Aristotle and Kant that of what has already become [*die des
> Gewordenen*]. Here intuition stands against analysis ... I would not want
> to change one word of the following statement [by Goethe]: 'The divine
> is active in the living, not in the dead; it is in that which is becoming
> and transforming itself but not in that which has already become and is
> now fixed [*Erstarrten*]. Therefore reason tends toward the divine, deal-
> ing only with that which is becoming and which is alive, while the
> understanding deals with that which has already become and is now
> fixed, so as best to use it'. (Spengler 1991, 68–9)

Inveighing against 'slogan[s], dry schema[s], personal 'ideals' which suf-
focate the 'immeasurable fullness, depth and animation [*Bewegtheit*] of
the living thing', Spengler calls on Goethe's support for the reductive
inappropriateness of the cosmopolitical term 'humanity'.[2] Apparently,
objecting to a comment by Luden, Goethe is cited as exclaiming:

> Humanity? That is an abstraction. There have only ever been people
> and there will only ever be people [*Die Menschheit? Das ist ein
> Abstraktum. Es hat von jeher nur Menschen gegeben und wird nur
> Menschen geben*]. (Goethe cited in Spengler 1991, 28–9)

An abstract concept such as 'humanity' is to be rejected as it appears to
confer a static, restrictive and essentialising identity on what would be
more accurately conceived of as a multitude or packets of singularities in
the process of transforming themselves on different planes, at different
speeds.[3] Such differential activity is evident everywhere in the natural
world, as Goethe explains in 'The Purpose Set Forth':

> No living thing is unitary in nature; every such thing is a plurality.
> Even the organism which appears to us as individual exists as a col-
> lection of independent living entities. (Goethe 1995, 64; 1998a, 56)

Nietzsche, who quotes this passage in his notes 'On Teleology', fully concurs with this perspective.[4] Indeed, in the *Nachlass*, he echoes Goethe when he unmasks terms such as 'the human' or 'the tree' as wishes to anthromorphosise the world, to subject natural phenomena, in all their various and varying guises, to the human, all too human need to control by assimilating the heterogeneous, so as to make sense of, so as to force 'sense' on, what would otherwise elude our mortal grasp. He writes: 'We produce bearers of characteristics, essences and abstractions as causes of these characteristics [*Wir produziren als Träger der Eigenschaften Wesen und Abstraktionen als Ursachen dieser Eigenschaften*]' (Nietzsche 1988b, 494).

In 'Towards a General Comparative Theory', Goethe similarly draws our attention to the rather lamentable way humans are driven, not only consciously and calculatively, but also instinctively, to relate the world to themselves, to their immediate needs and habitual interests. He writes:

> Man is in the habit of valuing things according to how well they serve his purposes. It lies in the nature of the human condition that man must think of himself as the last stage of creation. Why, then, should he not also believe that he is its ultimate purpose? Why should his vanity not be allowed this small deception? Given his need for objects and his use of them, he draws the conclusion that they have been created to serve him. ... Why should he not ignore a plant which is useless to him and dismiss it as a weed, since it really does not exist for him? (Goethe 1995, 53; 1959, 644)[5]

By the end of the essay he feels he has answered the question of why this anthropocentric way of interpreting nature is not only inadequate as a way of perceiving and interacting with the world, but is also ultimately detrimental to humans. He then concludes:

> Ultimately we will see the whole world of animals as a great element in which one species is created or at least sustained, by and through another [... *ja wir werden die ganze tierische Welt wieder nur als ein grosses Element ansehen, wo ein Geschlecht auf dem andern und durch das andere, wo nicht entsteht doch* [*sich*] *ernährt*]. We will no longer think of connections and relationships in terms of purpose [*Zwecke*] and intention [*Bestimmungen*]. This is the only road to progress in understanding how nature expresses itself from all quarters and in all directions as it goes about its work of creation [*und dadurch ganz allein in der Kenntnis wie sich die bildende Natur von allen Seiten und nach allen*

Seiten [äussert]]. As we find through experience, and as the advance
of science has shown, the most concrete and far-reaching benefits for
humans [*die reellste und ausgebreitetste Nutzen für die Menschen*] come
from an intense and selfless effort which neither demands its reward
at week's end like a labourer [*weder taglöhnermässig*], nor lies under
any obligation to produce some useful result for humankind [*für die
Menschheit*] after a year, a decade or even a century. (Goethe 1995, 56;
1959, 648–9 slightly adapted)

Having jettisoned a purposively driven approach to nature, which press-
gangs natural phenomena to serve human interests, it might seem
puzzling to see Goethe subsequently proposing that 'concrete and far-
reaching benefits' for humankind can be derived from his view of the
natural world. Having traced – via Nietzsche and Spengler – a refusal to
accept the abstract concept of 'humanity', it is also surprising to see him
thinking in such terms here. How are we then supposed to understand
his proposition? Is it to be understood as part of a pragmatic long-term
ecological strategy, a smart de-instrumentalisation of our relation to
nature? That is to say, are we being advised not to view nature as a mere
territory to be short-sightedly stripped of assets in order to best serve the
human species' long-term environmental needs? Our interest in securing
the ecological future of the planet would then amount to a surrepti-
tiously self-centred investment in our own survival. Or, to approach the
proposition from a different track – but one that would be difficult to
gauge as a 'concrete' benefit – should we interpret his claim spiritually? Is
he beckoning towards a Romantically inspired relationship to, a fulfilling
synthesis with, nature and its creatures? Support for this interpretation
could be rallied from Rudolf Steiner, who names Goethe as *the* thinker
whose ideas stimulated the creation of the Anthroposophy movement.[6]
Steiner claims to have developed the 'seed' inherent in Goethe's thinking, enabling him to explore 'the hidden, generative sources of reality
and to reveal them in a conceptual form fully accessible to intellectual
understanding' (Barnes in Steiner 2000, 282). After having spent fourteen
years editing Goethe's scientific works and researching in the Weimar
archives, Steiner presents Goethe as having developed the methodological foundations of a 'participatory science' which can lead to the 'healing
of the contemporary human being', who is perceived as suffering from
the alienating dualisms (subject/object, mind/body) of an overly mecha-
nised and abstract world (Steiner 2000, 301).[7]

I suggest that both these ways of understanding Goethe's methodological approach to nature – the pragmatic, deviously anthropocentric

and the anthroposophic – are mistaken.[8] The first is erroneous because it pre-supposes the nature of the species and its needs, whereas in this chapter I show how Goethe conceives of human nature as evolving, as at once transforming itself from within and being transformed from without. The smart adoption of a tactic of temporary de-instrumentalisation towards nature would foreclose such openness to radical change. The second, Steiner's therapeutic vision, can also be regarded as a misreading of Goethe for the following, and, we see, the related reason: Goethe developed an interesting, and, on some level, profound understanding of Kantian philosophy with which he considered himself as sharing several fundamental intellectual convictions. This intellectual affinity would pre-empt the assumption of some eventual conquest of spiritual wholeness and, indeed, it necessarily leads to an acknowledgement of the impossibility of ever being able to grasp things wholly in themselves. However, this renunciation should not be merely understood as a restricting and therefore a negative recognition of the limits of human faculties, but rather as an affirmative, even empowering, intensification of what it might be to be a human being in this world. That Goethe shares such a view will be demonstrated in this chapter.

Despite the tendency, illustrated earlier by the comments of Nietzsche and Spengler, to pitch Goethe against Kant, I hope to show that the former has more in common with the latter than is generally acknowledged. Indeed, compared to his remarks regarding the Romantic *Naturphilosophen*, such as Schelling, whom he sees as wanting to transcend natural phenomena in their bid to reach an anthroposodic-like cosmic wholeness,[9] Goethe tends to prefer Kant's view of the world and our place within it. His 'delicate empiricism' is more in tune with a philosophy which advocates a scrupulous vigilance to the ways we position ourselves in relationship to the empirical world and which steers a careful pathway between the excesses of absolute empiricism and absolute rationalism.[10] Ten years previous to the ambivalent acquaintance with Schelling, Goethe had returned from Italy to a Germany swept along by a similar 'tide, imbued in genius and wild in form'. He confessed to having felt that 'the subject of [his] study and [his] whole way of acquiring knowledge were being cast aside and crippled' (Goethe 1995, 19; 1998b, 539). He had consequently tried his best to publicly mark a distance between his current intellectual disposition and convictions, and the youthful *Sturm und Drang* effusions of works such as the popular *The Sufferings of Young Werther*. His sense of solitude and of being misunderstood was partially alleviated in 1794 by The 'Fortunate Encounter' with Schiller, whose intellectual exchanges, and rapidly flourishing friendship, facilitated and galvanised his reading and understanding of Kant. As Goethe relates in 'The Influence of Modern Philosophy', many of Kant's fundamental propositions echoed Goethe's own convictions, leading to a consolidation and refinement of his views of, and experiences in, the natural world and confirming his reservations about the ideas of the *Naturphilosophen* (Goethe 1995, 28–30; 1998a, 26–8). We now look at these ideas in more detail.

In 'Towards a General Comparative Theory', Goethe had already criticised the mechanistic understanding of living things, which conceives the relationship between creature and environment causally, and therefore reactively, evaluating creatures' attributes solely in terms of their being fit for any purpose. Hence, he proposed that, instead of asserting, for instance, 'the fish exists for the water' or 'water exists for the fish', it would be far more instructive and productive to see the relationship of the fish to its environment differently. Most preferred would be the following two alternative formulations. First, 'the fish exists in the water and by means of [*durch*] the water' and, second:

> the existence of what we call 'fish' is only possible under the conditions of an element we call 'water', so that the creature not only exists in that element but may also evolve there [*nicht allein um darin zu sein sondern auch um darin zu werden*]. (Goethe 1995, 54–5; 1959, 646–7)

The process by and through which an organism is shaped from without, as well as from within, has to be appreciated, he claims, rather than the water just being considered as a vessel for the fish, or the fish as merely suitably adapted to a particular environment. In addition, instead of conceiving of living forms as just using a capacity they were designed with for a particular purpose in mind,[11] Goethe promotes a view of life that is dynamic, interactive (changing, mutating, both progressing and regressing).

Goethe is fully aware of the reasons motivating the human need to posit a teleological end which is *external* to organisms: such ends consolidate the human's sense of being of a different nature from nature itself. If nature is represented mechanistically, human spontaneity and creativity shines forth all the more brilliantly. The 'generic' vision of the world, whereby life is divided into partial kingdoms, neatly classified into species serving pre-determined purposes, has the benefit of comfortably securing the human's superior position at the edge of nature. Humans have the tendency to see the world around them as ultimately existing for their own benefit – cows are for milk, bees are for honey – and they transpose this instrumentalised, but also physico-theological, way of thinking onto other organisms. Goethe illustrates the limiting conse-quences of this kind of thinking in the following example: the ox is typ-ically seen as having horns in order to defend itself. Goethe suggests that this formulation ultimately leads to a dead end for it provides no answer to the question of, for instance, why does a sheep not have any? Or if a sheep does have horns, why they wind themselves around its ears ren-dering them useless? (Eckermann 1981, 429). Goethe forcibly suggests that, instead of always starting questions with 'why?' (i.e. to what pur-pose?), it would be wiser to pose the question of 'how' [*wie*]?: 'how does an ox have horns'?[12] This alternative methodological approach is more productive inasmuch as it engages us with the activity of life, rather than trying to tie it down to causes and effects, to mechanical responses to functional demands. This method stimulates an interest in the ox's struc-tural organisation and necessitates a more comparatist study of different organisms, thereby instigating a relational examination *between* living forms, eventually leading maybe to the realisation of why, for instance, the lion does not and cannot have horns. In effect, Goethe advocates that we start out with a basic assumption of the inter-relatedness of life forms (their relations/ references [*Bezüge*] and affinities [*Verwandtschaften*].[13] He also places the emphasis more on each organism's *internal*, rather than external, finality. However, this finality is perceived as a mere episode in an ongoing process of metamorphosis. As Cassirer explained, Goethe's is a 'genetic', rather than a 'generic' approach to living forms (Cassirer 1991, 103).

In an 1830 letter to Zelter, Goethe identifies the major importance for him of Kant's Third Critique:

> In his *Critique of Judgement* old Kant did the world, and indeed me, a limitless service by firmly placing Art and Nature side by side and granting both of them the right to act purposivelessly according to great principles. Spinoza had already lent credibility to my dislike of absurd final causes. Nature and art are too big to be harnessed to pur-poses and they also don't need them, as relations [*Bezüge*] are every-where and relations [*Bezüge*] are life. (Goethe 1988b, 370, my translation)

For Goethe, Kant draws a pleasing parallel between life and art, although refusing to call nature an 'analogue of art' as this would lead to the under-estimation of natural phenomena by giving the impression that they are the external manifestations of an artist's creativity.[14] Kant's analysis of the way natural products organise themselves according to a recursive causality – they are both causes and effects of themselves – 'which has nothing analogous to any causality known to us', meets with his whole-hearted approval (Kant 1988, 23, section 65). Far from being an assemblage of pre-existing parts, living beings are more than the sum of their parts. There is an excessive quality to them, hence their unpredictability and elu-siveness.[15] Kant carefully considers the unsolvable question of the extent to which organisms are to be seen as educts – bringing forth pre-deter-mined characteristics and properties pertaining to their species – and to what extent they produce themselves 'separat[ing] and recomb[ining] raw material' in an original way which 'infinitely outdistances all the efforts of art' (Kant 1988, 19, section 64). Goethe gave the name 'morphology' to such study of 'structured form [*Gestalt*], and the formation [*Bildung*] and transformation [*Umbildung*] of organic bodies' (Goethe 1995, 57; 1959, 657).[16] Kant goes on to limit the scope of even a Newton's insight into a mere blade of grass, a move which could only delight Goethe, locked as he was in a life-long crusade against despotic, mechanistic explanations of natural phenomena (Kant 1988, 54, section 75).[17]

As well as the obstacles that arise from the instinctual inscrutability of living organisms, there are also basic hindrances to our understanding of natural phenomena that arise from the very terminological tools we employ to describe them. One important instance that Goethe draws our attention to is the difference between the terms 'structured form' [*Gestalt*] and 'formation' [*Bildung*]. The former is used to designate 'the complex of existence presented by a physical organism', but it abstracts from movement, fixes the organism, locks it up into a sealed identity. The use of this term leads to erroneous thinking as all forms – especially, but not just, organic ones – move, not one is permanent or completely static.[18] Hence Goethe's preference for the latter term '*Bildung*', as this draws attention not only to an individuating process which can be applied to an end product [a '*Hervorgebrachten*'], but also to something which is still being produced [a '*Hervorgebrachtwerdenden*']. If we are still to hold on to the term '*Gestalt*' then it must be with the proviso that the form/shape that is referred to is something which is held on to only momentarily [*nur für den Augenblick Festgehaltenes*], that the object is something which is still capable of constant, continued modulation (Goethe 1995, 63–4; 1998a, 55–6).

In 'Winckelmann and his Age', Goethe can be seen as elaborating on this idea of the inappropriateness and the negative repercussions of petrifying manifold things into sets, of grouping heterogeneous things together for (aesthetic and/or scientific) classificatory purposes:

> It is sad to have to think of anything as final and complete. Old armories, galleries and museums to which nothing is added are like mausoleums haunted by ghosts. Such a limited circle of art *limits our thinking*. We get accustomed to regarding such collections as complete, instead of being reminded through ever new additions that *in art, as in life*, we have nothing that remains finished and at rest, but rather something infinite in constant motion. (Goethe 1994, 113; 1998d, 116, my emphases)

Anticipating the *cause célèbre* of many modern experimental artists, Goethe here gestures towards a de-institutionalisation of art, the creation of alternative 'imaginary museums' as a way of edging towards the rediscovery of the dynamic and teeming proliferation of aesthetic and, by extension, life forms.[19] Indeed the parallel between life and art that Goethe saw Kant developing so admirably in *The Critique of Judgement* is reinforced in this passage. The attempt to do justice to the complexity of nature and to our relationship to, and within it, involves *an expansion of thinking*, akin to that experienced when confronted with the animated world of art, accompanied by an acute sense of our limited aptitude for understanding things in themselves.

Having shown how we miss the object of our scientific enquiry because of our tendency to petrify living forms in dead formula, Goethe obliges us, also in 'The Purpose Set Forth: On Morphology', to consider further how slippery our grip on living things actually is. Even the very contours of living forms, taken as guidelines for isolating the object which interests us, are constantly being eroded, discarded, renewed. Goethe describes how elusive the outer layer [*Hülle*], of living phenomena is, how the boundary between the inside and the outside of living things is blurred:

> Whether the covering takes the form of bark, skin or shell, anything that works in a living way must be covered over. And thus everything turned toward the external world gradually falls victim to an early death and decay. The bark of trees, the skin of insects, the hair and feathers of animals, even the epidermis of man, are coverings forever being cast off, given over to non-life. New coverings are constantly forming beneath the old, while still further down, close to this surface or more deeply hidden, life brings forth its web of creation [*das Leben [bringt] sein schaffendes Gewebe [hervor]*]. (Goethe 1995, 66; 1998a, 59)

Even what we take to be the outer container of things, animals, people, which we habitually rely on as a line of demarcation between ourselves and others, between the subject and object, is constantly being eroded, discarded, renewed. It is still very much caught up in a process and not a finished product with a fixed identity.[20]

Goethe also takes issue with the standard method of observing natural objects by 'dividing them into their constitutive parts'. Little understanding of the whole will be gained, Goethe warns, by decomposing the living forms of nature into lifeless pieces. Once having been pulled apart, it is impossible 'to restore a natural object and bring it back to life' (Goethe 1995, 63; 1998a, 54–5). Indeed, we are faced with an almost insurmountable problem in our encounters with the natural world: not only do we tend to isolate and separate nature into individual organisms and then proceed to dissect these artificial constructions each in turn so as to have an intellectual grip on them, but also it becomes apparent that we can only conceive of nature as a totality *by assemblage*, by mentally adding constituent bits together. Indeed, we are obliged, in Kant's words, to regard 'the real whole in nature as the effect of the concurrent dynamical forces of the parts'. That is to say, our 'discursive understanding' can only 'mechanically generate the whole', laboriously putting together bits which are only particular instances, partial aspects, of an englobing whole. An intuitive, quasi-divine understanding of the whole, capable of moving seamlessly from the 'synthetic universal' to the parts without encountering the contingent subsumption of particulars under a universal principle, is denied us (Kant 1988, 60–7 section 77). However, in the 'Excerpt from "Towards a Theory of Weather" ', Goethe persists:

> We can never directly see what is true, i.e. identical with what is divine; we look at it only in reflection [*Abglanz*], in example, in the symbol, in individual and related phenomena. We perceive it as a life beyond our grasp, *yet we cannot deny our need to grasp it.* (Goethe 1995, 145; 1998a, 305)

As well as concurring with and respecting Kant's disciplining restrictions on our possible knowledge of natural phenomena, Goethe believes that he has the 'sage of Königsberg['s]' ironic approval when he tests those same limits (Goethe 1995, 31–2; 1998a 30–1). The endeavour to be worthy of what lies beyond our limits, to be worthy of participating in the infinitely creative, globally interactive natural processes can be seen to parallel the imperative to strain ourselves to the utmost to be equal to the moral law. In his conversations with Eckermann, Goethe justified this Kantian extrapolation in the following way:

> The understanding does not suffice to grasp nature: the human must be capable of raising himself to highest reason in order to touch the divine that is revealed in primordial, physical as well as moral, phenomena [*Urphänomenen*], behind which it preserves itself and which in turn emanate from it.[21]
>
> The divine is only active in the living, not in the dead; it is in that which is becoming and transforming itself, not in that which has already become and is now fixed ...
>
> [Der Verstand reicht zu ihr [der Natur] nicht hinauf, der Mensch muss fähig sein, sich zur höchsten Vernunft erheben zu können, um an die Gottheit zu rühren, die sich in Urphänomen, physischen wie sittlichen, offenbaret, hinter denen sie sich hält und die von ihr ausgehen.
>
> Die Gottheit aber ist wirksam im Lebendigen, aber nicht im Toten; sie ist im Werdenden und sich Verwandelnden aber nicht im Gewordenen und Erstarrten.] (Eckermann 1981, 295, partially cited above)

This suggested parallel between our behaviour towards the natural world, between the way we position ourselves in relation to it and the moral domain, is essential to my proposition that there is a *cosmopolitical* interest to be gained from Goethe's 'scientific' writings and methodology. Crucial to developing this point further is an examination of Goethe's idea of the *Urphänomen*.

The term *Urphänomen* can be seen as functioning in a similar way to a Kantian 'thing in itself'. Both are negative limiting concepts [*Grenzbegriffe*], marking the limits of our understanding (we cannot grasp these noumena as they are not 'objects of possible experience') yet both, far more positively, 'denote a problematic space beyond these limits' (Caygill 1995, 393). Hence *Urphänomen* have an ambivalent, simultaneously negative and positive, significance for us. Indeed the very nature of the idea, as we will see, is complex, problematic and contradictory. Goethe's researches into the unfathomable potential of natural phenomena, their apparently infinite variety and creative will, and also the way they appear to share structural types, even 'a universal set of building rules' [*Baupläne*], led to the idea of *Urphänomenen*.[22] These archetypal phenomena (the primordial plant, the primordial animal) can be conceived as 'pregnant points' (Barnes in Steiner 2000, 267). These 'pregnant points' paradoxically both *contain* all phenomenal examples of plants and animals and are simultaneously *the place from which these phenomena emerge or could hypothetically emerge* (Goethe 1998c, 324).[23]

Kant also entertained the idea of *Urphänomen* when discussing anatomical morphology: he posits the possibility of there being a 'common primordial mother' [*gemeinschaftlich[e] Urmutter'*] who is the source of the variety of living forms:

> So many genera of animals share a certain scheme on which not only their bone structure but also the arrangement of their other parts seems to be based; the basic outline is admirably simple but yet was able to produce this great diversity of species, by shortening some parts and lengthening others ... This analogy of forms, which in all their differences seem to be produced in accordance with a common type [*einem gemeinschaftlichen Urbilde gemäβ*], strengthens the suspicion that they have an actual kinship [*Verwandtschaften*] due to a descent from a common parent [*Urmutter*] (Goethe 1998d, 435, section 509).

The 'heuristic fiction', to use Kant's term, of archetypes is reminiscent of Platonic ideas but, in contrast, their essence is dynamic not static.[24] In addition, they serve, not to take us away from an (imperfect) phenomenal world, but rather to delve deeper into its rich potentiality as we search (ultimately in vain but not entirely fruitlessly) for them.[25] It would take an *'intellectus archetypus'* to intuitively understand *Urphänomenen* as they lie at 'the limit of our perceptual ability', beyond the reach of our finite minds (Goethe 1995, xx).

Given the inadequacy of our ability to understand, Goethe suggested to Eckermann – as we have already seen – that the idea of *Urphänomenen* appeals more to, and better befits, 'highest' reason which tends 'towards the divine' (Eckermann 1981, 295; Goethe, 1995, xx). Such a reason would have to be more than merely mortal; it would be 'enhanced' in some way. Goethe confides to Eckermann that his incisive analysis of human faculties, of their potentiality and of their failings – including their lamentable inability to grasp 'how anthropomorphic' they are – arises from his investigations into natural science (Eckermann 1981, 295).[26] For his better awareness and knowledge of human beings, thanks are due to his dogged focus on natural phenomena, on the complex, interactive 'web of creation' p. 243, whose causality eludes our grasp and which can only be seen by us as *emerging*.[27] Consequently, Goethe maintains that subjective introspection – that lure of the Delphic injunction to 'know thyself'– leads only to a blind alley. In 'Significant Help Given by an Ingenious Turn of Phrase' he states:

> The human being knows himself only insofar as he knows the world; he perceives the world only in himself, and himself only in the world. Every new object, clearly seen, opens up a new organ of perception in us. (Goethe 1995, 39; 1998a, 38)

It is through the experiencing of nature that the nature of the human is revealed. However, human nature is not conceived of as already endowed with given, fixed qualities. Instead human nature is regarded as capable of change, packed with virtual potential, though also facultatively limited in ways it is important to recognise.[28] Thus we concomitantly explore the human, as an evolving creature stretching and straining within and against structural and facultative limits, when we consider, scrupulously, vigilantly, 'delicately', life forms and the possible extent of their (our) inter-relatedness through the 'heuristic' idea of the *Urmutter*.

However, despite human nature being revealed by nature, Goethe does not advocate a possible return to some 'originary' state of at-oneness with the natural world (i.e. unlike Steiner). The ideal of an eventual coalescence of our ways of thinking about nature and our experience of it, is posited not as a state of affairs to be retrieved from the past, but rather as a future development of the human mind, as yet far beyond our grasp, which is produced by a highly advanced culture:

> There is a delicate empiricism [*zarte Empirie*], which makes itself utterly identical with the object, thereby becoming true theory. But the enhancement of our mental powers belongs to a highly evolved age. [*Diese Steigerung des geistigen Vermögens aber gehört einer hochgebildeten Zeit an*]. (Goethe 1998d, 435 section 509)

If, with this regulative idea of reunion between theory and praxis in mind, we strive gradually to shed our anthropomorphic tendencies and to begin to observe and partake in the natural world without shooting purposiveness through everything we encounter, what might we be able to learn from nature? What 'concrete and far-reaching benefits' for humankind, to return to Goethe's claim cited at the beginning of this chapter, might be revealed from this reconfigured relationship to and with natural phenomena?

Goethe seems to point to an answer to this question in his conversations with Eckermann. Even if, in the scientific writings, he characterises nature as inventively self-modulating, giving the impression of playful excessiveness and frivolity, to Eckermann he insisted that nature is 'always true, serious, strict, always right'. If any 'mistakes and errors' crop up in our scientific encounters with natural phenomena, these are to be attributed solely to humans and not to nature itself. Consequently, if incorporated, though not unproblematically, as a model of what is 'true and pure' (though in itself amoral), nature can provide a focus, suggests Goethe, for human endeavours to 'rais[e] [oneself] to highest reason' (Eckermann 1981, 295, cited on p. 249). Such a striving and self-overcoming most probably results in the human being stretched out on the rack of mortal inadequacy and ultimately resigned to failure. However, this 'resignation' takes place, Goethe tells us, 'at the limits of humanity [*an den Grenzen der Menschheit*]' and not within 'the hypothetical limitations of me as a narrow-minded individual [*meines bornierten Individuum*]' (Goethe 1998d, 367 section 20).

Goethe advocates a pushing at the limits of what it is to be human so as to live up to a natural model, to which we already belong, of interactive global growth.[29] As such the definition of what is human, though nominally constitutive, remains contentless.[30] He suggests that we should participate actively – not contemplatively – in a dynamic whole which we are already more than a part of. Several of his 'Maxims and Reflections' develop this idea of an enhanced relationship to, and between, the world and us:

> The higher empiricism behaves towards nature as human understanding does to practical life. (Goethe 1998d, 437, section 523)
>
> Theory and Experience/ Phenomena stand against one another in continual conflict. Any reunion in reflection is an illusion; only through action [*Handeln*] can they be united. (Goethe 1998d, 433, section 497)
>
> The sciences should only act on the outside world through an enhanced praxis [*eine erhöhte Praxis*]: for they are actually all esoteric and can only become exoteric if improved by some doing [*durch Verbessern irgendeines Tuns*]. Any other participation leads to nothing. (Goethe 1998d, 430 section 474)

Goethe's stress on doing, on practical life and on a heightened form of empiricism is very different from other spiritualised, contemplative accounts of perceived holism.[31] Much closer to earth, grubbing around in the earth, studying the similarities and differences between various vegetables, flowers, bones and rocks, he looks towards the eventual coalescence of theory and praxis. This idea, which Goethe thinks is not un-Kantian, of 'enhanced praxis' would necessitate an improbably radical overhaul of humanity as a species but it can nevertheless function as an 'ultimate end' towards which we strenuously orientate ourselves. In *Groundwork for a Metaphysic of Morals* Kant seems to be encouraging a similar approach to ourselves and to the world around us when he writes:

> ... the idea of a purely intelligible world, as a whole to which we our-selves belong as rational beings (although from another point of view we are members of the sensible world as well), remains a serviceable and permitted idea for the purposes of a rational belief, though all knowledge ends at its boundary; it serves to produce in us a lively interest in the moral law by means of the splendid ideal of a univer-sal kingdom of *ends in themselves* (rational beings) to which we can belong as members *only if we are scrupulous to live in accordance with maxims of freedom as if they were laws of nature*. (Kant 1964, 130–1)

This possible parallel between the future of humanity as an ethically driven whole, as an evolutive cosmopolitical entity, and nature's capac-ity for self-organisation and transformation, is one that has preoccupied contemporary complexity theorists.[32] For example, Brian Goodwin boldly identifies the anthropomorphic values that might be deduced from such a grafting of the world of practical reason (wherein we are free to act according to maxims) onto the dynamic natural world conceived as governed by underlying laws, though amoral ones.[33] He writes:

> A science of qualities is necessarily a first-person science that recog-nises values as shared experiences, as states of participative awareness that link us to other organisms with bonds of sympathy, mutual recognition and respect. (Goodwin 1997, 220)

Stuart Kauffman also provides us with an account which at once demonstrates how the human cannot be seen as the source of 'purpose and value' in the natural world, thereby not only dislodging the human from its traditionally central place within it, but also reiterating how nevertheless 'we are at home in the universe', not just the products of a 'chain of accidental mutations' (Kauffman 1995, 4–6). He draws the following cosmopolitical conclusions from his re-enchanted worldview:

> ... the most important problem confronting humanity [is] the emer-gence of a world civilisation, its profound promise, and the cultural

dislocations this transformation will cause. To undergird the pluralistic global community that is aborning, we shall need, I think, an expanded intellectual basis – a new way to think about origins, evolution, and the profound naturalness of life and its myriad patterns of unfolding. This book is an effort to contribute to that new view, for the emerging sciences of complexity ... offer fresh support for the idea of a pluralistic democratic society, providing evidence that it is not merely a human creation but part of the natural order of things. (Kauffman 1995, 5)[34]

The order that emerges 'at the edge of chaos' in the natural world provides, we are told, some hope for the 'global community' that has been in the making at least since 1795/6, when Kant wrote his 'Perpetual Peace' essay. Goethe can be seen as making a valuable contribution to this Kantian project with his advocacy of an exploration of ourselves, of our potential as inter-related living beings, through a re-evaluation of our relationship to other life forms. His methodology of 'delicate empiricism' and of 'enhanced praxis' is not just a theory about how to interpret nature, but it is also a philosophy of life. Goethe provides us with indications about how to live affirmatively and productively; he also claims it is incumbent on us to live up to 'highest reason' in our dealings with other living beings as we are indissociable parts of one en-globing and dynamic whole.

Notes

1. The guarded nature of the sentence is intended to signal that I suspect Nietzsche of overstating his diametrical opposition to Kant's philosophy. I see the two thinkers as having more in common than Nietzsche lets on. For instance, in section 337 of *The Gay Science* entitled 'The Humaneness of the Future [*Die zukünftige Menschlichkeit*]', he evokes the prospect of a 'marvellous growth', a 'new feeling', wherein the 'history of humanity as a whole [*die Geschichte der Menschen insgesamt*]' reverberates within and through the supra-individual. To experience intensely the ever accumulating sum of the world's past sufferings and joys, to feel the aristocratic 'sense of obligation' to humanity [*der Menschheit*], without succumbing to the arbitrary, sometimes debilitating and ineffectual sentiments of compassion and pity, is a 'burden' to be heroically striven for. He exclaims: 'We of the present day are only just beginning to form the chain of a very powerful future feeling, link for link – we hardly know what we are doing' (Nietzsche 1974, 267–8; 1988a, 564–5). Despite his professions to the contrary, this vision resonates with Kant's writings on cosmopolitics. I explored the nature and implications of this *rapprochement* between Kant and Nietzsche in '*Nietzsche and Kant's "Secret Utopia": Global Ethics and the Humanity of the Future*' (paper presented at the Nietzsche Society Conference, University of Sussex, September 2004 unpublished).

2. For Kant's sophisticated exploration of the terms 'human', 'humanity', 'humaneness', and their interrelation with other (terrestrial and extraterrestrial) life forms and with technology, see Morgan 'Kant, Cosmopolitics and the Interplanetary Perspective', forthcoming.

3. Here Goethe's analysis goes way beyond Spengler's who homogenises singularities into generalisations about different cultures.

4. In his remarks 'On Teleology', Nietzsche makes the following comment on this statement by Goethe: 'Very important for the source of Goethe's philosophy of nature, from a Kantian proposition'. The proposition in question is one to be discussed later in this chapter relating to the inscrutable causality of organisms, in which 'everything is reciprocally both end and means'. This remark by Nietzsche that couples Goethe (whom he explicitly admired), with Kant (whom he presents in a lamentably reductive and negative way) gives us a rare example of his sympathetic insight into Kantian philosophy and into its consolidating influence on Goethe.

5. See also Goethe's remarks to Eckermann about how the cork tree does not exist so that we can plug our wine bottles (Eckermann 1981, 229).

6. Steiner also perpetuates what I see as the myth of Kant and Goethe's diametrical opposition when he writes: 'Indeed we can say without hesitation that all of German thinking runs along two parallel lines, one permeated by Kant's way of thinking and the other closer to Goethe's thinking ... ' (2000, 140). He later adds: 'Goethe was unable to gain much from this [Kant's] worldview' (142).

7. See also Barnes' 'Participatory Science as the Basis for a Healing Culture' in this volume of Steiner's essays. For an account of other nineteenth- and twentieth-century German holistic movements, often inspired by Goethe's writings, indeed advocating a 'back to Goethe!', see Harrington (1996).

8. In fact, it is wrong to try to present Goethe's writings on nature as a 'methodological approach'. His views of nature are indissociable from what I would call a radical philosophy of life.

9. See the letters to Schiller 6 January 1798; 30 June 1798 in Goethe (1988a 324, 353) and Boyle (2000, 597–600).

10. See Kant (1983, 92–3, B74–5): '... neither concepts without an intuition in some way corresponding to them, nor intuition without concepts, can yield knowledge ... . Thoughts without content are empty, intuitions without concepts are blind'. See also Morgan (2000, 145–50) for an account of how Goethe reiterates many of Kant's concerns in his methodological writings, especially in the 1792 essay 'The Experiment as Mediator between Object and Subject'.

11. This would be an encasement theory of organic life [*Einschachtelungslehre*], whereby a creature's existence consists of a developmental unpacking or mere activation of qualities and properties with which the creature was originally endowed by a 'primordial intentional force'. For a discussion of the inadequacy of such a theory, see Kant (1988, 82–6, section 81).

12. Similarly, in an 1831 letter to Zelter, Goethe explains that his interest in Niebuhr's history books on the Romans and their agricultural laws lies not in the content (not in the 'what', not in the stuff) but in the 'how', in *how* Niebuhr explains those selfsame laws, in *how* he makes those complicated relations clear: it is the historian himself and *how* he operates which interests the reader Goethe. Here Goethe displays a free relation to the past and a wish to find methods to live productively by (Goethe 1988b, 417). This approach to

the past impressed Nietzsche and obviously influenced his 'On the Uses and Advantages of a History for Life'. For his *Nachlaβ* see Nietzsche (1988b, 664).

13. For an exploration of how 'Verwandtschaften' feature in Kant's writings, see Morgan (2000, 106–58).

14. See Goodwin (1997 184–5) for the importance of Kant's analysis of organisms' 'purposiveness without purpose' and of the parallel between life and art: 'Kant was so struck by the complex and subtle coherence of organisms that he likened the developmental process, the transformation of a simple initial form such as a fertilised egg into the adult form, to the creation of a work of art, which also has an inner coherence expressed in the dynamic unity of its emergent parts ...'.

15. Both Goethe and Kant celebrate the spontaneity of nature, but neither would go as far as someone like Nietzsche who sees 'nature as chance' (Nietzsche 1990, 82). For Goethe life is intrinsically dynamic, undergoing transformation but in accordance with laws or principles, not arbitrarily, hence his appeal for bio-mathematicians from d'Arcy Thompson to contemporary figures such as Ian Stewart. Kant certainly has fundamental objections to conceiving matter as living (see Kant 1988, 46–7 section 73), whereas Goethe finds it far less difficult to envisage the possibility of hylozoism as he admits in 'Campagne in Frankreich' (Goethe 1998b, 314). Indeed, it is the proclamation of this unorthodox belief in hylozoism, the rude (unpredictable, not pre-determined) eruption of life from previously lifeless matter, which so dismays Goethe's kind hosts, the Jacobis and their polite friends in 1792, convinced as they are that nothing can come into being other than what was already there (which for Goethe leads inevitably to the conundrum 'what came first the chicken or the egg'). Their cold response to this revolutionary theory heightens Goethe's sense of isolation at a time when, psychically and physically traumatised by his own experience of the revolutionary wars (with the fear, the squalour of masses of refugees on the move, the violence, waste and uncertainty), he was repulsed by events in and emanating from France and the radical transformation they represented. There is a paradoxical mismatch at this point between Goethe's views on biology, his views on its ever-emerging will to power and his socio-political resistance to change (and incomprehension of upper-class friends' receptive response to the French Revolution, their enthusiasm for a newly adopted '*Streben nach Demokratie*' [Goethe 1998b, 317]). Kant, on the other hand, who cannot countenance the prospect of hylozoism, was a consistent support of the French Revolution. Given the parallel between the natural world and human society evoked in this chapter, this intriguing divergence between Kant's and Goethe's political views probably merits further exegesis.

16. Goethe's importance for D'Arcy Thompson, whose own work has been 'rediscovered' by contemporary biologists such as Ingber (1998), is made explicit in the following lines: 'our own study of organic form, which we call by Goethe's name, morphology, is but a portion of that wider Science of Form which deals with the forms assumed by matter under all aspects and conditions, and, in a still wider sense, with forms which are theoretically imaginable' (D'Arcy Thompson 1995, 269).

17. See Tantillo (2002, 188ff) for a summary of Goethe's battle against 'Newtonian and Cartesian' ways of understanding nature.

18. See, for instance, Goethe's eloquent essay on the long life of granite (Goethe 1998a, 253–8).

19. An example of one such art movement is the Independent Group who, inspired by D'Arcy Thompson's work (who was in turn inspired by Goethe), set up an exhibition at the ICA called 'On Growth and Form' in 1951 and another called 'Parallel of Life and Art' in 1953. See Walsh (2001, 21–7, 89–107).
20. As is reiterated in 'A Friendly Greeting': 'Nature has neither core/ Nor outer rind,/ Being all things at once [*Natur hat weder Kern/ Noch Schale,/Alles ist sie mit einemmale*]' (Goethe 1995, 38; 1998a, 35).
21. Despite the suggestion in this passage that humans 'must be capable' of raising themselves sufficiently to understand *Urphänomene*, Goethe highlights elsewhere how temporality renders impossible such a feat. To Herder he declares that one would need a whole lifetime to trace *Urphänomenen*, that is, as finite beings who take years to mature, it is already too late to grasp the essence of natural things (Goethe 1998c, 205), also cited in Lacoste (1997, 29).
22. For the contemporary currency of the term 'Baupläne' see Ingber (1998).
23. As such '*Urphänomene*' are akin to what scientists now call 'phase space', 'the space of the adjacent possible'. See Stewart (1998, 118–19).
24. See also Tantillo (2002, 66) for how Goethe's theory of forms differs from Plato's.
25. See Goethe's account of his heated discussions with Schiller about the status of the *Urpflanze* (Goethe 1995, 20–1; 1998b, 540–2).
26. See Goethe (1998d, 530 section 1220) for humans' inability to see their own will to anthropomorphisation.
27. See Stewart (1998, 7): 'emergence is not the absence of causality but rather a web of causality so complex that the human mind cannot grasp'.
28. See Eckermann (1981, 298, 347) for the importance of recognising limits and an explicit reference to Kant in this context.
29. See Lacoste (1997, 55): 'un modèle synthétique global'.
30. As such Goethe's notion of the human is akin to Kant's enigmatic and intriguing formulation: 'the supersensible substrate of humanity' (Kant 1988, section 57).
31. For example, Aldous Huxley's narcotically enhanced entry into the suchness of things and the mind at large (documented in Huxley 1994).
32. For an analysis of 'self-overcoming' [Steigerung] as representing 'nature's [including human nature's] desire to tend towards greater complexity' see Tantillo (2002, 58–103).
33. Goodwin tells us that his *How the Leopard changed his Spots* is written 'very much in the Goethean spirit' (Goodwin 1997, 123).
34. See also Kauffman (1995, 304): 'I am heartened by the possibility that organisms are not contraptions piled on contraptions all the way down, but expressions of a deeper order inherent in all life. I am not certain that democracy evolved to achieve reasonable compromises between people with legitimately conflicting interests, but I am heartened by the possibility that our social institutions evolve as expressions of deep natural principles'.

Bibliography

Archibugi, D. (ed.) (2003) *Debating Cosmopolitics*, London: Verso.
Boyle, N. (2000) *Goethe: The Poet and the Age*, Vol. II, Revolution & Renunciation, 1790–1803, Oxford: Oxford University Press.
Boyle, N. (1991) *Goethe: The Poet and the Age*, Vol. I, The Poetry of Desire, Oxford: Oxford University Press.

Breckenridge, C. et al. (ed.) (2002) *Cosmopolitanism*, Durham and London: Duke University Press.

Cassirer, E. (1991) *Rousseau, Kant, Goethe: Deux essais* trans. J. Lacoste, Tours: Belin.

Caygill, H. (1995) *A Kant Dictionary*, Oxford: Blackwell.

Cheah, P. and Robbins, B. (1998) *Cosmopolitics: Thinking and Feeling beyond the Nation* Minneapolis, MN: University of Minnesota Press.

D'Arcy Thompson (1995) *On Growth and Form* abridged by J. T. Bonner, Cambridge: Cambridge University Press.

Eckermann, J. P. (1981) *Gespräche mit Goethe*, Baden-Baden: Insel Verlag.

Goethe, J. W. (1998a) *Naturwissenschaftliche Schriften I*, Hamburger Ausgabe Vol. XIII, München: dtv.

Goethe, J. W. (1998b) *Autobiographische Schriften II*, Hamburger Ausgabe Vol. X, München: dtv.

Goethe, J. W. (1998c) *Autobiographische Schriften III*, Hamburger Ausgabe Vol. XI, München: dtv.

Goethe, J. W. (1998d) *Schriften zur Kunst, Schriften zur Literatur, Maximen und Reflexionen*, Hamburger Ausgabe Vol. XII, München: dtv.

Goethe, J. W. (1994) *Essays on Art and Literature*, The Collected Works Vol. III, ed. J. Gearey, Princeton, NJ: Princeton University Press.

Goethe, J. W. (1995) *Scientific Studies*, The Collected Works Vol. XII, ed. and trans. D. Miller, Princeton, NJ: Princeton University Press.

Goethe, J. W. (1988a) *Briefe* Hamburger Ausgabe, Vol. II, 1786–1805, München: d.t.v.

Goethe, J. W. (1988b) *Briefe* Hamburger Ausgabe, Vol. IV, 1821–1832, München: d.t.v.

Goethe, J. W. (1959) *Schriften zur Natur und Erfahrung: Schriften zur Morphologie I*, Stuttgart: Cotta.

Goodwin, B. (1997) *How the Leopard Changed Its Spots: The Evolution of Complexity*, London: Phoenix.

Harrington, A. (1996) *Reenchanted Science: Holism in German Culture from Wilhelm II to Hitler*, Princeton, NJ: Princeton University Press.

Held, D. (2002) *Democracy and the Global Order: From the Modern State to Cosmopolitan Governance*, Oxford: Blackwell.

Huxley, A. (1994) *The Doors of Perception & Heaven and Hell*, Glasgow: Flamingo.

Ingber, D. (January 1998) 'The Architecture of Life' in *Scientific American*. Available on web at http://www.sciam.com/1998/0198issue/0198ingber.html#further.

Kant, I. (1994) *Political Writings* ed. H. Reiss, trans. H. B. Nisbet, Cambridge: Cambridge University Press.

Kant, I. (1988) *The Critique of Judgement* trans. J. C. Meredith, Oxford: Oxford University Press.

Kant, I. (1983) *Critique of Pure Reason* trans. N. K. Smith, London and Basingstoke: Macmillan.

Kant, I. (1964) *Groundwork of the Metaphysic of Morals* trans. H.J. Paton, New York: Harper Torchbooks.

Kauffman, S. (1995) *At Home in the Universe: The Search for Laws of Complexity* Harmondsworth: Penguin.

Lacoste, J. (1997) *Goethe, Science et Philosophie*, Paris: Presses Universitaires De France.

Morgan, D. (forthcoming) 'Kant, Cosmopolitics and the Interplanetary Perspective' in D. Morgan *Cosmopolitics and the Future of Humanism,*

Morgan, D. (2001) 'The Discipline of Pure Reason: Dosing the Faculties' in *Tekhnema,* Issue 6, 'Teleologies- Scientific, Technical & Critical', Paris: American University of Paris.

Morgan, D. (2000) *Kant Trouble: The Obscurities of the Enlightened,* London and New York: Routledge/ Taylor & Francis.

Nietzsche (1990) *Twilight of the Idols/ The Anti-Christ* trans. R. J. Hollingdale, Harmondsworth: Penguin.

Nietzsche, F. (1988a) *Die fröhliche Wissenschaft* in Kritische Studienausgabe Vol. III, ed. Colli and Montinari, München/Berlin: dtv/ de Gruyter.

Nietzsche, F. (1988b) *Nachgelassene Fragmente 1869–1874,* Kritische Studienausgabe Vol. VII, ed. Colli and Montinari, München/ Berlin: dtv/de Gruyter.

Nietzsche, F. (1974) *The Gay Science* trans. W. Kaufmann, New York/Toronto: Vintage Books.

Spengler, O. (1991) *Der Untergang des Abendlandes,* München: dtv.

Steiner, R. (2000) *Nature's Open Secret: Introductions to Goethe's Scientific Writings* trans. J. Barnes and M. Spiegler, Sussex: Steiner Press.

Stengers, I. (1997) *Cosmopolitiques,* 7 Vols, Paris: La Découverte.

Stewart, I. (1998) *Life's Other Secret: The New Mathematics of the Living World,* Harmondsworth: Penguin.

Tantillo, A. O. (2002). *The Will to Create: Goethe's Philosophy of Nature,* Pittsburgh: University of Pittsburgh Press.

Van Eynde, L. (1999) *Goethe, lecteur de Kant,* Paris: Presses universitaires de France.

Walsh, V. (2001) *Nigel Henderson: Parallel of Life and Art,* London: Thames & Hudson.

Index